Change and Continuity in Infancy

Jerome Kagan

with the collaboration of

ROBERT B. MCCALL,

N. D. REPPUCCI, JUDITH JORDAN,

JANET LEVINE, *and*

CHERYL MINTON

New York · London · Sydney · Toronto

Change
and
Continuity
in
Infancy

JOHN WILEY & SONS, INC.

Library of Congress Catalogue Card Number: 71-152498

ISBN 0-471-45419-2

Printed in the United States of America.

10 9 8 7 6 5 4 3 2 1

*"I have steadily endeavored to keep my mind free
so as to give up any hypothesis, however much beloved
(and I cannot resist forming one on every subject)
as soon as facts are seen to be opposed to it.
Indeed, I have had no choice but to act in this
manner, for with the exception of the Coral Reefs,
I cannot remember a single first-formed hypothesis
which had not after a time to be given up or greatly
modified. This has naturally led me to distrust
greatly deductive reasoning in the mixed sciences."*

CHARLES DARWIN

*"Truth," said Balthazar to me once,
blowing his nose in an old tennis sock,
"Truth is what most contradicts itself in time."*

BALTHAZAR, LAWRENCE DURRELL

Acknowledgments

I have been helped enormously by many people, but especially by my five collaborators: Robert McCall, N. D. Reppucci, Judith Jordan, Janet Levine, and Cheryl Minton who were, in every way, coinvestigators. Without their wisdom, loyalty, and guidance the work might never have been completed. Marshall Haith has been a constructive and loving critic and, with William Kessen, provided enormously helpful critiques of the manuscript. I acknowledge my deep appreciation to Doris Simpson whose skill, patience, and loyalty are without parallel. Others who were associated with the project for a substantial period are: Elizabeth B. Anderson, Suellen Brander, Gayle Henkin Brent, Marian Cleveland, Rosalind Folman, Claire Fishman, Barbara Henker, Amy Hen-Tov, Milton Kotelchuck, Dorothy Largay, Robert Lentz, Roseanne McCall, Edith Marsden, Caroline Mechem, Frederick J. Morrison, Michael Novey, Judith Ross, Michael Ross, Leslie Pearson Rovainen, Suzanna Sak, Henriette Salek, Jon Terry Saunders, Jane M. Schneider, Terry Stagman, Richard Stein, Betty Chang Sun, Charles Super, James Weiffenbach, and Lois Welch.

Financial support for the work came from Research Grant MH8792 from the National Institute of Mental Health, U.S. Public Health Service; contract number PH43-65-1009 from the National Institute of Child Health and Human Development, and a research grant from the Carnegie Corporation of New York.

J.K.

Preface

The illusion that we can specify in time or location the beginning of an idea or major effort is one that we require to keep our understanding of the present tidy. This book originated in the fall of 1960 when Howard Moss and I were studying the results of an analysis of the Fels longitudinal data that resulted in the publication of *Birth to Maturity,* in 1962. We were both persuaded that there were profound differences among infants which time and experience did not easily subdue. It was also clear that a satisfying understanding of these phenomena, both their origins and final consequences, could only be attained through a series of related longitudinal studies whose observations remained close to the child, avoiding the distortions that are an inherent part of a mother's descriptive comment or the longhand notes of a visiting observer. Howard Moss left Fels to join Richard Bell at NIMH and, during the last eight years, both have clarified some of the issues raised by the earlier investigation. I remained at Fels and, with Michael Lewis, began to inquire into the attentional processes of the young infant. There were two reasons for this choice. We wanted to develop sensitive procedures to examine individual differences among infants and to learn more about their mental life. We became enchanted with the second problem and Lewis has made major contributions to our understanding of early cognitive development. When I came to Cambridge in 1964, I was attracted to two problems: the original affection for temperamental differences in the young child and the new excitement with early cognition. I could not put either one aside and the longitudinal study reported in this book reflects the pursuit of both goals.

November, 1970   *Jerome Kagan*

Contents

Change and Continuity in Infancy

Basic Conceptions

Each generation of psychologists seems to discover a fresh set of phenomena and a sparkling new object of study. The introspectively tutored adult was favored during the beginning of this century and the content of consciousness was the preferred theme. The exploring albino rat captured the stage from the brooding adult when the academy decided that public responses and biological drives were more critical than feelings, sensations, or thoughts. The human infant has become one of the stars of this decade and the focus of inquiry has returned to unseen mental processes, but under the modern title of cognitive structure.

The ease with which loyalties to species or subject matters are broken is to be expected in a discipline as young as psychology. The behavioral sciences are in the inherently frustrating formative period during which they are selecting the phenomena they wish to pursue in depth and the concepts they must quantify and place in propositional form. The behavior of a typical psychologist during the last century resembles that of a child who has had a blanket thrown over him as he stood in a large room containing a variety of interesting objects. His task is to determine, without removing the opaque cover, what is in the room. It would be proper strategy to walk until he hit something, put out a hand, and explore the object to see if a quick determination was possible. If a few moments of exploration proved fruitless, it did not matter; there were many other objects to be probed. Our temporarily blinded hero would pass from object to object, exploring quickly, hoping for a clue that might define one event permanently, but always prepared to pass on if the initial inquiry was not rewarding.

This horizontal progress is not an unfair description of psychology's first 100 years. We probe a subject, an idea, or a phenomenon until we become frustrated conceptually or methodologically, and then search for another love object. We turned from introspecting adults when we were unable to solve the subjectivity problem; we turned from rats running mazes when we could not solve the reinforcement problem and were unable to generalize from turn sequences in alleys to human problem solving. We turned from personality study when we failed to develop sensitive procedures to measure motives, anxieties, or conflicts. And now we affirm the child.

THE CONCERN WITH CHILDHOOD

Interest in the young child, especially the infant, draws its force from four divergent sources. The commitment to historical explanation has always influenced domestic empiricism and experimental studies with rats, cats, mice, and monkeys have often posed developmental questions. Harlow and his colleagues wondered about the effect of infant experience with terrycloth mothers on adult social behavior (Harlow, 1962, Harlow & Harlow, 1966), while Denenberg (1964, 1966) and Levine (1962) inquired into the effect of mild handling of week-old mice on adult open-field behavior. This historical bias, which is not shared by all psychological groups, is sustained by a strong belief in the persistence of well-learned habits, an obvious heir of Hullian behaviorism, and a characteristic American optimism that affirms that whatever has happened to an organism can either be undone or done differently with the next generation. The influence of psychoanalytic theory, although waning rapidly, also directed interest to the child. As the seminal theory of personality development, it issued strong statements about the long-term effect of family experiences during the first five years. Third, the deep concern with educational progress in the child of poverty, a phenomenon that has always been in the background and has suddenly become prominent, has catalyzed a heady series of investigations into the mental life and experiences of very young children. There is general agreement that the consistent social class differences in the academic skills and motivation of school-age children can be previewed as early as age 3, although the patterns of prior events that mold these differences are largely unknown. The candidates that carry the explanatory burden include subtle damage to the central nervous system during the prenatal and perinatal periods, daily exposure to an environment that does not optimally nurture the development of motivation to acquire academic skills, attachment to adult caretakers, and expectancy of success in problem situations. Implicit in some of these explanations is the prejudice that the lower class child is missing a critical set of experiences during his first five years. If he were to enjoy these experiences, all would be well.

The belief in sensitive periods in development, which lurks in the essays that seek to interpret this social dilemma, has been the fourth force behind the zeal for child watching (Caldwell, 1962). Impressive empirical demonstrations with animals require the invention of some special theoretical term to explain why the timing of experience is crucial. The primate studies, the work on infantile stress in mice, and the imprinting phenomena in precocial birds are but three instances of the generalization that the first habits learned in an environment are more resistant to change than those acquired later—a primacy effect in the behavioral realm. Moreover, physiological changes during the early postnatal period have more enduring effects than the same changes imposed on a more mature organism. Since the effects of the specific experience on later behavior depend on the time when the experience occurred, it is necessary to posit a concept like sensitive period. The weak meaning of the phrase implies that psychological or physiological reactions to environmental events are different at different times. The strong meaning implies that a particular experience or process must occur within a limited time period if the organism is to develop behaviors or structures necessary for normal functioning. There is less evidence for the stronger definition than there is for the weaker one, but Riesen's (1961) classic demonstration of the role of patterned light during the initial postnatal days on the development of visual capacity is one undisputed instance of the usefulness of the strong form of the hypothesis. Since most of the demonstrations of sensitive period phenomena involve very young organisms, attention naturally has turned to the human infant.

The Focus on Infancy. Most psychologists are awed by the amount and rate of change in physical and psychological growth that occur during the first 30 months of life, and wish to understand this drama. The newborn is transformed from a crying, squirming, reflexive creature to a coherent, symbolic, coordinated, and planful child in less than 30 months.

And a set of convenient milestones mark the journey—the smile of recognition at 4 months, fear of a stranger at 8 months, crying to separation at 10 months, two-word sentences at 18 months, and conceptual conflict at 24 months. Robert Fantz' (1966) demonstration that with remarkably simple methods one could tell what a baby was looking at and, perhaps, what he preferred to watch was an important catalyst in recruiting interest in the mind of the infant. To everyone's surprise the very young infant was not perceptually innocent. The 2-week old stared longer at checkerboards and bulls' eyes than at stimuli of homogeneous color, and as early as 4 months looked longer at a picture of a human face than at most nonsense figures. Fantz' early work provided hope that we might be able to determine what a baby perceives and, in turn, come closer to probing his mind. Subsequent results from independent laboratories are relatively consistent and make a sensible beginning to the story. These early empirical successes have recruited many to the excitement of the first year, perhaps because we recognize that simple forms often reveal profound insights into nature's secrets. Biology's success with E. coli, drosophila, and neurospora are not forgotten easily, and the maxim that basic principles will be more easily given up by study of simple forms is a well-rehearsed catechism. The infant is likely to display, in relatively undisguised fashion, basic processes operative throughout the life cycle. The role of physical contrast in attention; habituation to repeated events; and reaction to discrepancy are all seen in less noisy contexts in the infant laboratory. Finally, the aesthetic appeal of the infant is not an irrelevant factor. He is not tainted by the myths of his culture, he has no desire to please the experimenter, he smiles frequently, and, he often supplies beautiful curves.

The two classes of behavioral scientists who study the infant have slightly different aims, but often use similar strategies. One group wishes to understand the basic principles of learning and perceptual dynamics. A second wants to understand the causes and consequences of variability in infant reaction patterns, and is committed to the historical prejudice that seeks previews of later behavior in the psychological display of the infant. This commitment takes its nurture from the overwhelming variability among infants from the first day. There are quiet and active babies, irritable and contented babies, excitable and placid babies, smiling and dour babies, heavy and light babies, premature and term babies, hypoxic and full breathing babies. Everyone acknowledges the obviousness of these differences, but only a few believe they play a permanent role in guiding the psychological organization of the older child. This controversial hypothesis has promoted inquiries into the stability or derivative form of dimensions of difference among infants. This book summarizes a 2-year longitudinal study of a large group of firstborn, white infants and reaches some tentative conclusions about the degree of permanence of early attributes and the differential growth of cognitive structures.

COGNITION IN INFANCY

Study of perceptual dynamics in infancy has led naturally to the question of whether the infant learns anything when he merely looks at an object or listens to a sound. This issue has generated considerable debate because of an unstated belief that the infant was seriously different from the adult. If an adult were to look at a photograph of Lake Atitlan for the first time he would learn and retain, for some time, the fact that it has an irregular perimeter. The adult would not have to feel the photo, swim in the lake, or carefully trace the lake's outline with his eyes. At a more conceptual level, if an adult hears a scientist state that an operon is a concept used by molecular geneticists to explain the suppression of structural genes, he is likely to learn the meaning of this concept. Bandura (1963, 1968) and his colleagues have shown that a 3-year-old child who is afraid of dogs will approach them after watching a short series of films in which children play with dogs. Finally, the work of Solomon and Turner (1962), Miller (1969), and John (1968) indicates that a representation of experience may be established without corresponding action, and these structures can lie latent for a long time without mediating overt behavior. These examples are sufficient to warrant faith in the common sense proposition that a child or adult can acquire a perceptual structure, a concept, or alter the hierarchy of his overt behaviors by looking or listening. Motor action is not necessary.

Studies of psychological growth in the human infant prior to the 1960's seemed opposed to this view. Test items assessing "infant intelligence" were devoted almost exclusively to overt behaviors—age of sitting, walking, hand-eye coordination, smiling, removal of a napkin from a toy, prehension of a button. The implicit assumption was that the child's level of intellectual development covaried with his precocity on motor and sensorimotor acquisitions. This intuitively reasonable belief was supported by Jean Piaget, the major cognitive theorist of this century. Piaget (1954) stated explicitly that the infant's intellective structures were mental interiorizations of overt actions, and more recently Bruner (1968) argued that the nature of infant cognition must be sculpted, in part, by the child's skill behaviors. Piaget and the infant testers probably arrived at their faiths independently for neither tended to study the other's writing during the first half of the century, and there has been minimal contact among the loyal cadre of these groups. Such independent accord is usually a guide to truth. How can we understand this commitment to the diagnostic value of action in assessing mental growth? The reasons are probably different. The mental testers were probably moved by pragmatic considerations, Gesell's (1941) clearly written procedures, and the dominance of behaviorism and operationalism. There was no way to assess what the infant was thinking, but there were ways to measure what he was doing. It is more difficult to understand Piaget's affinity for this materialistic view of infant intelligence. Piagetian theory is profoundly cognitive and his epistemology would lead one to expect a more mentalistic view of infant psychology.

Although motor actions and sensorimotor coordinations are obviously important in the infant's instrumental adaptation to the environment, they may not be always necessary for the establishment of cognitive structures. The maturity of sensorimotor coordinations may be imperfectly correlated with the maturity of cognitive structures. We concur with Russell that "from any occurrence that a man notices, he can obtain knowledge" (Russell, 1940). A child seems to be able to acquire cognitive representations of an event merely by looking at it, for if an 8- or 12-week-old infant is shown a stimulus repeatedly, duration of gaze gradually decreases (Fantz, 1964). If a transformation of that habituated stimulus is presented, the infant immediately shows a marked increase in looking and often a change in autonomic reactivity. The infant under 3 months of age does not have to touch or manipulate a stimulus to learn something about its structure. Investment of attention is sufficient, and it is likely that the infant learns much about his environment through merely attending to it. Although action is not necessary, it can facilitate learning because activity is accompanied by an increased alertness and, therefore, a greater likelihood of noting salient aspects of an object. Action is clearly an effective aid to the acquisition of cognitive structures. If the structure to be learned involves a totally new overt response, then the behavior probably must occur. A new action that is not in the child's repertoire must be practiced if it is to become part of that repertoire. But transfer of an existing response to a new stimulus does not seem to require the display of the behavior (Solomon & Turner, 1962; John et al., 1968). The present work is primarily concerned with the development of schemata rather than sensorimotor coordinations, and our research procedures were designed to provide some insight into these acquisitions.

The Concept of Schema. A schema is a representation of an event that preserves the temporal and spatial arrangement of its distinctive elements without necessarily being isomorphic with the event. This definition is in close accord with Bartlett's (1932) original statement. The concept of schema is similar in implication to the notion of cortical neuronal model postulated by neurophysiologists to explain, among other things, the phenomenon of habituation. The schema need not involve an action component, and is not synonymous with an image, symbol, or word, although schemata can be *about* these entities. The major function of a schema is to allow the organism to recognize and assimilate information. An empirical fact may help the reader appreciate the meaning intended. We recently asked 4-year olds to look through a set of 50 pictures illustrating objects, people, or scenes, many of which he had never seen before and could not label when requested. The children devoted no more than a few seconds to each picture and flipped through the 50 illustrations in three to four minutes. The child was then shown 50 pairs of pictures, one of which was the picture viewed earlier, the other was new, and he was asked to point to the picture he viewed earlier. The average 4-year old correctly recognized about 45 of the 50 pictures although he could only recall three or four of the set. Some children recognized all of them two days later. Since some of the pictures illustrated objects the child had never seen (an unusual lathe or an engineer's slide rule) it is unlikely that his awesome performance could be totally explained by assuming that each picture elicited a language label. Since he devoted only a few seconds to scanning each picture, it is unlikely that he had a well-defined image of the scenes.

What hypothetical entity can we call upon to explain the child's ability to recognize over 90% of the scenes, for neither language, nor action, nor image provides a satisfactory explanation. The concept of schema stands for the cognitive structure that permitted recognition. Each picture contained a unique arrangement of salient elements and the schema preserved that configuration, without necessarily preserving a simple isomorphism with the event. A normal 4-month-old, family-reared infant possesses a schema for a human face. The salient elements represented in the schema are probably the symmetric arrangement of the two eyes within an oval boundary. This inference rests on the observation that changes in these aspects of the stimulus, in contrast with changes in other components, are most likely to provoke a special reaction in the infant. It is not necessary that the schema preserve the exact spatial arrangement of these elements, only that it represent the relation among those salient elements. It is unfortunate that when psychologists speak of a "schema" for a face, they are forced to use a language of entities distributed in space and time.

The relation between psychological event and cognitive schema bears, of course, a close analogue to the relation between sensory event and neural patterns of discharge within receptor, intermediate nuclei, and cortex. Amplitude and frequency of a tone are represented within basilar membrane, cochlear nucleus, geniculate, and temporal cortex. Correlatively, the temporal relations among the critical phones in the phrase "Stop that," bear a lawful relation to cognitive processes somewhere in the mind. Schema refers to the process that *permits a child to understand the meaning of that phrase.* The sensory physiologists have gained some preliminary understanding of the complex relation between external stimulus and neural event. The cognitive psychologist remains considerably more puzzled.

Although the principles that describe the relation between an event and its resulting schema cannot be stated at this time, it is important to appreciate that the concept of schema, as used here, is to be differentiated from the motor actions that may be initiated in the service of a schema. Motor actions have greater limitations on their variability than schemata, because they are usually serial rather than parallel processes. Furthermore, motor actions are subordinate to mechanical constraints, and must be accommodated to the external context. The child with a mental representation of a tower will initiate different motor actions if he is given blocks or pegs. The blocks are easily arranged in a tower form, but not the pegs, and the child may line the latter items up, side by side, in a derivative form. It is usually difficult to guess the cognitive structures that mediate a particular action, just as it is not clear why a child's temperature is 101°F. We have no principles that permit preliminary translation from cognition to behavior. Moreover, ". . . understanding leads to no particular behavior. Even when there is sematic agreement, the specific forms in which it occurs differ, and these may be of trivial importance. Thus there is no way to link either understanding or interpretation with particular behavior." (Deese, 1969, p. 516.)

It is not suggested that it is impossible to measure cognitive processes with public operations. The body of this text is an empirical investigation of schemata in infants using the quantifiable variables of fixation time, vocalization, smiling, and heart rate change. However, it is argued that the relation of these variables to cognition is extraordinarily complex. We do not reject the assumption that cognitive structures can be operationalized; but approach this task with humility.

The Role of a Schema in the Isolation Phenomenon. The usefulness of the concept of schema can be illustrated by applying this construct to the behavioral disruption that follows isolation. If monkeys or dogs are reared in isolation from birth they show extreme fear and behavior disruption when removed from isolation and exposed to a situation different from the one in which they had been raised. The investigators imply that the animal left a situation of minimal stimulation or minimal stimulus variability and entered one with greater stimulation or stimulus variability. This phrasing may be misleading. A dog removed from an isolation cage and placed in an area containing no other living creatures also shows the typical effects of fear and disorganization (Fuller, 1967). It is not reasonable in this instance to imply that the animal went from a situation of minimal stimulation to one of greater stimulation. Rather, the animal went from one environment to a different environment. It may be more profitable to conceptualize the animal's experience in terms of an encounter with an environment that is discrepant from his established schema.

Although it is difficult to offer an unambiguous operational definition of a schema, there are three general assumptions about a schema that are relevant to the emotional distress displayed by animals raised in isolation. First, the longer the exposure to a particular constellation of events the better articulated the schemata for those events. The articulation of a schema refers to its stability and is reflected in the consistency with which a given class of events engages the same schema. Second, exposure to an event discrepant from the original stimulus that generated the schema alerts the organism and potentially sets the occasion for fear. A discrepant event is not synonymous with a novel one. A discrepant event shares some salient elements with the familiar; a novel event shares no salient elements with the familiar. If a face is the familiarized event for which a schema has been created, a face with one eye is discrepant; a randomly generated black and white geometric design is novel. A discrepant event alerts the organism and provokes him to cope with it, either through assimilation, withdrawal, or attack. If the organism cannot cope with the discrepant event, usually because he has no response to make toward it, he is likely to become fearful. This view is consonant with Hebb's (1946) classic paper on the bases of fear, as well as more recent empirical data, for chicks kept in plastic hoods showed no signs of fear when first allowed visual experience (Moltz & Stettner, 1961).

The third assumption about a schema that is relevant to the isolation data is that the greater the variability of the rearing environment, the less vulnerable to fear the organism will be when discrepant events are encountered. A highly variable environment provides the organism with discrepant experiences, permits the development of a set for discrepancy, and furnishes opportunities to learn ways of coping with it. Monkeys, for example, reared with a terrycloth surrogate mother who "moved" according to an irregular and unpredictable schedule were markedly less fearful than monkeys reared with the traditional, stationary, surrogate mother (Mason, personal communication).

The phenomena of stranger and separation anxiety are further examples of the association among variability, discrepancy, and fear. The 8-month-old infant possesses a good schema for his mother's face and may display fear to a stranger's face. But the fear usually lasts only six to eight weeks. It vanishes presumably as a result of continued exposure to other faces and acquisition of responses that allow the infant to deal with the discrepancy. Existing data indicate a positive relation between degree of contact between mother and infant, and occurrence of anxiety to strangers during the second half of the first year. The closer the contact between the infant and a single caretaker the more likely the infant will display anxiety to a stranger (Schaffer & Emerson, 1964; Collard, 1968), and first-born infants are more likely to cry and show signs of fear to a stranger than later born infants (see Collard, 1968; Waldrop & Bell, 1966).

Separation anxiety, which usually peaks at 10 to 13 months in American infants, refers to the distress displayed when the primary caretaker leaves the infant. The distress seems to be a partial result of discrepancy, for the infant is more likely to cry and crawl to the locus of the mother's exit if she leaves by an *unfamiliar* rather than a *familiar* door. In a recent study of 11 month old infants in a home setting, mothers were instructed to leave their infant from an exit they normally used or from one they rarely used (e.g., a closet or cellar door). The infants were more likely to cry, study the exit locus, and crawl toward the exit when the mother left from an unfamiliar than from a familiar door (Littenberg, Tulkin, & Kagan, 1971). Observations of infants in rural settings in cultures where infants are carried on their mothers' bodies during most of the day (Uganda, Mexico, Guatemala) reveal earlier onset of distress when the child is removed from the mother than occurs in Western infants (Ainsworth 1967; Brazelton & Roby, personal communication).

The event that elicits the distress is not an increase in stimulation, but a change from the usual; a discrepancy from an established schema. The isolation effect in mammals may occur because the animal acquires a schema for the distinctive elements of the rearing environment, as well as a set of responses to that environment. The longer the animal remains in the isolated context the firmer the schema and the stronger those habitual responses. Removal from isolation is synonymous with exposure to a discrepant environment to which the animal does not have coping reactions, and this experience is the occasion for fear.

The animal's specific reaction is a function of the responses that are, by inheritance or experience, prepotent to the internal mosaic of sensations that accompany fear. There should be important differences among infants of various species in their initial reaction to discrepancy. In most species, infants react with fear to events discrepant from a schema, but each may be programmed to react differently to the discrepancy. Fuller has shown that beagles become less and terriers more active when they leave isolation, and encounter the discrepant environment. The increased activity among terriers, in contrast to the decreased activity among beagles, parallels genetic differences in normal activity levels between the two species, for beagles are ordinarily less active than terriers (Fuller, 1967).

An anecdotal observation is relevant. One of our graduate students raised a female macaque monkey from birth. This animal was with the student continually for the first five months and had as much experience and exposure to human faces as any human infant. When the monkey was shown a set of clay masks of human male faces that we presented to our infants, the monkey displayed extreme and repetitive fear (retraction of the lips and ears, baring of the teeth, and motor trembling). A human infant rarely shows a reaction this severe to a model of a face. Extreme fear and avoidance seem to be stronger, prepotent responses to discrepancy in the infant monkey than in the infant human, as different activity levels characterize the preferred reactions of terriers and beagles.

This interpretation of the bases for distress and fear has a different flavor from the three most popular explanations of the isolation data (Fuller, 1967). One stance assumes that the behavioral effects are the result of the animal failing to learn some essential structures—a deficit interpretation. A second group of interpretations views stimulation as falling on an intensity or variability continuum, and argues that the isolated animal acquires an adaptation level for "low amounts" of stimulation. As a result he is not prepared for intense or variable stimulation and becomes frightened when removed. A third interpretation is that isolation prevents the animal from habituating to stimulus complexities "so that attending to pertinent components while disregarding others is made difficult" (Fuller, 1967, p. 1652). The position taken here is that neither amount, intensity, nor variability of stimulation provides a theoretically profitable way to conceptualize the phenomenon. The animal who leaves the isolated area encounters a discrepant environment to which he does not have a response. He is alerted, but cannot cope with the situation, and this combination occasions distress. The emphasis is placed on the relation between his schemata and the events in the new environment, not on the absolute variability or intensity of the new situation.

Schemata differ in degree of articulation of salient elements, accessibility, and position in a hierarchy; they do not differ in intensity. External stimulus sources differ in intensity. This is not a trivial distinction. If the behavioral disruption is viewed as a product of "input overload," one searches for stimulus intensity differences between isolation and nonisolation conditions. If disruption is seen as a product of lack of congruence between schema and environment, one examines the distinctive qualities of the environment. These views lead to obviously different empirical strategies.

The popularity of the interpretation of the isolation effect in terms of a continuum of stimulus intensity or variability is a forceful illustration of two major vectors that determine inference and explanation. Inferences regarding the cause of a phenomenon are governed first by the basic premises of the inventor. Premises are held with different degrees of faith and inferences that are inconsistent with or contradict basic beliefs are usually not selected if they are noted, or more typically, are not even brought to consciousness. Most 18th-century physicists were sure that light was corpuscular, and were prevented from experimenting with the idea that it might be a wave. A creative idea is only possible when traditional premises do not seize the mind too strongly. The traditional view in experimental psychology and psychophysics describes sensory events as falling along an intensity continuum. The faith that passive organisms are activated by stimulus events varying on an intensity dimension finds its clearest statement in Hull's construct of stimulus intensity dynamism (Hull, 1951).

The empiricist's predilection for manipulation is the second constraint on quality of inference. If an inference is to be followed by action, or if one only considers inferences that can be tested in the empirical arena, then the exploratory hypotheses are likely to be seriously constrained. The scholar will be searching, unconsciously to be sure, for hypothetical causes that can be *manipulated* in an experiment. Stimulus intensity or variability is more easily manipulated than schema for an event, for there is no obvious operational strategy that guarantees that a schema has been altered. The scientist's mind usually wanders in those inference spaces harboring ideas that are amenable to empirical intervention.

THE PRESENT RESEARCH

The investigation summarized in this text rests on the assumption that the child is an active, attentive creature who is continually and spontaneously acquiring schemata for aspects of his environment. Many of the procedures were instituted on the assumption that infants differed in the degree of articulation of schemata for human faces, forms, and speech, and that reactions to discrepancies from the ecologically regular form might provide a clue to schema articulation and, by inference, to quality of cognitive structures. We expected infants to differ in cognitive organization and wished to study the stability of these dimensions of difference.

THE MEANING OF STABILITY

Although demonstration of stability is one prerequisite for theory building, the fact of stability of a disposition or its derivative is necessarily ambiguous as to cause. Suppose, as the data of Cameron, Livson, and Bayley (1967) and Moore (1967) indicate, that there is a correlation between amount of vocalizing in 4- to 6-month-old girls and a reliable index of verbal ability at 2 or 4 years. How is this association to be interpreted? One might view this correlation as evidence for a constitutional basis of intelligence. The formal argument would state that the same central intellective process caused both the frequent vocalizing at 4 months and the high intelligence score. This is *endogenous* continuity (i.e., a particular internal process remained stable over time). However, it is equally reasonable to conclude that an environmental force, such as the mother's reciprocal interaction with her child, produced both the high vocalizing score in infancy and the older child's rich vocabulary. There need be no causal relation between the vocalization at 4 months and the later verbal resources. Each is an independent correlate of different sets of maternal behaviors. The stability was in the mother's behavior. This is an example of *exogenous* stability, for the stable "process" was in the external environment. The text shall consider many provocative instances of stability, but, in most cases, we will not be able to differentiate between those that involve intraorganismic dimensions and those that reflect continuity of external forces.

The Value of Assessing Behavioral Continuities. The issue of continuity is linked to three themes in developmental psychology. First, knowledge of those responses that show stability will facilitate prediction of future behaviors and permit early diagnoses of psychological syndromes that are dangerous to the child or society, or desirable syndromes that should be accelerated and protected. Second, continuity studies help to validate major theoretical positions. Knowledge of continuities in behavior permits a test of the psychologist's hypothesis that frustration of oral needs in infancy leads to depression in adulthood; or the behavioral prediction that partial reinforcement of aggressive action in childhood produces greater resistance to extinction of aggressive behavior during adolescence. The validation of these theoretical predictions requires studies of behavior over time. A third rationale for continuity studies is the one that will be pursued most thoroughly here. Studies of continuity facilitate understanding of the significance of responses at particular ages. Contemporary psychology does not understand the meaning of its most simple phenomena. What is the meaning of cooing at 3 months, the smile at 4 months, separation anxiety at 10 months, attempts at mastery at 1 year, or early attainment of what Piaget (1952) calls the object concept? What covert processes do each of these public acts reflect? What genotypic program produced them and what form will that genotypic program take in the future? An important working assumption of this investigation is that study of the predictive consequences of a well-delineated response aids our understanding of the significance of the original act, and allows us to fill in the many blank spaces in our dictionary of behavior.

Homotypic and Heterotypic Continuity in the Child. The endogenous versus exogenous distinction noted earlier refers to whether the source of the stability is in the child or in the environment. A second distinction concerns the nature of the dependent variable. Some continuities involve the same or very similar responses. Girls who cry frequently at 1 year may cry excessively at 3 years; infants who thrash actively at 4 months may be highly motoric at 2 years. The basic response modality is the same at both ages. This phenomenon has been called phenotypic continuity in the past, but geneticists have chided us for using a biological term with a perfectly clear meaning and giving it a different connotation. Thus the terms homotypic and heterotypic shall be substituted for what was formerly called phenotypic and genotypic continuity. Homotypic continuity refers to stabilities in the same response modality. Heterotypic continuity refers to stabilities between two classes of responses that are manifestly different, but theoretically related.[1] For example, if crying to strangers at 8 months indexed precocious schema development for human faces, it might predict a large vocabulary at 5 years of age, but not irritability. The relation between these two responses is theoretically reasonable and involves manifestly different behaviors.

The Fallacy of Homotypic Continuity. Although most theories neither demand nor assume that continuities refer only to manifestly similar responses, the practicing empiricist has sometimes been more cautious than necessary and has searched for stability of response systems that looked alike. They have sought evidence for stability of IQ or school achievement scores, activity, irritability, social responsiveness, dominance, dependency, or compulsive behavior. This strategy derives from the implicit assumption that a particular behavior is maintained over time by the same forces that promoted its initial acquisition and display. This assumption is not always defensible, especially during the first decade.

An 8-month-old infant usually cries when he is hungry, or when confronted by a stimulus that disconfirms an expectancy. An 8-year-old child usually cries when he wants to be freed from a parental restriction, is afraid of physical harm, or anticipates punishment. The act of crying, although characterized by salty tears and facial grimaces at each age, is emitted in the service of dramatically different forces and there is no reason to expect continuity between frequency of crying in infancy and early childhood. The act of boasting by a 12-year-old boy or a 32-year-old adult man, on the other hand, is often an attempt to maintain behavioral congruence with sex role standards for masculinity. In this latter instance, there is good theoretical cause to expect this behavior to show moderate stability over

[1] R. Q. Bell uses the terms isomorphic and metamorphic to make the same distinction.

this 20-year period, for the motivating conditions that elicit the act often remain stable. Thus, some behaviors display stability of manifest form, and others do not.

The Cryptograph of Heterotypic Continuity. The more intriguing form of continuity bears close resemblance to the physicist's principle of energy conservation. A liter of water in a closed system is converted to steam and recondensed to liquid. Although the manifest character of the substance changes markedly, the physicist assures us that the amount of energy in the system did not change. A copper bar in a clear solution of acid suddenly turns into the deep blue of copper sulfate, but the chemist knows that the amount of copper remains the same. Many social scientists believe in the conservation of selected motivational and affective states that assume different public disguises. For example, a 6-year-old child with strong anxiety over potential maternal rejection may be afraid to leave home and, as a result, refuse to go to school. At age 12, when display of a phobic reaction to school is regarded as regressive by both parent and child, the child may substitute excessive obedience to parents as a way of alleviating anxiety over potential rejection. If the parents valued school achievement the child might exhibit intense efforts at academic mastery. The basic source of anxiety present at age 6 remained part of the child's repertoire of motives. However, at age 6 the desire to reduce anxiety over possible rejection led to avoidance of school; whereas, at age 10 it elicited a zealous attitude toward schoolwork. In the case noted above there are theoretical guides to diagnose the meaning of the phobia at the early age and the school achievement at the later age. More often, there is no theory of the response, and psychologists are forced to search for behavioral similarities, rather than continuities in expectancies, motives, standards, sources of anxiety, or richness of cognitive structures that might be dressed in different behavioral guises at different times.

Examples of heterotypic continuity without homotypic stability are few in number, but sufficiently persuasive to warrant more confident study of this brand of continuity. Emmerich (1964) has reported that aggressive, extraversive 3-year-old children become socially poised 5-year olds; whereas the well-behaved 3-year olds often become anxious and withdrawn kindergarten children. The aggressive behavior of the 3-year old was not maintained but perhaps his expectancy of acceptance from both peer and adult was the stable underlying dimension that produced the manifestly different responses at 3 and 5 years. Behavioral passivity with adults in a 10-year-old boy does not predict passivity in the 25-year-old adult. But the passive 10-year old is likely to avoid the selection of both a masculine vocation and masculine interests (Kagan & Moss, 1962). The stable process may have been "anxiety over ability to assume the masculine role."

The public forms of this anxiety were different at 10 and 25 years of age. Similarly, girls who liked athletics during the period 10 to 14 years of age were highly motivated in college and experienced conflict over behaving in a passive and dependent manner with men, but they were not very athletic. If one assumes that rejection of the traditional feminine role is the continuous internal process mediating both the preadolescent and adult behavior, the continuity is reasonable.

Pedersen and Wender (1968) observed a group of children in a nursery school setting and quantified variables describing the degree to which the child showed long periods of sustained, solitary involvement with a task, in contrast to the degree to which he sought out adults for contact and recognition. Four years later, when these children were about $6\frac{1}{2}$ years old, each was given verbal and performance subscales from the Wechsler Intelligence Scale for Children. There was no relation between verbal IQ and the child's earlier behavior in the nursery school. However, children who had played alone for long periods of time performed much better on the blocks, picture arrangement, and mazes subtests of the performance scale than the children who were continually seeking out adults. There is no manifest similarity between the social behaviors at $2\frac{1}{2}$ and the test behaviors four years later. However, if a construct such as tempo of information processing remained stable, it could produce long periods of sustained play with toys at the earlier age and the tendency to reflect over the quality of one's hypotheses on the performance scale at $6\frac{1}{2}$ years of age. Two manifestly different behaviors are associated over time because each is the product of an internal process that is stable.

A recent investigation by Bronson (1967) provides an additional example of heterotypic continuity. The subjects, members of the Berkeley Guidance Study, were assigned scores based on interviews and observations during four childhood periods (5 to 7 years, 8 to 10 years, 11 to 13 years, and 14 to 16 years of age). Subjects were assessed again when they were 30 years old and Q-sorts were prepared for each subject. Boys rated as placid and controlled when they were 5 to 7 years had very conventional thought processes, regarded themselves as objective, and had relatively narrow interests at age 30. There is no obvious manifest similarity between the childhood behavior and the adult attitudes or cognitive dispositions. If we assume, however, that the placid-controlled boy is a heavily socialized child, with a strict set of inhibitions on nonconformity, then this specific stability over 25 years is theoretically reasonable.

Three Classes of Continuity in the Child. In summary, three different types of continuity are possible—complete continuity, heterotypic continuity, and homotypic continuity. When continuity is complete, both underlying psychological process and manifest form of behavior remain stable. This class of stability is most likely to occur after puberty when the rate of change of basic components of psychological organization is slowing down. The motives for group acceptance and mastery have become established, and the desire to match behavior to internalized standards is usually strong by early adolescence. The 13-year-old boy who is competitive and involved in athletics because of a desire to match behavior to a sex role standard is likely to display similar behavior a decade later. The desire to maintain congruence with sex role standards as well as the specific instrumental behaviors that gratify this desire remain stable for a long time. Complete continuity between times t_1 and t_2 is most likely to occur when (a) the t_1 observation occurred sometime after puberty, (b) the psychological process was operative at both ages (e.g., desire to maintain congruence with sex role standards; desire for social recognition; expectancy of hostility from others), and (c) the overt behaviors were not subject to inhibition or suppression because they violated age or sex role norms.

Heterotypic continuity can occur during any era of development as long as there is a core process that ties one epoch of development to the next. Heterotypic continuity occurs most often during the first decade, when response systems are changing rapidly. The child is learning more effective ways of gratifying motives, and family and peers are insisting that the child inhibit age and sex role inappropriate responses. The third class, homotypic continuity, is a form of "fool's gold." In this case the topography of the behavior remains stable, but the response is issued in the service of different motives, standards, expectancies, or sources of anxiety. There are several varieties of this species. Allport's (1961) concept of the functional autonomy of behavior is one variant. The old story of the man who goes to sea to avoid the stress of a harried home life and comes to adopt the mariner's way for 20 years contains, as its moral, the idea that one motive may initiate a particular act, but a different motive can maintain that act with no obvious break in display of the behavior. A related category includes the case in which a behavior is initially learned and maintained in the service of one motive, drops out of the behavioral repertoire for a period, and reappears at a later date in the service of a different set of forces. The earlier example of "crying" is illustrative of this class. The 6-month-old child typically cries to strange events. The 6-year old uses the cry as an instrumental strategy to avoid a coercive restriction; the 36-year old cries as a result of task failure. The events that released the act of crying are markedly different at each of these ages, and there is no compelling theoretical basis for expecting that the infant who cries easily to novel events will be the adult who will cry to task failure.

It may seem gratuitous to endow any status to homotypic stabilities that are not based on a stable underlying process. However, this is a rash judgment. The public reacts more to the behaviors it witnesses than to the hidden intentions it may infer. Behaviors are maintained for long periods of time by social reward and punishment, despite important shifts in basic expectancies, standards, motives, and sources of anxiety within the person. The uneasiness we feel toward the mica-thin mask of sincerity that dresses our culture reflects an acknowledgment that behavioral veneers can remain stable despite marked psychic changes within the organism.

Continuity in Mother's Behavior with Child. The discussion up to now has focused on continuities in the child's behavior, rather than continuities in the mother's actions. The relationship between mother and child is a delicate ballet. But it has been traditionally supposed that a mother's behavior with her infant was primarily a function of her motives, conflicts, and theories of child rearing. Continuity in the mother's behavior was assumed to be dependent on the stability of elements in her personality. This assumption is too simple. The mother's behavior is, of course, guided by her motives and anxieties, but it is also under the direct control of her child. The polar dimensions of maternal *acceptance-hostility* and *autonomy-restriction* have been studied with great fervor by American psychologists. Empirical evaluation of the continuity of these dimensions has not been impressive, although the evidence suggests better continuity for an acceptance-hostility attitude than for restriction-autonomy.

However, before drawing conclusions about these attitudes, let us analyze the meanings of these phrases. The operational definitions for maternal acceptance or rejection are probably different for various cultural groups. Mothers in the isolated rural areas of northern Norway rarely talk to their children, and move them away from doorways with an indifference that is characteristic of the treatment shown an out-of-place pair of shoes. An American psychologist would be prone to label this behavior as rejecting if he saw it in a middle class Chicago mother. But it may be a mistake to view this public act as indicative of rejection in the rural Norwegian mother.

Rejection is an attitude of dislike and hostility toward the child. It is not immediately obvious which specific behaviors should be regarded as the most sensitive operational indexes of that attitude. Thus, study of the continuity of a rejecting or accepting attitude will have to discover first the classes of behavior that reflect the attitude. They should differ across cultures and across age within any culture. There is likely to be minimal homotypic continuity of the behaviors, and, as a result, assessment of the continuity of the attitude requires first a solution to the problem of the relation between the attitude and the behavior.

The restrictive-permissive dimension is usually defined in terms that are closer to concrete behavioral events. The controlling mother is defined by her behavior; she consistently punishes deviations from her standards, prevents the child's exploration of new areas, and punishes excessive independence of action. However, the degree to which a mother controls her child is, in part, a function of the degree to which he *requires* control. The mother-child dyad is a feedback system in which the mother typically reacts to the child in a way that is congruent with her internalized ideal for him. If the child's attributes are congruent with the mother's ideal, her control will be less firm than if his characteristics deviate from her standards. The mother's contemporaneous behavior toward her 5-year old, therefore, is often the reaction to his behavior at that time or during the previous 12 months, rather than an early antecedent of the behavior he is displaying.

Aside from Schaefer's suggestion that the attitude of affection-hostility is more stable than restriction-autonomy from infancy through preadolescence, there has been very little study of the mother over relatively short time periods in order to establish the forms that continuity of attitudes or behavior might take. A recent report by Moss (1967) is a rare exception. Moss observed mothers and infants at 3 weeks and 3 months in the natural context of the home. He recorded a variety of discrete behavioral categories during a typical day. The maternal behaviors that showed the greatest stability between 3 weeks and 3 months involved social contact with the infant (affectionate contact yielded an r of .64; looks at infant yielded an r of .37; talks to infant yielded an r of .58; smiles at infant yielded an r of .66). Communicative contact with the infant is a common theme in these actions. The maternal behaviors that showed minimal stability were: holding the infant distant, total amount of holding of the infant, burping the infant, and stressing the musculature of the infant. These reactions were less stable because they were elicited by the infant and became less frequent with age. The 12-week-old child requires less close, physical handling than the 3-week old and the decreased maternal contact is clearly a function of the child's decreasing need for such ministrations. Moreover, the 3-week-old boys cried more than the girls, and, consequently, elicited more physical contact from mothers. However, the mother had extinguished her "tending" behavior by the time the boy was 3 months old, presumably because she learned that her son was not easily quieted by her maternal nurturance. His refusal to quiet led her to desist in her attempts to placate him. As a result, stability of this maternal action was minimal. Maternal contact with the infant in order to minister to his needs is not stable because the mother's behavior is controlled, in large measure, by the infant. If he changes dramatically over time, so does the mother's behavior.

The tendency to smile and vocalize to the infant is more closely tied to the mother's motives, for her tendency to bend and smile is less under the control of his actions than is her tendency to hold, diaper, and rock. And there is better continuity for the former behaviors. Other examples of the infant's power to shape the mother are seen in Schaffer and Emerson's (1964) assertion that some infants like being "cuddled," while others resist this care. The mother's tendency to fondle the infant is related to the child's receptivity to these actions. The dialogue between mother and infant is subtle. Stabilities in maternal behavior depend on the degree to which the child's behavior controls the mother and the degree to which these infant acts change over time. If the child's behavior remains relatively stable, the mother's behavior is likely to do the same. Since the child undergoes dramatic shifts during the opening year of life, one should not expect marked homotypic stability for many maternal behaviors during this period.

Conditions Favoring Continuity or Discontinuity. There are three hypotheses that relate to the three classes of continuity discussed above.

Principle 1: Homotypic continuity is likely to be less common during the first 10 years of development than heterotypic continuity. The form and eliciting conditions of behavior change so dramatically during the early years of life that continuity of early behaviors such as crying to separation, tantrums to frustration, or withdrawal from a stranger is not to be expected. The major motives and sources of anxiety of 2-year olds center around desire for the mother's presence, nurturance, and preservation of the familiar. The 10-year old, on the other hand, is principally concerned with power, congruence with sex role standards, mastery of instrumental competencies, and acceptance by peers. These critical developmental differences in hierarchy of motives militate against strong evidence for complete or homotypic continuity. However, there is some evidence suggesting the presence of congenital or early acquired predispositions toward passive-withdrawal versus active attack to stress or threat. If this intraindividual dimension were stable it would have different manifest forms during the first decade and would more likely show heterotypic than homotypic stability.

Principle 2: Discontinuity in behavior and internal process is most likely to follow major changes in the psychological ecology of the child, such as birth of a sibling, alteration in the family structure (i.e., divorce, separation), or school entrance.

Principle 3: There are critical juncture points in development where reorganization of behavior and process are likely to occur. Heterotypic discontinuities are most likely to occur at these nodal points. One such node is the period around the second birthday—between 18 and 24 months. Language becomes a dominant mode of interaction with and interpretation of the environment at this time. The child's commerce with objects and events becomes dominated by his symbolic labeling of them, and assimilation of new experience contains a large language component. The child under 2 years who has been motorically advanced and psychologically alert has probably been well adapted to his environment. This child may suddenly become less well adapted if he is growing in an environment that does not stimulate his language development. Adults now begin to expect symbolic reactions, not only sensorimotor coordinations. A child who has been motorically retarded, on the other hand, may suddenly become alert, and appear intelligent because he is in an environment where his language development has been accelerated. There is no strong relation between level of precocity of sensorimotor coordinations during the first year and quality of language resources at 3, 6, or 12 years; no homotypic continuity between adaptive motor skills during infancy and symbolic resources during the school years. It is unclear as to whether there is any heterotypic continuity over this period, and, if so, what the nature of these continuous processes might be.

A second focus of discontinuity occurs between 5 and 7 years of age. Most children undergo a marked change in quality of cognitive functioning at this age. The changes seem to relate to the tendency to inhibit irrelevant acts and to select appropriate ones; the ability to maintain set on a problem; the appreciation of the requirements of a problem. S. H. White (1966) has summarized some of the major psychological and biological events that change during this short period. The child stops adopting position habits in his solution of problems and develops his own sense of left and right. Reversals in letters and forms become less frequent and the child is now able to detect the simultaneous touching of both face and hand. He becomes more planful in his play and in his attack upon problems. One of the processes common to many of these changes is an increase in reflection, an increased tendency to pause to consider the differential validity or appropriateness of a response, the ability to select the right response rather than emitting the one that happens to sit on top of the hierarchy when an incentive stimulus appears. This natural shift toward increased reflection, selection, and ease of attention maintenance is demanded by the school as well as the family environment. The child who is not capable of adopting this reflective posture will encounter more negative sanctions for his impulsive actions than he did during the preschool years. The child who has difficulty maintaining appropriate inhibition because of central nervous system deficit or intense psychological conflict will have to develop a new set of defenses to attenuate the anxiety that will inevitably occur. These new defenses are likely to lead to discontinuities. It is interesting to note that these psychological changes are accompanied by changes in biological processes. The juvenile growth spurt occurs at this age. The amplitude of the visual evoked potential rises until age 6, and then begins to plateau. Finally, children suffering from convulsive seizures during childhood are commonly given medication until about 6 years of age, for this is the time at which febrile convulsions tend to disappear. It is hopefully more than coincidence that the changes in psychological functioning are paralleled by equally dramatic changes in biological parameters during this 24-month period.

Another characteristic of the period between 5 and 7 years is the common observation that the 5-year-old child's veneer of defenses against anxieties is thin, and evidence of serious sources of anxiety is usually visible. The preschool child who is anxious over separation shows it by clinging to his parent and protesting his reluctance to leave the home or the familiar. Children who are anxious over violation of cleanliness, sexual, or aggressive standards will exhibit a tension that is obvious to most observers. During the next three or four years, however, defenses grow rapidly, and although the basic conflict may still exist, the behavioral topography of the child does not always reveal the hidden problem. Children who are manifestly frightened, withdrawn, or regressed at age 5 sometimes appear relatively mature and minimally anxious at 10 years of age. The behavioral profile has changed dramatically. For some, however, the underlying process has not been altered to an appreciable degree. When a serious stress is imposed, the conflict is revealed.

SPECIFIC CONCEPTIONS FOR THE PRESENT RESEARCH

Curiosity as to the meaning of variability in selected infant behaviors and the differential stability of these reactions was the basic incentive for this investigation. As a result, we assumed the attitude of a naturalist, focused on a specific set of goals, but always listening with the third ear, prepared to note unsuspected invariants whenever they appeared and perpetually vigilant for surprises. This general aim was supplemented by three specific *a priori* issues that guided our procedures. These involved (a) a search for early anlage of reflection-impulsivity, (b) sex differences in psychological organization, and (c) social class correlates of cognitive development. Elaboration of each of these themes will help the reader appreciate the design of the study.

Conceptual Tempo and Reflection-Impulsivity. The dimension called reflection-impulsivity describes the child's decision time and quality of performance when he is faced with a problem that has many solution alternatives (i.e., response uncertainty). Some children and adults are impulsive; they arrive at and report their decision quickly and typically make more errors than the reflective who broods an excessive amount of time about the validity of his solution hypothesis. The longer decision times of the reflectives are typically accompanied by more accurate performance.

Most of the empirical work that has involved school age children indicates that the tendency to be reflective or impulsive generalizes across a variety of tasks, as long as the task contains response uncertainty (Kagan, 1966a). The short-term stability of the reflection-impulsivity dimension is illustrated in a study in which second grade children were tested for 10 weeks successively on variations of the Matching Familiar Figures Test in which the number of variants was increased by 1 each week. The first week the child was shown a standard and 2 variants, the second week a standard and 3 variants, and so on until the last week when the child was shown a standard and 12 variants. The average correlation for response time across the 10 weeks was $+.70$. The reflective children remained reflective, the impulsive children remained impulsive across the 2½-month period (Yando & Kagan, 1970). This classification also displays long term continuity. A group of 104 boys and girls in grades 3 or 4 were individually administered one version of the Matching Familiar Figures and a different version one year later. The correlation between response time on the two administrations averaged .62 (Kagan, 1966a). A third study of stability involved 102 children who were given the Matching Familiar Figures Test in their first year of school and tested again 1 and 2½ years later. The stability correlation over the 1-year period was .50; over the 2½-year period it was $+.31$. The tendency to display fast or slow decision times to this response uncertainty problem is moderately stable among school-aged children (Messer, 1968).

Generality of the Dimension. The correlations between response time on this Matching Familiar Figures task and decision time on a Haptic Visual Matching Test were consistently high across many samples of children in the first three grades (Kagan 1965, 1966a); correlations for response time on each task ranged from .61 to .87. The tendency to show long versus short decision times in selection of a hypothesis also generalizes to tasks in which the child must generate his own hypotheses. Ink-line drawings of incongruous scenes were presented tachistoscopically to a group of young children in the second and third grades. Each child made a minimum of 108 descriptions across all 6 scenes and the response latency from exposure of picture to first significant verbalization was recorded. Response time on the tachistoscopic recognition task was positively correlated with response time to the MFF ($r = .40$, $p < .01$) (Kagan, 1965).

Impulsive children are more likely to make errors of commission in a serial recall task while reflective children rarely do so. Impulsive children make more errors in reading English prose than reflective children, and the multiple correlation with word errors as a criterion and verbal IQ and response time on the Matching Familiar Figures as separate predictors was +.51 for boys and +.59 for girls. The reflection-impulsivity dimension also predicted errors on inductive reasoning problems. First grade children previously classified as reflective or impulsive were given tests of inductive reasoning. On one test the child was told three attributes of an object and he had to guess the object (e.g., What is yellow, melts in the sun, and you eat it? What has doors, wheels, and moves?). In a second procedure the child was shown three pictures in a fixed order that portrayed the beginning of a story sequence. The child was then given four pictures and asked to select the one picture (from the four) that illustrated the next thing that was most likely to happen in the story. On both procedures the impulsive children responded more quickly and made more errors than the reflective children (Kagan, Pearson, & Welch, 1966).

Studies of the eye-tracking patterns of reflective and impulsive children are consonant with the suggested interpretation of their molar behavior. Reflective children are more likely to make homologous comparisons than impulsives. A homologous comparison is a visual comparison of similar details across the variants (the dog's tail in variant 1 is compared with the tail in variant 2). Reflective children tend to examine all the variants before responding, whereas the impulsive children look at only one or two, and then offer a solution (Drake, 1968). The reflectives are generally cautious and explore all alternatives before offering a solution; the impulsives adopt a much riskier strategy. The impulsive child's graphic reproductions are less complete and he is likely to omit from a drawing of a house a detail he reported orally when asked to describe the picture. The impulsive child talks faster and will answer a question posed in a natural conversation with greater haste than a reflective.

The major determinants of the reflection-impulsivity dimension are presumed to be anxiety over error and height of standards surrounding quality of performance on problem tasks. A child who has high standards and is afraid of making a mistake will be reflective; a child who has low standards and is not anxious over failure will be impulsive. Lower class children are generally less fearful of making a mistake on intellectual tasks and are usually more impulsive than middle class children. Even within a lower class sample, impulsivity is negatively correlated with school achievement (Cohen, 1969). We wished to ascertain, first, how early one might detect signs of anxiety over error, and to determine if these early signs were predictive of the reflection-impulsivity dimension in the 2-year-old child. We also believed that there were subtle biological bases of reflection-impulsivity that were operative during infancy and potentially predictive of this dimension. There is some evidence for this speculative conjecture.

The literature on human behavioral genetics is scattered and it is difficult to find major islands of agreement across investigations. One generalization, however, continues to be confirmed in independent studies. A tendency toward inhibition versus spontaneity shows replicable heritability (see Gottesman, 1963). In general, identical twins are more similar in degree of inhibition than fraternal twins (Scarr, 1966) and the processes that mediate this inhibition-spontaneity dimension may share variance with those that produce an extreme degree of reflection or impulsivity. Reflection is the result of an inhibition of the reporting of a first hypothesis and a subsequent search for a better solution.

An encounter with a new situation usually activates an immediate response. Some children act on this first hypothesis; others acknowledge its possible relevance but inhibit it and search for a more appropriate response. This disposition is potentially relevant to a variety of situations, including the duration of involvement with a toy and habituation of attention. The child who activates a representation of some terminal state that might be effected with a toy is likely to continue playing with the object until that end state is reached. Hence he is likely to continue his involvement longer than a child who does not generate some goal to be reached. The latter child's play is typically guided by the superficial characteristics of the object. A piece of clay is broken into smaller pieces and then left. But the child who activates a representation of a horse may begin sculpting the clay into that form. This dimension may also be relevant to rates of habituation to meaningful visual events that do not permit manipulation. The child who relates an external event to a richly articulated representation of the stimulus—that is, a schema—may maintain interest longer than one who reacts to the stimulus primarily on the basis of its physical qualities.

These speculations led to the hope that differences in duration of continued attentional involvement with objects or visual stimuli during the first year would be partially predictive of the reflection-impulsivity dimension during the third year of life. Earlier work at the Fels Research Institute had revealed individual differences among 6- and 12-month-old infants in the duration of attention to visual stimuli and duration of sustained attentional involvement with a toy. These tendencies showed moderately positive associations. Some infants terminated involvement rapidly to both visual stimuli and toys; others maintained interest on both. Our hope was that the latter group would be more likely to show a reflective posture during the preschool years. Some support for this notion came from the longitudinal study of Pedersen and Wender (1968) mentioned earlier. The 2½-year-old children who spent long times involved with toys did well on the performance scales of the Wechsler Intelligence Scale for Children. It was suggested that their better performance scores resulted, in part, from a reflective tempo. The concern with duration of involvement in play and duration of sustained attention to visually presented stimuli during the first year was based on the hope that these variables would share some variance with the conceptual tempo dimension assessed during the preschool and early school years.

Sex Differences in Early Infancy. The remarkable change in the behavioral scientist's attitude toward the etiology and significance of sex differences parallels the change in attitude toward the role of biological factors in the development of language and the origins of severe psychopathology. Environmental shaping had been viewed as the sole cause of sex differences in behavior. But psychology has suddenly witnessed a strong swing favoring biologically based differences in the organization and patterning of response systems. The female is more resistant to mortality following serious disease and more males die during each decade of life than females (Hamburg and Lunde, 1966). Moreover, matching for birth weight, more male premature infants die in the first weeks of postnatal life than females (Braine et al., 1966). These sex differences in biological integrity may result, in part, from the female's extra X chromosome. The second X could protect the female against lethal alleles on the X that are recessive, for the female has a possibility of being heterozygous, while the male will display the effect if he carries the recessive allele. The hypothesis of genetic mosaicism in the female (i.e., half of the somatic cells have a paternal X active; the other half a maternal X active) would attenuate the seriousness of any disease producing locus on the X chromosome. There is evidence that this occurs in several blood diseases, which are more often fatal among males than females.

The concern with unlearned sex differences in behavior comes, in the first instance, from observations of primates in natural settings and, in the second, from dramatic changes in animal behavior produced by hormone balance experiments (see Maccoby, 1966; Jensen, Bobbitt, & Gordon, in press). Observers have reported consistent differences in dominance behavior in infrahuman primates, even when the animals are raised in isolation and have no opportunity to learn these habits directly or through modeling. Infant male rhesus become independent of their mothers earlier than females, and it appears that the mother helps to establish this earlier independence by turning away from her male infant more often (Jensen, Bobbitt, & Gordon, unpublished). Moreover, male macaques seemed more influenced by early privation than females, and exhibited more biting, hitting, and grabbing of the mother (Jensen, Bobbitt, & Gordon, in press).

Sex differences in initial response hierarchies lead to different reactions to the same environmental intrusion. Castrated male mice respond to the injection of androgen with increased fighting; castrated females do not show increased fighting, but display increases in components of mating behavior (Tollman & King, 1956). And either normal or castrated female rats are more likely to build a nest than normal or castrated males, following exposure to young pups (Rosenblatt, 1967). At the human level there is evidence suggesting earlier orienting to people and more intense signs of fear in the young female than in the male (Collard, unpublished). Although one might explain these differences on the basis of social exposures it is possible that thresholds for fear reactions are different in the female. When five pure strains of mice were subjected to 200 avoidance conditioning trials, the female of every strain made more successful avoidances than the males (Collins, 1964).

At a more subtle level of analysis, Jay (cited in DeVore, 1965) reports that in the langur of North India certain vocalizations are more common in one sex than in the other. The sound made by grinding of canines and the sound that resembles a "belch" are observed more frequently in males; the squeal and the scream more common in females. Hall and DeVore report that among baboons, the bark and the roar in time of threat are typically observed in males, not females; the muffled growl observed in estrous females but not in males. Particular facial-motor patterns also show sexual dimorphism. Grinding of teeth and "grinning" during copulation are common among males, but rare among females. Of 47 motor responses observed in the baboon, 14 were more frequent in the male and rare or absent in the female; whereas only 2 were preferentially displayed by the female. This difference suggests that distinct motor patterns displayed in time of excitement, threat, courtship, or pleasure may display sexual dimorphism, with skeletal motor reactions more likely to index special psychological states in the male than in the female. This idea corresponds with the observation that 6-month-old boys are more likely to reach behind a barrier to obtain an attractive object. The girls more typically look away from both barrier and object (Kaye, 1969).

Thus, sex differences in rate of development, vulnerability to disease, prepotent response patterns, and threshold for fear have some empirical support. The obvious sex differences in the behaviors of preschool boys and girls are partially the product of differential socialization. But it is possible that the hierarchy of responses displayed during the first year may have biological determinants and exert more than a trivial influence on the socialized behaviors displayed later.

Sex differences in older children and adults have been documented many times and more often involve patterning of responses rather than mean scores. A typical finding is that boys and girls have similar means and standard deviations on a set of test scores, but the patterns of inter-correlations among the variables are different. These pattern differences are often difficult to interpret. For example, girls and boys have equivalent error and time scores on the Matching Familiar Figures. However, the error scores are generally independent of social class and IQ for boys, but correlate about —.30 for girls. The data to be reported later reveal many other examples of this phenomenon.

There are two possible interpretations of sex differences in patterning of variables. One possibility is that the responses have different meanings. A girl may obtain good grades in order to please her mother; a boy in order to prove his masculinity. An infant girl may vocalize when she is excited by new stimulus events; an infant boy when he is restless.

A second possibility is that a particular event influences different response systems in the sexes, although the central process is the same. To illustrate, threat to self-esteem leads preferentially to withdrawal in the girl, but to aggressive attack in the boy. The favored explanation of this difference is that the sexes have learned different ways of dealing with anxiety. However, discovery of sex differences in preferred reaction pattern during the early weeks of life would imply basic differences in the organization of responses.

Different reactions within a species to the same environmental intervention are common in work with animals (Fuller 1967). As has been noted earlier, terriers who have been reared in isolation and who are normally active, show a major increase in activity following removal from isolation. Beagles, who are normally less active, show a decrease. The experience of isolation amplified the genetic differences in activity displayed by dogs raised under normal conditions. The studies of pure-bred mice strains yield comparable results. Each strain has a prepotent set of responses to varied conditions and an experimental intrusion produces different behavioral effects. If we had a clearer understanding of the differential hierarchy of responses in males and females we might be better able to interpret the empirical data. The present research hoped to provide some information on this issue. If response organization is fundamentally different in the sexes, study of the infant is a likely context to discover it before the overlay of acquired motives disguises the phenomenon.

A few *a priori* hypotheses about sex differences can be stated succinctly. Infant girls were expected to be cognitively precocious over boys because biological studies suggest that girls' physical growth is advanced

(Bayley, 1940). Girls were expected to show fear earlier and in more intense form because one of the occasions for anxiety is the detection of a discrepancy, and no available response to make to it. If the female infant is precocious perceptually, she should have a better articulated schema for events in her life space and, consequently, be more receptive to the detection of discrepancy. If she is too young to deal with the discrepant event, she will be subject to more frequent experiences of distress during the opening year of life. The girls' precocity may be paid for in more frequent bouts with fear. Girls were also expected to show earlier signs of language acquisition and less motor activity than boys.

Finally, we anticipated less variability on psychological dimensions for girls and, as a result, stronger relations between particular familial experiences and behavior among the girls. Physical growth studies suggest that there is less variability of many growth parameters for girls than boys (Acheson, 1966). If girls were less variable on psychological dimensions, the social environment would be acting on a more similar group of girls than boys. If there were fewer girls than boys who were extremely active, then there should be greater covariation for girls between a specific social experience and its expected effect on the child. Infants who are at the extremes of a temperamental dimension should react less predictably to a maternal action than those who are less extreme. Stated more concretely, an extremely lethargic child should be less responsive to a parent's smiling than an infant of average arousal. Consider the following analogy: a hand is to be placed on two pieces of clay. One lump is of homogeneous softness and pliability; the second of variable plasticity. Some parts yield easily, others with difficulty. If the hands come down on the clay with the same force they will make different impressions, and the homogeneous piece will take on a more faithful reflection of the force that was imposed on it.

The detailed study of a large group of firstborn, Caucasian boys and girls provided an opportunity to gather information on the pattern of sex differences during the first year. The belief that organization is different in the sexes led us, of course, to keep the sexes separate in all data analyses.

Environmental Correlates of Development: The Influence of Social Class. A final inquiry centered on the role of environmental experiences on cognitive structures and behavior. The search for the analge of conceptual tempo or early sex differences in patterning of behavior is essentially an intraorganismic issue that subordinates environmental forces. Developmental psychology is in a frustrating position; it believes that the caretaker's handling of an infant changes the infant's schema and behavior, but it is unable to state specific funcational relations because of inadequate data and weak theory. The early approach to this problem was bold, and would have been a major gain had it been successful. The strategy of the 1950's was to interview parents of preschool or school-age children—by questionnaire or face-to-face interview—and assume that any covariation between parent and child behavior was causal. After 20 years, it is apparent that this strategy has two flaws.

First, parents are poor informants of their contemporaneous behavior and even poorer reporters of their past reactions with their children. They unconsciously distort or forget details and often are totally unaware of actions that would be directly relevant to the child's development. A mother does not know how many times she hit her child; how inconsistent her response to the child's crying; how loud her voice when she chastised him; how often she smiled when he mastered a skill. Psychologists coded what the mother was able to report and concluded that these reported dimensions were central variables in the mother-child relationship. Such a conclusion reminds one of the amateur naturalist armed with fishnets that had holes 7 inches in diameter who, after collecting fish specimens for 6 months, concluded that the ocean contained no fish less than 7 inches long. A mother's memory of an event three years in the past bears too little relation to reality to be used with confidence. Robbins interviewed mothers of infants about their contemporaneous handling of the infant. Several years later, the mothers were again asked about specific behaviors during the infant period. There was little relation between the two reports. The mothers had forgotten what happened and when it happened. The distorted reports could best be understood if one expected the mothers' reports to be congruent with acceptable child-rearing practices (Robbins, 1963). One reason for our ignorance of the developmental dynamics of parent-child interaction rests with methodological inadequacies (Radke, Yarrow, Campbell, & Burton, 1970).

A second problem is theoretical. Even if one observes a mother directly, her behavior at any moment is intimately tied to the reactions of her infant. As indicated earlier, nurturant behavior is often a reaction to the child's signals of distress. Since boys at 3 weeks sleep less and fret more than girls they tend to receive more contact and care than girls (Moss, 1967). The mother's attitudes about child rearing, her involvement with her baby, and her anxieties also determine her actions. Japanese mothers believe that babies must be quieted and soothed, and they hover around the infant, ministering to him at the slightest protest. American middle class mothers are afraid of creating a passive and spoiled baby and, therefore, leave him alone in his room, and allow him to cry a few minutes before soothing his distress. The two maternal patterns produce different habits and it is not surprising that American one-year-old children cry and vocalize much more than Japanese infants of the same age. Mother and baby shape each other in a sometimes harmonious, sometimes erratic dance (Caudill and Weinstein, 1966, 1969).

As the child grows and his behavior patterns become more fixed, the parents' behaviors increasingly become a reaction to the child rather than an initiated action. This phenomenon makes it impossible to infer causality from contemporaneous adult-child interactions. In a recent follow-up study, mothers of boys, who were 8 to 10 years old when the mothers were first asked about how early they emphasized independence and mastery training, were questioned about similar issues when the boys were 14 to 16 years old. There was a negative correlation ($r = -.39$) between encouragement of independence during early childhood and encouragement of similar behaviors during adolescence (Feld, 1967). If the mother's early encouragement had been successful the mother should have stopped "pushing." The mothers who had not accelerated their sons, on the other hand, might be responding to the boy's lack of independence with increased pressure at the later age. The parent's behavior toward the child at any given time is always partly controlled by the child's contemporaneous behavior.

A longitudinal design is therefore useful in research that seeks to determine familial antecedents. We have commented on this problem in earlier writings and suggested that only when the caretaker's behavior is clearly antecedent to the child's actions can associations between caretaker and child behavior be used as a theoretical base for positing a functional relation. The induction of even low level generalizations is an overwhelmingly complicated task, and no single investigation can do more than begin to provide a small slice of insight into this problem.

We made observations of the mother and child in the home when the infants were 4 and 27 months of age. The 4-month observations focused on a narrow range of mother-child variables, for the intent was to study the consistency and promptness of the caretaker's response to the child's distress, and the distinctiveness of the mother's vocal and tactile stimulation of the child. In addition we compared the development of children from various socioeconomic backgrounds for we assumed that caretaking practices varied with these backgrounds.

This is only one strategy that can be taken in elucidating cause-effect sequences in development. The best posture is to posit, *a priori,* a causal dimension and study its subsequent effects (e.g., the effects of prematurity, type of feeding, length of time with the mother). This attitude led us to code distinctive vocalization from mother to infant during the 4-month observations because face-to-face vocal interaction between mother and infant should have a major effect on the child's establishment of a face schema and his future vocalizations to human faces. This directed search for the effects of a class of experiences is the most desirable, but is only possible when there are strong hypotheses. If theory is weak, however, as is true of developmental theory, an inductive tactic can be useful. The inductive strategy states: pick criterion groups that are known to be divergent on critical dimensions in later childhood. Study the infants in these criterion groups before they display the criterial behaviors, and infer the invariant dimensions in the handling of infants that might help to explain the "to be developed" behavioral differences 3 or 4 years later.

There are several independent dimensions that could be chosen to establish criterion groups. Social class is the most relevant dimension for cognitive development. One of the most replicable findings in psychology is the association between social class, on the one hand, and school grades, IQ scores, or quality of performance on problem-solving tasks, on the other (Werner, 1968). Differences in quality of speech, vocabulary, comprehension, and number ability are awesome during the school years, but can be seen as early as 3 years of age. It is of more than casual interest to determine how early these differences can be detected and the pattern of the class differences.

Membership in a social class represents a continuing mosaic of experiences and it is not obvious which sets of conditions are most influential for intellectual variables. Previous work suggests a few generalizations. The poorer vocabulary of the lower class child seems to be a product of less extensive stimulation of language development. But it is not clear why the lower class child's motivation seems less intense, or why he performs less well on nonlanguage tasks. It is sometimes assumed that the lower class parent gives less praise for mastery of sitting, walking, standing, or problem solving than the middle class parent. As a result the development of a motive for mastery does not grow. It has also been speculated that a lower class parent does not provide the variety of experiences that middle class children encounter. These hypotheses are in need of verification and early observations of class differences in mother-infant behavior should be illuminating. One intriguing and enigmatic fact is that the correlation between social class and indexes of intellectual development is consistently higher for girls than for boys. On the one hand, the restricted variability attributed to the girls may lead to a more faithful effect of experience—the ball of clay analogy. But an alternative interpretation states that mothers of different social classes differ more in their handling of daughters than in their actions toward sons.

We chose to study the patterns of differential development in children from different class backgrounds with the hope that we might provide some beginning answers to the questions posed above.

The text that follows summarizes our attempt to study the development of a large group of children during the first few years in order to ask about continuities in development, sex differences in the patterning of responses, the correlates of social class, and anlage of conceptual tempo. These goals, however broad, constrained our perceptions, methods, and choice of response variables. We tried, however, to remain receptive to surprises and reasonably optimistic, trusting nature to reveal to us, if even briefly, a bit of the secret beauty of growth.

II

Methods

As indicated in Chapter I, the investigation centered on four basic themes: early anlage of conceptual tempo, class and sex differences in attentional processes, and continuities in cognitive development. The development of schemata for human faces and human forms during the first year was one of the critical variables under study and the degree of articulation of a schema for a face—or any event—is not always faithfully reflected in the infant's gross motor behavior. The single hypothesis that guided much of the procedural decisions was that events moderately discrepant from established schema would elicit special reactions different from those elicited by stimuli that either matched schema or were totally novel. The pattern of reactions to the transformation was presumed to be indicative of the degree of articulation of the infant's schema for the event. An infant with a poorly articulated schema for a face should produce different patterns of fixation, smiling, vocalization, activity, and cardiac deceleration to a photograph of a face than one with a well articulated schema. The absence of sensitive procedures for indexing the fragile and dynamic phenomenon of distribution of attention is one of psychology's most serious frustrations. The response variables chosen seemed appropriate on intuitive grounds as well as historical precedent.

The rationale for selection of stimuli followed from our concern with individual differences. We wished to determine which children were advanced and which retarded in the development of schema for familiar events. The stimuli had to fulfill two criteria—all children had to have frequent exposure to the stimulus class used, and the stimuli should be interesting. These two constraints made the choice of human faces and human forms reasonable, if not obvious. Previous work had demonstrated that during the period 4 to 13 months, human faces and human forms elicited more sustained attention than most other stimuli, certainly more than meaningless geometric designs, regardless of their degree of complexity or contour contrast (McCall & Kagan, 1967).We also hoped to study development of schema for speech and our procedures permitted measurement of the infant's reactions to human speech. The paradigm for the laboratory presentation of stimuli was simple and consistent. We presented the infant with a set of stimuli (usually four in a set) that represented a standard and several transformations of the standard. We quantified the infant's reactions to repeated, single representations of the members of this set.

The interest in conceptual tempo dictated the use of a free play situation in which mobility and tempo of the child's play were the variables of interest. A smaller group of infants was visited for a day in their homes when the infants were 4 months old during which time mother and child were observed, and visited for two days in their homes when the children were 27 months old. The purpose of these procedures was to see if particular patterns of maternal practices covaried with the child's behavior in the laboratory or with the social class of the mother.

The decision to begin the assessment at 4 months, rather than earlier, was based on evidence indicating that important changes in psychological functioning occur at about 12 weeks. These changes are accompanied by parallel developments in the biology of the central nervous system. The Moro reflex begins to vanish, the occipital EEG assumes voltages and rhythms that resemble those of the older child; the latency of the visual evoked potential approaches adult values (Ellingson, 1967). In addition, amount of crying decreases while babbling, cooing, and playing show dramatic increases between 12 and 16 weeks. The infant shows a clear appreciation of three dimensions and habituation to repeated events becomes a reliable phenomenon. Finally, the likelihood of eliciting a smile in response to a human face is greatest at 4 months across many cultural settings. These varied and profound changes, which occur between 8 and 12 weeks of age, suggest important reorganizations in central nervous system functioning. The brain seems to awaken and take control from more primitive systems. After 3 months, attention to external events should be more clearly a function of the relation of the event to acquired schema than of general alertness or the contrast value of the stimulus. Distribution of attention should be more obviously a cognitive phenomenon. Since development of cognitive functioning was the focus of our inquiry, 4 months seemed like a wise place to begin the exploration.

SAMPLE

The total sample consisted of 180 infants (91 boys and 89 girls), Caucasian, firstborn, and living within a 30-mile radius of Cambridge, Massachusetts. Fortunately there was little attrition during the first year and the total sample rarely dropped below 160 for the major variables. The range of educational level ran from 8 years through a graduate degree. The range of maternal ages was 17 to 38 with a median of 23 years. The profile of dominant religious affiliation for the families was 70% Protestant, 22% Catholic, and 8% Jewish. We divided our sample into four groups based primarily on educational attainment of the parents and secondly on occupation of father. When we refer to the child's social class in this report we shall be referring to these four levels of educational attainment. The lower middle class (LMC) consisted of families where one or both parents did not finish high school and neither parent had more than 12 years of education. In all cases the father was an unskilled laborer. There were 16 boys and 16 girls in the lower middle class group. The middle class$_1$ group (MC_1) consisted of parents who had graduated high school but not college. The father was employed as a skilled laborer or in a white collar job and there were 25 boys and 19 girls in this group. The middle class$_2$ group (MC_2) included parents who had attended or graduated college but who had no advanced degree. The father was typically an entrepreneur or employed in a white collar job (30 males and 31 females in this group). In the upper middle class group (UMC), both parents were college graduates and one or both were in graduate training or had an advanced degree. There were 20 boys and 23 girls in this group. Reference to the upper or lower half of the social class distribution in this text means that we were comparing LMC and MC_1 children with MC_2 and UMC children.

All the mothers were volunteers. Advertisements in local newspapers described a study of infant psychological development and invited the mother to call for information and an initial appointment. Many of the lower middle class group had to be solicited directly and persuaded to volunteer. The staff visited outpatient clinics, consulted published birth lists, and called on potential parents to enlist their cooperation. About a third of those solicited volunteered to cooperate. Thus the sample is neither random nor representative of the entire Boston area. However, if we assume that a mother who volunteers for such a project has a more than average interest both in her child and in science, we obtain a partial control on parental motivation. The mother was paid a nominal amount for each visit to the laboratory and her transportation expenses—typically a taxicab. Appendix Table 1 contains the descriptive statistics for the sample.

Each infant came to the laboratory at 4, 8, 13, and 27 months for a series of assessment procedures. Each infant was typically seen within 10 days of these dates. At 4 months of age the infant was placed supine in the crib illustrated in Figure 2-1; at 8 and 13 months the child sat in a highchair illustrated in Figure 2-2. We tried to minimize irritability and maximize alertness by bringing the infant to the laboratory following a nap and feeding and never testing a child unless both mother and staff thought he was alert and happy. If the infant became distressed during an episode, the episode was interrupted and not resumed until the child was once again in a positive state. If the interruption was only a few minutes long, the episode was resumed at the point where it was interrupted. If the child napped or was fed, then the episode was initiated from the

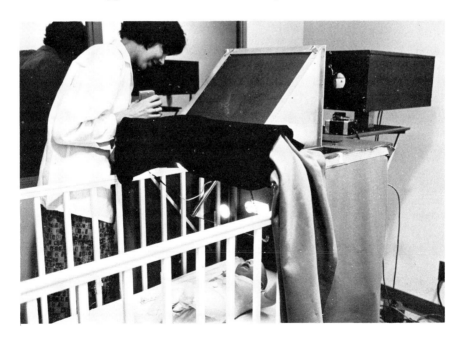

Figure 2-1 Apparatus for 4-month assessment.

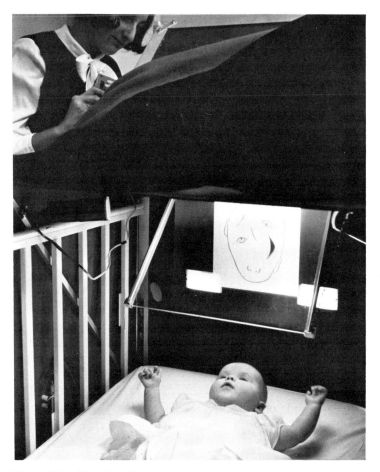

Figure 2-1 (Continued)

beginning. If the child continued to be irritable, the mother and infant went home and returned on another day. Interruptions were rare at 8, 13, and 27 months and were only a problem with the 4-month-old infants.

PROCEDURES AT 4 MONTHS

Two-Dimensional Faces. Each 4-month-old infant was first shown a series of 16 achromatic slides of human faces (4 presentations of 4 different faces illustrated in Figure 2-3). We shall refer to them in the text as PR (photo regular), SR (schematic regular), PS (photo scrambled), and

SS (schematic scrambled). PR was a photograph of a male face; SR was a schematic outline of a regular face; PS and SS were collages of the photograph and schematic regular faces. Each stimulus was presented for 30 seconds with a 15-second rest interval between each stimulus, during which the visual field was partially illuminated, (brightness of 2.5 footcandles). The stimuli were presented 20 inches from the plane of the child's face, measured 6½ × 8½ inches, and occupied a visual angle of about 20 degrees. The pictures were projected by a slide projector electronically programmed for the correct intervals of stimulus presentation and interstimulus periods. The 16 stimulus presentations were preceded by one "warm

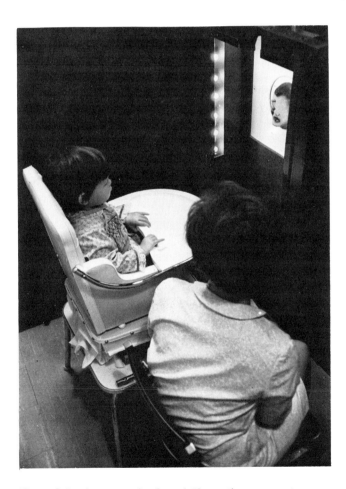

Figure 2-2 Apparatus for 8- and 13-month assessment.

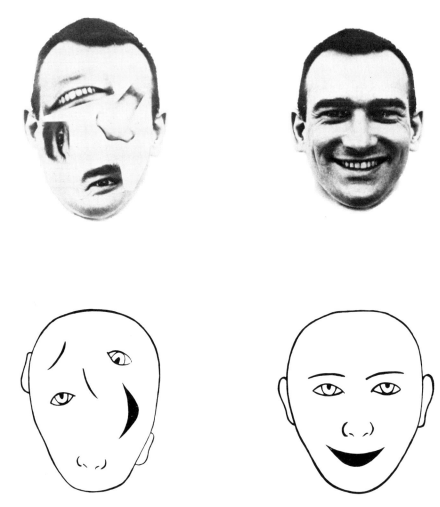

Figure 2-3 Achromatic faces shown at 4 and 8 months.

up" stimulus (an achromatic photograph of a male with one eye—a cyclops face). Two different orders of presentation were used.

Three-Dimensional Clay Faces. After a short recess (usually 5 minutes) the child was shown a series of different three-dimensional, sculptured faces ($4\frac{1}{2} \times 6\frac{1}{2}$ inches) painted flesh color (4 presentations each of 4 different faces, which are illustrated in Figure 2-4) in two different orders. We shall refer to them as REG, SCR, NE, and BL. REG was a *regular* male face; SCR was a *scrambled* representation of the face with eyes, nose

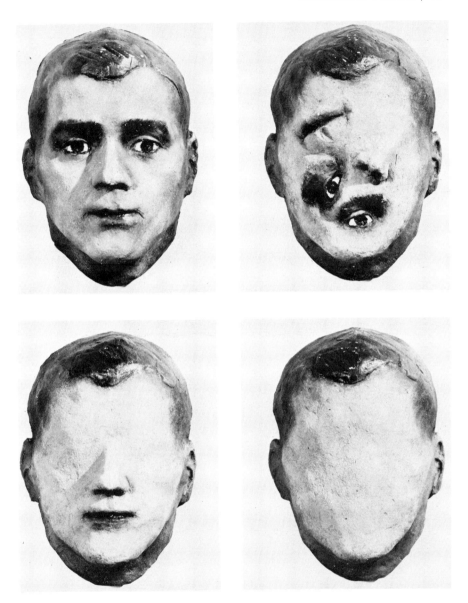

Figure 2-4 Three-dimensional clay faces shown at 4, 8, and 13 months.

and mouth rearranged; NE was a regular face with *no eyes,* and BL was a *blank* face with neither eyes, nose, nor mouth.

As in the two-dimensional episode, each stimulus was presented for 30 seconds with a 15-second rest interval between each stimulus during which the visual field was homogeneously white. This series was also preceded by a three-dimensional "warm up" stimulus which was an amorphous form. (Brightness was 1.6 footcandles and faces occupied a visual angle of 17 degrees.)

Variables Coded. The major variables coded during both visual episodes were: duration of each fixation of the stimulus, frequency of smiling, time vocalizing (positive babbling), time fretting or crying, and a continuous monitoring of the child's heart rate. The four behavioral variables were coded by two observers who were posted on either side of the child's crib looking through observer holes down on the child's face (see Figure 2-1), although the infant could not see the observer. Average interobserver reliabilities (across different infants) for each of these variables were high (.97 for fixation, .71 for vocalization, .86 for smiling, and .80 for fretting. A Grass polygraph equipped with a Lexington Instruments cardio-tachometer recorded the infant's heart rate. The major variable coded was the magnitude of the cardiac deceleration during the first fixation. This value was obtained by subtracting the three lowest heartbeats during the first fixation from the three lowest heartbeats during the five seconds prior to stimulus onset (or prior to the first fixation when first fixation did not coincide with stimulus onset).

Gross Motor Activity. The behavior of a small group of subjects (36 boys and 30 girls) was recorded on audiovisual tape during the administration of the two visual episodes. These infants comprised the last third of the sample since the audiovisual recorder was not in operation for the first 10 months of the study. We shall not give detailed consideration to these data. However, since they will be discussed briefly in Chapter VII, a word of explanation is in order. Three basic responses were coded as discrete variables: turning of the head back and forth, thrashing of the arms, and mass movements in which trunk and limbs moved simultaneously. Each infant was given a score for each stimulus according to the following code:

½ point: Nonvigorous thrash of one arm.
1 point: Turning of the head; vigorous thrashing of one arm; nonvigorous thrashing of two arms; nonvigorous mass movement.
2 points: Vigorous thrashing of two arms; vigorous mass movement.

Three independent female coders were used in the scoring of the records. Each infant received a score for the total administration of two-dimensional faces and another score for the three-dimensional faces. In order to attenuate the systematic biases in each coder's scores, each coder's distribution of scores was divided into quartiles. Infants in the lower quartile for a particular coder's distribution received a score of 1; infants in the second quartile, a score of 2; infants in the third quartile, a score of 3; and infants in the fourth or top quartile, a score of 4. Each S, therefore, received a score of 1, 2, 3, or 4 for each of the two visual episodes.

PROCEDURES AT 8 MONTHS

Each infant came to the laboratory with his mother when he was 8 months of age and was subjected to four procedures in the following fixed order: two-dimensional faces, auditory sentences, three-dimensional faces, and a free play period.

Two-Dimensional Faces. The child was seated in a highchair behind a gray wooden enclosure that had lights on the top (see Figure 2-2). The child's mother sat to his right and slightly behind him and his face was eye level with the screen. The two-dimensional faces were the same achromatic slides the child saw at 4 months. In this case, each stimulus was presented for 15 seconds with a 15-second rest period between each stimulus. The stimuli were shown in the same order to all subjects (brightness was 2.1 footcandles, and faces occupied a visual angle of 17 degrees).

Three-Dimensional Clay Faces. Subjects were shown the same 4 faces for a total of 16 trials (4 illustrations of each stimulus). Each stimulus was on for 30 seconds (unlike the 15-second exposure for two-dimensional faces) with a 15-second rest period between each stimulus. All Ss received the same order. (Brightness was 1.9 footcandles, and the faces occupied a visual angle of 13 degrees.)

Auditory Episode. Between the administration of the two- and three-dimensional faces, a new procedure was presented. The child listened to a tape recording that contained 4 different recitations read by a male voice, each 20 seconds long with a 10-second silent period after each presentation. Each of the 4 episodes was presented 3 times for 12 trials. The order was the same for all children. The 4 episodes were: (a) a meaningful set of sentences read with high inflection: "Hi, baby; how are you, baby? Hi, smile for me. That's good, that's nice. Good baby. Come on, say Mommy, say Daddy"; (b) the same set of meaningful sentences read with *low* inflection; a set of nonsense words read either with (c) high inflection or (d) low inflection: "Og, sesalk; lof perks mit, sesalk? Og, mitlaf del em. Thef doog; thef skase; doog sesalk. Mok loo, yas yemal; yas logok."

The speaker baffle was located to the right of the child's head. Thus, the child had to orient his head in order to attend to the speaker, and this was noticeable to an observer.

Variables Coded. Two observers sat in front of the enclosure peering through portholes at the child's face. For the visual episodes, the variables recorded were: length of each fixation of the stimulus, vocalization, smiling, fretting, and cardiac rate. For the auditory episode, the variables coded were: orientation to the speaker, fretting, smiling, vocalization, and cardiac rate.

Gross Motor Variables. As at 4 months, a small group of infants (34 boys and 31 girls) were recorded on audiovisual tape. In most instances the subjects were the same ones recorded at 4 months. Three independent observers viewed the taped visual record and coded 5 different variables according to the following code:

½ point: Nonvigorous thrash of 1 arm
1 point: Vigorous thrash of 1 arm; nonvigorous thrash of 2 arms
2 points: Vigorous thrash of 2 arms; twisting of the body; rocking of the body; leaning out of the chair.

Each infant was assigned a total score for each of the 3 episodes. As at 4 months, each coder's distribution of scores was divided into quartiles and subjects assigned scores of 1 through 4 depending on the quartile into which their scores fell for each episode. The coders had no knowledge of the 4-month data when these records were quantified.

Free Play. Typically, a recess occurred after the auditory episode and before the administration of the three-dimensional faces. Following the administration of the three-dimensional faces, electrodes were removed from the child and he was taken to a room 11 × 11 feet in a different part of the building (see Figure 2-5). The room was marked off into 12 rectangles (3 × 3 feet). The mother was seated in a corner of the room and a standard set of age appropriate toys was arranged in a fixed order in a circle around the child. The toys were a wooden bug, a red plastic dog, a pail, a set of wooden blocks, a wooden mallet, a pegboard, a shaft of plastic quoits, a toy lawnmower, and a furry dog. The child was placed in the center of these toys which formed a circle around him, and was allowed to play for 15 minutes. His mother was instructed neither to talk to the child nor to interact with him unless he became upset.

The main variables coded were: number of squares traversed (index of locomotor activity), and the number of times the infant changed activities during the 15-minute free play episode. For the first 50 infants, continuous description of the infant's behavior was dictated into a tape recorder and the record transcribed verbatim. This manuscript was scored

Figure 2-5   Site of free play session at 8 and 13 months.

by two independent coders for number of act changes, where an "act change" was defined as a change in manipulative involvement from one toy to another. For example, if the child began the session by banging blocks, and then turned to manipulate the quoits, an act change was scored. Act changes were only scored when the infant initiated contact with one of the nine toys. Changes were not scored if the infant played with parts of his body or with his mother. Since the intercoder reliability was high ($r = .91$), act changes were scored as they occurred for the remaining subjects.

At the end of the play period, the mother was instructed to rise from her chair and leave the room, closing the door behind her. We coded the child's reaction to the separation for two minutes. The major variables of interest were occurrence of fretting or crying and the latency to these distress responses.

PROCEDURES AT 13 MONTHS

The assessment at 13 months included 3 visual episodes, the same auditory episode that was administered at 8 months, and a free play period in the same room with the same toys used at 8 months of age. As at 8 months, the infant sat in a highchair behind a large wooden enclosure, with his mother slightly to his right and behind him.

Episode 1: Human Forms I (HF I). The first episode contained 4 three-dimensional representations of an adult male (12 inches high $\times$ 3 inches wide) as illustrated in Figure 2-6. The four stimuli were regular man in trunks (REG); the same form with head placed between the legs at knee

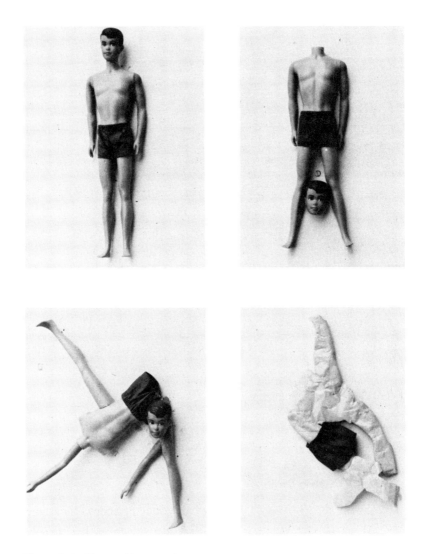

Figure 2-6 Human Forms I shown at 13 months.

level (HBL); the form completely scrambled with the limbs, trunk, and head in an asymmetrical arrangement (SCR); and a free form of the same general area, color, and texture as the three previous stimuli, but with no obvious resemblance to a man (FF) (see Figure 2-6). Each stimulus was shown for 20 seconds with a 15-second interstimulus interval during which the field was blank. Each stimulus was presented three different times, resulting in a total of 12 trials for the series. Three different orders of administration were used. The major variables coded were the same as those assessed at 8 months: duration of each fixation, vocalization, smiling, fretting, and cardiac deceleration during the first fixation.

Episode 2: Auditory Episode: Human Speech (AUD). The same 4 stimuli administered at 8 months were played to the children in the same order used 5 months earlier. Each stimulus was 20 seconds long with a 10-second silent interval between each stimulus. Orientation to the speaker, smiling, vocalization, and cardiac deceleration were coded during the entire episode.

Episode 3: Three-Dimensional Clay Faces (3D). After a recess of 10 to 15 minutes during which an infant was taken from the room and brought into a lounge area, he returned to the laboratory and was shown 5 different three-dimensional faces, 4 of which were identical to those shown at 4 and 8 months of age. The fifth face contained only a pair of eyes in the correct position, with nose and mouth absent. This stimulus was called Eyes Only (EO). Each stimulus was presented 3 times for a total of 15 presentations. Each stimulus was presented for 20 seconds with a 15-second period between presentations; 3 different presentation orders were used. The variables coded were the same as those listed for HF I.

Episode 4: Human Forms II (HF II). The last visual episode involved additional transformations of the male form used in Human Forms I. Three different transformations were prepared—a man with 3 identical heads (3H); an animal's head on the man's body (AH) and a human head on an animal's body (HH) (see Figure 2-7). Each stimulus was presented for 20 seconds with a 15-second rest period between each stimulus, and each stimulus was presented 3 times, 12 trials in all. As with HF I and three-dimensional faces, 3 different orders were used and the same variables were coded.

General Postural Variables. An audiovisual film record was made of the majority of the 13-month children, (56 boys and 55 girls out of a total of 160 cases had good audiovisual records at 13 months), and this record was used to code additional variables. A manual was prepared to allow quantification of two major classes of variables: (1) discrete motor acts that might index boredom, excitement, or interest, but requiring minimal inference by a rater; (2) ratings, for each episode, of activity, alert-

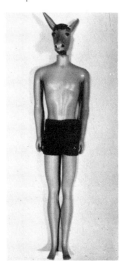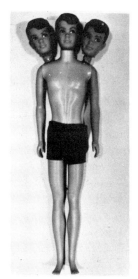

Figure 2-7 Human Forms II shown at 13 months.

ness, negative affect, positive affect, and habituation rate. The discrete postural categories are defined below.

Twisting: Child makes a *full body twist* either to the right or to the left involving the head and the trunk; if the child simply moved his head, a twist was not coded.

Arm waving: Child lifts one or two arms into the air and brings them down on the highchair, usually several times, but only once was necessary for coding.

Lean forward to stimulus: Child leans forward in the highchair while his eyes are fixated on the stimulus and points to or attempts to touch the stimulus. If the child was not looking at the stimulus when he leaned forward, this variable was not scored.

Quieting: Child noticeably decreases his level of motor activity when the stimulus is presented; the child stopped moving or stopped playing with an object, and attends to the stimulus.

The definitions of the *rating* variables appear below.

Activity: This rating was based on the frequency of motor activity during the session, taking into account the vigor as well as frequency of the activity. Scores of 1 to 1.4 reflected low or minimal motor activity; scores of 1.5 to 1.8, some periods of activity but a predominance of quiescence. Scores of 1.9 to 2.2 reflected a moderate flow of motor activity through most of the session; scores of 2.3 to 2.6 reflected some inactive periods but a predominance of frequent, intense motoricity; scores of 2.7 to 3.0 continuous, highly intense periods of motor activity.

General alertness: This rating indexed the child's overall sensitivity to the immediate environment, as inferred from his general reaction to change (i.e., child looks up when the stimuli are changed; child glances at the screen several times during the offset period; child reacts to an extraneous noise in the room, usually by quieting and becoming vigilant).

Negative affect: This rating assesses the child's irritability, dourness, fretting, or apprehension to the episodes, as inferred from frequency of crying and whining, or grimacing or whining in an attempt to leave the testing situation, or extended quieting unaccompanied by fixations, indicating boredom.

Positive affect: This rating measured the child's elation, humor, or excitement to the stimulus situation, as inferred from frequency and intensity of smiling and laughing, and intensity of pointing or leaning to the stimulus.

Speed of habituation: This rating indexes the rate at which the child became bored, as inferred from the rate of decrease in fixation time to succeeding stimulus presentations.

The coding of the audio-visual records was done by a graduate student (Fred Morrison) who had no knowledge of the child's social class, any of the earlier data obtained at 4 and 8 months of age, or any of the hypotheses of the investigator. All the coder knew at the time of the scoring was the child's sex and name. A sample of eight subjects was randomly selected to evaluate intercoder reliability of these variables and a second student independently coded the same variables. Interrater reliabilities were above $+.85$ for all variables.

Free Play. After a short recess during which the electrodes were removed the child and the mother went to the same playroom (11×11 feet square) used at 8 months and the child's behavior was observed for 17 minutes. The toys were the same ones used at 8 months and included: wooden bug, red plastic dog, pail, wooden blocks, mallet, pegboard, shaft of plastic quoits, toy lawnmower, and furry dog. As before, the room was marked off in 12 equal area rectangles in order to allow coding of locomotor activity (number of squares the child traversed). The mother sat in one corner of the room and was instructed not to interact with the child unless necessary. The major variables coded were: number of squares traversed, total number of times the child changed activities (act changes), the specific toys played with, and a description of each of the activities that were unusual, or nonstereotyped. After the 17-minute free play period, the mother, child, and toys were put on one side of the wire barrier which traversed the width of the room. On a signal the mother gently placed the child over the barrier. This episode lasted a maximum of five minutes but was terminated if the child became extremely upset. The major variables coded included: latency to fretting, latency to crying, and a description of the child's behavior.

PROCEDURES AT 27 MONTHS

Initially the examiner established rapport with the child and then attached electrodes in order to code heart rate telemetrically. The examiner attached two "bandaid" electrodes to the child's chest. These electrodes were connected to a 4 ounce telemetric heart rate receiver that was placed in a pouch and buckled on the child's back. After the child was relaxed, both mother and child were escorted to a large room decorated as a living room, one wall of which contained 4 large one-way mirrors (see Figure 2-8). Brown masking tape on the floor divided the room into 35 equal squares (3 × 3 feet).

Episode 1: Free Play. Mother and child were left in the room for an initial 5-minute adaptation period. At the end of this period 10 toys (musi-

Figure 2-8   Site of free play at 27 months.

cal toy, mallet, play dough, doll, wagon, colored wooden blocks, large clear plastic box, butterfly flutterball, plastic train, and toy rifle) were arranged in a standard pattern on the rug. *E* gave the mother two magazines and asked her to remain on the couch and not to initiate any interaction with the child, but to be as natural as possible within the constraint of these instructions. The mother and child were left alone for 30 minutes.

Coding: The major variables coded during the 35-minute adaptation and free play sessions were: (a) locomotor movement (number of squares traversed in each of the seven 5-minute time periods); (b) time in the 4 squares next to the mother; (c) time in physical contact with mother; (d) duration of each uninterrupted activity with the toys; (e) number of distinct acts; (f) verbalizations; (g) smiling.

Two observers independently coded the duration of each activity and the behavioral variables by depressing buttons attached to an Esterline Angus chart recorder. A third observer dictated a detailed account of the child's play onto magnetic tape. In addition, a television film record of the entire play session was recorded. The tape and television film record were used to check on the reliability of the observers and to settle any major differences in scoring between them. The reliability coefficients for the duration of each sustained activity for each of 20 children ranged from .72 to 1.00, with a mean coefficient of .97. Since these figures were inflated by the high agreement between coders on durations over 100 seconds, reliability coefficients were obtained for acts less than 100 seconds in length. The range of coefficients was from .64 to 1.00, with a mean coefficient of .88. The intercoder reliabilities for the other behavioral variables ranged from .89 to .95.

Episode 2: Distribution of Attention to Visual Stimuli. When the free play session was finished, the toys were removed from the room and the child was seated on a comfortable chair in front of a viewing screen. The chair was raised 18 inches from the floor by a black platform base that was approximately 10 feet from the screen. A KLH speaker was located immediately below the screen. The mother sat to the child's right and the examiner sat to the left and slightly to the rear of the child. The room was darkened and a series of 23 colored slides with accompanying narration were presented. Ten of the pictures contained either a visual or auditory violation (e.g., a man was wearing a bright red dress, a girl sleeping in a bathtub) but 13 stimuli were ecologically valid. Each stimulus was presented for 15 seconds; the first 7 seconds *without* an auditory accompaniment, the next 3 to 7 seconds with an auditory accompaniment, and the remaining 1 to 5 seconds again without auditory narration. There was a 4-second interstimulus interval.

Coding: An observer behind a one-way vision screen coded fixation of each stimulus, smiling, turning toward the mother, and turning toward the examiner. The examiner, who was sitting next to the child, wrote down all the child's verbalizations. Finally, the child's heart rate was monitored telemetrically throughout the episode. The behavioral variables of fixation time, smiling, and orientation to the adults were simultaneously recorded on chart paper with heart rate and fixation time on contiguous channels. Thus heart rate change could be quantified with respect to onset of fixation of the stimulus. Appendix Table 2 contains a description of the stimulus and accompanying narration.

Episode 3: Embedded Figures Test (EFT). After a juice "break," the *E* and child sat on small chairs at a table, with mother seated by the table. The examiner first taught the child the requirements of the task; namely, that he had to find a picture exactly like the standard. The test series consisted of 6 sets of figures. Each set contained the standard stimulus and 3 different sets of variants of increasing difficulty. There were 2 different types of perceptual problems. In the first 3 sets of figures (dog, horse,

Figure 2-9 Child being administered item from Embedded Figure Test.

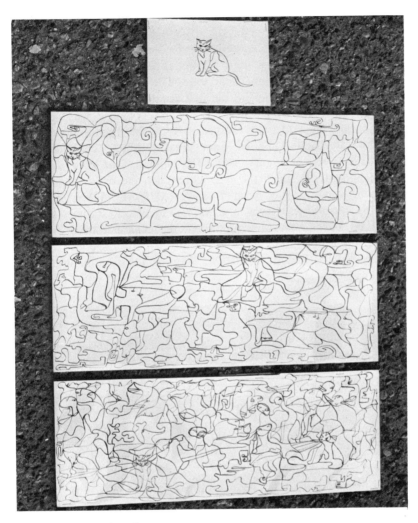

Figure 2-9 (Continued)

and bird), the problem was to match to a standard. Each illustration of variants contained a number of colored figures that resembled the model, but only one was identical to it. In the second set of 3 problems (cat, car, and flower) the model was a black and white line drawing *embedded* in progressively more noisy and complex backgrounds (see Figure 2-9). The child had to find the model in the embedded array. If the child was incorrect, the examiner asked the child to find a better one. The examiner continued until the child was correct or was reluctant to continue with the problem.

Coding: The major variables coded were: length of time the child looked at the stimulus before making his initial response, accuracy of the response, smiling or laughing, and heart rate. The only heart rate variable coded was degree of deceleration to the first scanning of the test stimulus. Intercoder reliability for response time to first response was so high ($r = .99$) that only one coder was used for most of the children.

Episode 4: Decision Time to Conceptual Conflict. The "conflict" apparatus is illustrated in Figure 2-10. The child had to learn to touch the yellow light and not touch the red light. When the child touched the yellow light, he was rewarded with a candy (M & M). When the child was wrong, no reward was given and he was incorrect. If the child did not seem to be learning the discrimination, the examiner tried in every way to combat position preferences or unique hypotheses. Once the examiner felt confident that the child was learning the discrimination she

Figure 2-10   Child in conceptual conflict situation.

switched to a fixed schedule of light presentation (Gellermann, 1933). When the child had made 5 consecutively correct trials, the conflict series began. The first conflict trial (called Negative 1) was a pair of red lights—a situation of uncertainty with no correct response. The child then received two standard red versus yellow discrimination trials, followed by a second conflict of two yellow lights (Positive 1); a second situation of uncertainty with both responses correct. Two more standard discriminations were presented followed by a pair of red lights (Negative 2); two more standard discriminations and then a second double yellow trial (Positive 2). There were two more standard discriminations, and then a double conflict in which two yellow and two red lights were presented simultaneously, one of each color on each side.

The response times to the conflict trials were reliably larger than the mean response time to the 5 criterion trials or to the immediately preceding nonconflict trials, indicating that this procedure was inducing conflict.

Coding: The variables coded were: duration of fixation of the lights before making each response (response time), and the accuracy of the response. These two variables were coded by only one observer from behind a one-way vision screen since intercoder reliabilities on an initial sample were high ($r = .99$).

Episode 5: Distribution of Attention to Human Forms and Faces. The child was taken from the living room to the same laboratory where he had been shown the forms and faces at 8 and 13 months. The first episode was Human Forms I (HF I); the second was the set of clay faces. Each series was administered as it was at 13 months. However, each stimulus was only shown twice rather than 3 times, as occurred at 13 months. The same 3 orders of presentation used at 13 months were used at 27 months and each child received the same order at 27 months that he had seen at 13 months.

Coding: The major variables coded for both episodes were: length of each fixation of the stimulus, smiling, cardiac rate, and a record of all the child's verbalizations.

VISIT TO THE HOME

Within two weeks of the laboratory session an observer who had no knowledge of the child's laboratory performance visited the mother and child at home on 2 separate days. Typically the total observation of the mother and child was 6 hours with a range of 4 to 7 hours. The observer, who was known to these mothers for over 2 years, easily established rapport with them. She told the mother she was going to observe the child's behavior in the home and the mother was to act naturally and enter into her normal duties. The observer wrote down, in detail, all sequences involving a child's violation of a socialization standard set by the mother, or classified *a priori* by the experimenters as a socialization standard. The standards included: aggression, violation of the integrity of household goods, cleanliness, toileting, intrusion into the mother's activity, explorations, excessive dependence, tantrums, genital play, disobedience, inappropriate table manners, or placing himself in a physically dangerous context. In addition, maternal commands and the child's reactions to these commands were recorded. We recorded the mother's reactions to the child's violations of socialization standards, including verbal prohibitions, facial or bodily communication of punishment, threat of loss of love, removing the child or the object, ignoring the child, acts intended to encourage the child, and the child's counterreactions.

Vocabulary Tests. Some time during one of the visits to the home 2 vocabulary tests were administered. The first was a vocabulary recognition test composed of 22 items in which the child had to choose among 3 alternatives. He was presented with 3 colored pictures, each on a 6 × 3½ inch laminated card, and asked to touch the object named by the examiner (e.g., pictures of a knife, fork, and spoon were presented and the child was asked to "touch the fork"). Full credit was given only when the child touched the correct picture first, and half credit given if he touched the correct picture second. The vocabulary naming test was composed of 15 items in which a single colored picture on a 6 × 3½ inch laminated card was shown to the child. The examiner asked the child, "What is this?" Examples include a key, a policeman, and a zipper. Full credit was given only when the child responded accurately first. Half credit was given if, after an initially incorrect response, the child responded accurately or if any answer was close to accuracy, for example, "coffee" or "broken" for broken coffee cup; "man" for a policeman, "light" for a light socket. Maximum possible scores on the vocabulary recognition and naming tests were 22 and 15 respectively. (Test items appear in Appendix Table 3.)

TREATMENT OF DATA

The primary behavioral data at 4, 8, 13, and 27 months (fixation time, vocalization, smiling, fretting) were continually recorded on chart paper moving at a fixed speed. All time scores (fixation, vocalization, fretting) were reduced to the nearest half-second. Smiling was coded as a discrete variable and magnitude of cardiac deceleration was assessed directly from the polygraph charts. Since fixation time and the heart rate data appeared in spatially contiguous channels, it was easy to restrict the deceleration index to first fixations. Appendix Table 4 contains the maximum sample sizes for the major variables at the first three ages.

The entire corpus of data was, of course, enormous and frequent checks were made for reliability of scoring. Every heart rate record was checked by an independent coder in order to insure that the deceleration values were reliable. All raw scores were put on punch cards and the distribution parameters for each variable examined. On the basis of these distributions and theoretical considerations a set of primary variables was constructed and placed on magnetic tape for computer analyses. The major analyses on the entire sample made use of product moment correlations within and across ages; analyses of variance, t-tests and occasionally, chi-square tests. On several occasions, extreme groups on one variable were compared on a second variable. Most of the time we selected the top and bottom thirds of one distribution, less frequently the top and bottom quartiles, and compared the reactions of these extremes on another independent variable. The choice of where to cut the distribution was determined after an examination of the distribution of scores on the cutting variable, and without knowledge of the scores on the other, dependent variable. Selection of cutting points was controlled by the natural division in the values. In no case did we compute the differences for all possible cutting points and then select the division that produced the most significant results. In all analyses of extreme groups the division described in the text was the only one computed. All probability values reported in the text are for two-tailed tests.

III

Fixation Time

The intuitively obvious and most public index of attentiveness in the visual mode is orientation toward an event. The duration of the initial fixation seems to be a more sensitive index of the interest value of a stimulus than the length of succeeding fixations; but total fixation time is likely to reflect the power of the stimulus to maintain the child's attention. Fixation time, like any response, has multiple determinants and the power of each changes with age. High rate of change (physical contrast or movement), discrepancy from schema, and activation of hypotheses are three such determinants that assume differential salience during the first 2 years of life.

THE FIRST DETERMINANT OF FIXATION TIME: CONTRAST AND MOVEMENT

Ontogenetically, the earliest determinant of duration of orientation to a visual event is inherent in the structure of the central nervous system. The infant naturally attends to events characterized by a high rate of change in their physical characteristics. Stimuli that move, have discrete elements, or possess contour contrast are most likely to attract and hold a newborn's attention. Hence, a 2-day-old infant is more attentive to a moving or intermittent light than to a continuous light source; to a design with a high degree of black-white contour contrast than to one of homogeneous hue (Berlyne, 1958, Haith, 1966; Salapatek & Kessen, 1966; Fantz, 1966; Fantz & Nevis, 1967; Carpenter, 1969). The newborn's visual behavior seems to be guided by the following rules:

1. If alert, and light is not too bright, eyes open up.
2. If eyes open but see no light, search.
3. If see light but no edges, keep searching.
4. If see contour edges, hold and cross them. (Haith, 1968.)

The behavioral addiction to contour and movement is concordant with neurophysiological studies of ganglion potentials in vertebrate retinas, which indicate that some ganglion cells respond to movement, some to onset of illumination, others to offset, and others to both. Contour edges should be "attention getting" for the sharp change in stimulation created by an edge elicits specialized firing patterns that should produce both orienting and sustained attention (Kuffler, 1952, 1953).

Hubel and Wiesel, (1959, 1962) have shown, further, that neurons in the striate cortex subtend retinal fields in the cat's eye and have "on and off" areas that are mutually inhibitory. These cells behave in a way that would lead to increased contrast between a figure and its background as a result of mutual inhibition of the center and the periphery. These neurophysiological data imply that the infant should be attracted to the eyes of a human face because of the sharp contrast between iris and sclera.

The infant's preference for contour is monitored by the size of the object for there is an optimal area that maintains attention at a maximum. Four-month-old infants exposed to meaningless achromatic designs with varied perimeters were most attentive to the moderately large designs (McCall & Kagan, 1967) and, among young infants, duration of fixation to a meaningless achromatic design is a curvilinear function of the square root of the absolute amount of black-white border in the figure (Karmel, 1969).

There is some controversy over whether contour or complexity exerts primary control over attention in the early months, where complexity is defined in terms of either redundancy or variety in the figure. Existing data support the more salient role of contour over complexity. McCall and Kagan (1967) found no relation, in 4-month olds, between fixation time and number of angles in a set of achromatic meaningless designs. Further,

McCall and Melson (1970) found that fixation time in 5-month-old infants was independent of complexity, where complexity was defined as degree of asymmetry and irregularity in the arrangement of 9 squares. But in a subsequent study in which complexity was held constant, and area and contour length of the squares were varied, fixation times were clearly related to both contour and area. Finally, infants' average evoked cortical potentials to geometric patterns were independent of redundancy, but displayed an inverted U-relation with density of contour edge (Karmel, White, Cleaves, & Steinsiek, 1970).

Nature has apparently equipped the newborn with an initial bias in the processing of experience. He does not, as the 19th-century empiricists believed, have to learn what he should examine. Moreover, there may be similarities among infants of varied species with respect to those stimuli that have natural salience. Many species of birds display fear to stimulus patterns characterized as "solid in appearance, circular, and composed of concentric elements," a description that resembles a human face (Blest, 1957). Monkeys also show fear to facelike patterns containing eyes staring at them directly. Human infants, however, are more likely to react to a facial pattern with increased interest, rather than with avoidance or fear. It is tempting to go beyond this datum and suggest that the apparent curiosity of the human child may be a partial derivative of man's stronger tendency to approach salient stimuli, in contrast to the stronger avoidance posture of infrahuman forms.

The comparative data invite the interesting speculation that the stimulus attributes that attract an animal's attention may be more similar across vertebrate species than the subsequent, prepotent response pattern provoked by processing the events. Species within a family or order may differ primarily in the response used to obtain a goal, rather than in sensory process or mechanisms of habit acquisition or maintenance. Rats in a Skinner box nose the manipulandum, birds peck at it, children hit it with their hands, and mules would probably kick it. Evolution more often acts on external morphology than on physiological function. ". . . it is extremely difficult to understand the growth of human functioning systems without bearing in mind that man's structure imposes a shape on human skills just as crucially as do the bizarre proportions of science fiction characters." (Bruner, 1968, p. 67.)

Since the topography of a response depends on morphological constraints, we might expect species to differ more dramatically in overt behavior than in the mechanisms of stimulus or information processing. The behavior elicited by exogenous stimulation of the hypothalamus, for example, is dependent on the behavioral systems that are natural for the species, as much as by the specific nuclei stimulated (Valenstein, Cox, & Kakolewski, 1968, 1969). Symbolic communication provides a nice illustration. Humans naturally make sounds and, consequently, communication is typically mediated by spoken language. Chimpanzees do not usually make sounds and attempts to teach them to talk using sounds have failed. But chimpanzees can move arms, fingers, and hands and recent attempts to teach them to communicate using gestures as signs have been remarkably successful, much more successful than earlier attempts that concentrated on shaping sounds into symbols (Gardner & Gardner, 1969). Comparative analysis of preferred reactions to contrast and movement may aid understanding of the differences in the behavioral topography of varied species, especially the bases for the early attachment of the mammalian infant to its mother.

THE SECOND DETERMINANT OF FIXATION TIME: DISCREPANCY FROM SCHEMA

The initial unlearned disposition to maintain long attentional epochs to events with movement and contour eventually competes with a new acquired determinant. Discrepancy between an event and the child's acquired schema for that event becomes an obvious determinant of fixation time between 8 and 10 weeks of age. As indicated in Chapter I, a discrepant event is one that shares some salient elements with the original event that generated the schema, and is to be distinguished from a novel event that shares few or no elements with the original.

The modern neurophysiologist emphasizes the role of both discrepancy and novelty in evoking the orienting reflex. Orientation to an event is not occasioned by a stimulus, in the customary sense of the term, but rather by a *change* in its intensity or pattern. The organism compares the present with the past, where the past is represented by a schema. Although an orientation reflex can be produced by *any* change in adaptation level, duration of sustained attention—following the initial orientation—is presumed to be a curvilinear function of degree of discrepancy of an event from the "schema." As suggested in Chapter I, a schema is a cognitive representation of an event that preserves its spatial and temporal pattern of distinctive elements, and permits the organism to recognize aspects of past experience. A schema is a functional property of mind, similar in meaning to the older term engram. The schema represents the unique configuration of the salient elements of the experienced event. The salient physical elements of visual events include rate and direction of movement, color, shape, orientation, and number, variety, form, and arrangement of internal elements. The elements of the external event bear a special relation to each other and to the context, and this relation must be preserved in the schema, although the form of that preservation is not a simple isomorphism. Hence, the face is not adequately described by noting its color, outline, and number and type of internal elements. The face is a gestalt and one must add a statement about the spatial relations among the eyes, nose, and the relation of each to the outline of the whole.

The primary determinant of the salience of an event, however, rests not only with the physical properties, but also with the past experience of the perceiver. The salience of a red light on an oscilloscope is obviously dependent on past encounter with this machine, and the corpus of research on acquired distinctiveness of cues attests to the difficulty of writing down universal *a priori* rules about salience of stimulus elements. Elements that are signals of pleasure, pain, or reduced uncertainty quickly acquire distinctiveness. Hence, the greater the information value of the element, the more likely it will play an important role in the schema. But information only has meaning with respect to some receiver. We must know the cognitive structures of the receiver in order to state the informational value of the stimulus. The principles that govern the information value of elements are among the most challenging and critical problems in contemporary psychology. Major theoretical progress waits upon their solution. Despite the primitiveness of our understanding of the concept of schema, it is useful in organizing our discussion of the infant's reaction to external stimuli, as the cloudy concept of gene was useful to biologists at the turn of the century.

The Discrepancy Principle. The second determinant of sustained attention is the relation between a perceived event and the infant's schema for that class of events. This hypothesis is called the *discrepancy principle.* The discrepancy principle states that an event that is moderately discrepant from the one that generated a schema (e.g., alterations in the temporal and spatial configuration of the original stimulus) will elicit longer fixations than minimally discrepant events or events that bear no relation to the schema. A curvilinear relation is hypothesized between fixation time, on the one hand, and degree of discrepancy between the perception of an encountered event and the schema for the original event, on the other (Berlyne, 1960; Charlesworth, 1966; Hunt, 1963, 1965).

The long fixation to a stimulus that represents an optimal discrepancy may derive from the fact that it takes time to match the event to an existing schema, as it requires time to search for a particular word when one is in the state we call "tip-of-the-tongue." As long as the search for the match continues, attention remains riveted on the event. Familiar events find their match quickly and elicit short fixations. Novel events, with no resemblance to a schema, have a similar result for a different reason.

There is some empirical support for the discrepancy principle. At 4 months of age achromatic illustrations of faces elicited fixation times that were twice as long as those displayed to random shapes of varying numbers of turns (McCall & Kagan, 1967), but this difference was minimal at 1 week of age. Three and 4-month-old infants study a regular schematic face longer than one with the same components disarranged, (Wilcox, 1969; Haaf & Bell, 1967), and fixate a partly disarranged scrambled face longer than a completely disarranged one (Haaf & Bell, 1967). But prior to 2 months infants display equivalent fixations to a schematic illustration of a regular face and a completely disarranged version of that face. It is only after 8 to 10 weeks that they look longer at the former than the latter (Fantz & Nevis, 1967; Wilcox, 1969; Lewis, 1969). This differential fixation to a regular representation of a face over an equally complex nonfacial pattern is clearest between 4 and 6 months of age, when infants display relatively long fixations to faces. After 6 months, fixation times to photographic representations of faces drop by over 50% (to values of 3 to 4 seconds), and are equivalent to both regular and irregular faces (Lewis, 1969). We interpret this developmental pattern as evidence for the discrepancy hypothesis. Prior to 3 months, before the infant has a good schema for a face, photographs of either regular or irregular faces are so discrepant from the infant's schema that they elecit equal attention. Between 3 and 5 months, the schema for the caretaker's face becomes better articulated and the perception of a photograph of a strange face is optimally discrepant from that schema. During the latter half of the first year, the schema for a face becomes so well articulated that photographs of regular or irregular faces, although discriminable, elicit relatively equivalent epochs of attention.

A second source of support for the discrepancy principle comes from research designs in which an originally meaningless stimulus is presented repeatedly (usually 5 to 10 presentations), followed by a transformation of the standard (Fantz, 1964; Schaffer & Parry, 1969). Fixation times are typically longer to the transformation than to the last few presentations of the habituated standard (McCall & Melson, 1969). For example, 4-month-old infants were shown a stimulus composed of 3 objects in a triangular arrangement (e.g., a plastic flower, a doll, or a bird) for 5 repeated trials. On the sixth trial, infants saw a transformation of the standard in which 1, 2, or 3 of the original elements were replaced with new objects. Most infants displayed longer fixations to the transformation than to the preceding standard. When the analysis was restricted to the 42 infants who displayed either rapid habituation or short fixations to the last 4 presentations of the standard (trials 2 through 5), an increasing monotonic relation emerged between amount of change in the standard (1, 2, or 3 elements replaced) and magnitude of increase in fixation from the last standard to the transformation (McCall & Kagan, 1970).

In a similar investigation, infants 2 to 52 weeks old were shown a particular geometric pattern (called the standard) after each exposure of a changing set of visual stimuli. After 22 trials (i.e., the infant saw the standard on 22 separate occasions) he was shown a pair of stimuli; one was novel, the other was the standard. Infants under 12 weeks did not display differential fixation times to the 2 stimuli. Infants over 12 weeks looked longer at the novel member of the pair (Fantz, 1963). However, the effect of discrepancy on fixation time may emerge as early as 8 weeks. Four-week-old infants were exposed for 30 minutes daily to one of 2 colorful stimuli while they lay in a bassinet. The stimuli (colored tassels of yarn or a cluster of flowers) were exposed over a period of 4 weeks. When the infants were 4 and 6 weeks old they were presented with the pair of stimuli for 8 trials; one was familiar, the other was discrepant. The 6-week-old infants looked longer at the familiar than at the unfamiliar stimulus; the 8-week olds looked longer at the unfamiliar stimulus (Weizmann, Cohen, & Pratt, 1969).

The most persuasive support for the curvilinear form of the hypothesis comes from an experiment in which a new schema was established experimentally. Each of 84 firstborn, Caucasian infants, 4-months old, was shown a novel, three-dimensional, horizontal stimulus that consisted of 3 elements, each of different shape and hue. This stimulus was repeated for 12, 30-second presentations. Each infant was then randomly assigned to one of 7 groups. Six of these groups were exposed to a stimulus at home that was of differing similarity to the standard that was viewed initially in the laboratory. The mother exposed the stimulus in the form of a mobile for 30 minutes a day for 21 days when the infant was alert and happy. The 7 experimental groups are described briefly below (see Figure 3-1).

Group control standard: These infants were exposed to the same stimulus they saw in the laboratory at 4 months.

Group subtraction: These infants were exposed to a 4-element stimulus constructed by adding one extra stimulus element to the 3-element standard seen in the laboratory.

Group serial rearrangement: These infants were exposed to a stimulus in which the 3 elements of the original standard were rearranged in the horizontal plane.

Group 90-degree rotation: These infants were exposed to a stimulus in which the 3 horizontal elements in the standard were rearranged in a vertical plane.

Group asymmetric rearrangement: These infants were exposed to the 3-element stimulus rearranged in an asymmetric form.

Group extreme discrepancy: These infants were exposed to a totally

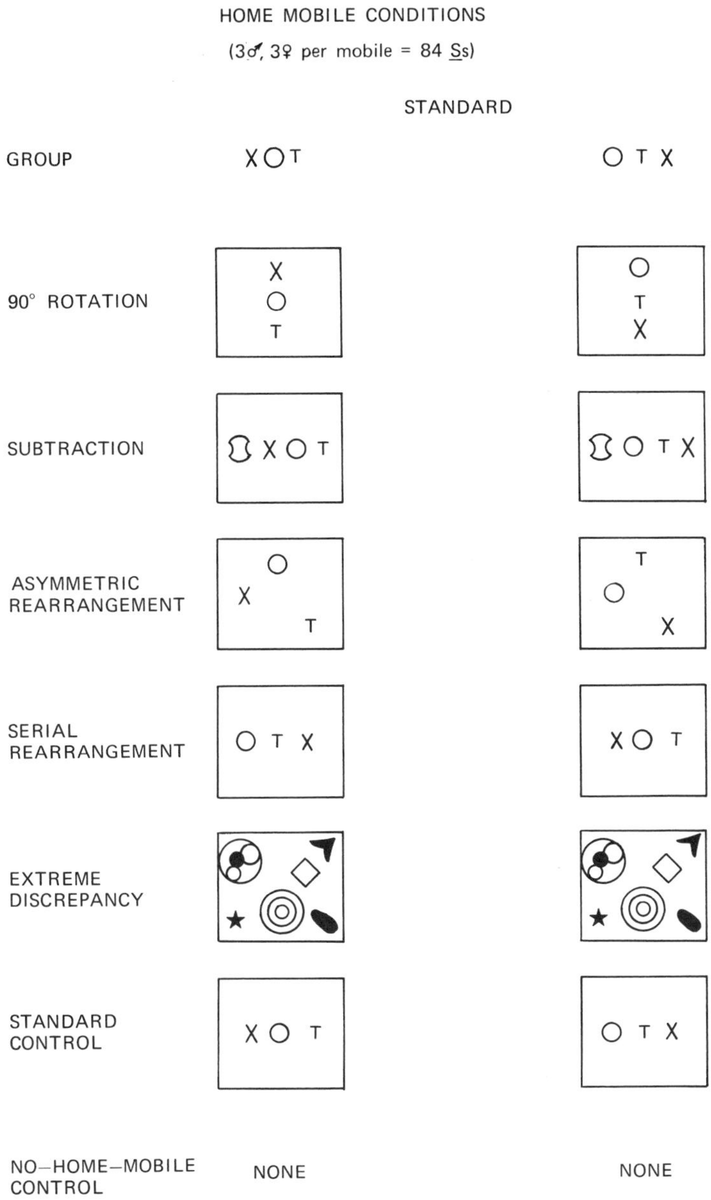

HOME MOBILE CONDITIONS

(3♂, 3♀ per mobile = 84 Ss)

STANDARD

GROUP	X◯T	◯ T X

Figure 3-1 Stimuli used in experimental mobile study.

novel mobile consisting of many more elements of different shapes and colors than those of the standard.

Group no mobile control: These infants were exposed to no stimulus during the 21-day experimental period.

Three weeks later each subject returned to the laboratory and was shown for 12 repeated presentations the same stimulus viewed in the laboratory initially at 4 months. The principal dependent variable was the change in fixation time between the first and second test session (each subject was his own control). Figures 3-2 and 3-3 illustrate these change scores for first and total fixation time for the first trial of the series, as well as the mean for the first 6 trials.

Since the infants who saw no mobile at home during the three intervening weeks *showed no change* in first or total fixation time across the two visits, we can conclude that no important maturational changes occurred that might have influenced the distribution of attention to the standard stimulus on the second visit. The change scores for the six experimental groups must reflect the effect of being exposed to the various mobiles at home. The infants exposed to mobiles that were minimally discrepant from

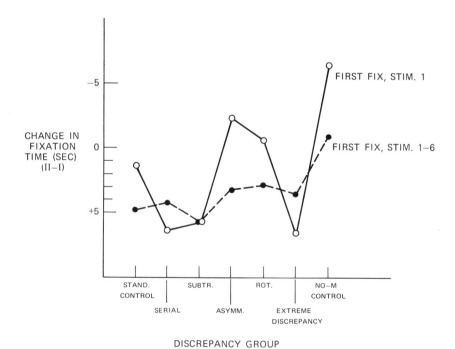

Figure 3-2 Changes in first fixation time for experimental groups.

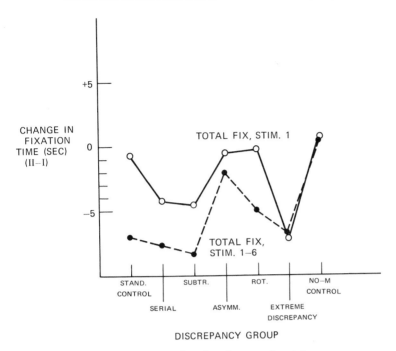

Figure 3-3 Changes in total fixation time for experimental groups.

the standard (control standard, subtraction, serial rearrangement) as well as those exposed to the mobile maximally discrepant from the standard (extreme discrepancy) showed the largest decrease in fixation time from visit one to visit two. The infants exposed to the two moderately discrepant mobiles, on the other hand, showed the smallest drop in fixation. An analysis of variance across all seven groups for change in total fixation time was significant ($F = 2.32$, df 6,56; $p < .05$ for interaction of group by visit). Moreover, comparisons between asymmetric and rotation, on the one hand, and either the three minimal discrepancy groups or the extreme discrepancy group were significant. These data lend support to the hypothesis of a curvilinear relation between duration of attention and stimulus-schema discrepancy (Super, Kagan, Morrison, Haith, & Weiffenbach, press). Although the existing data are far from conclusive, they are at least persuasive of the hypothesis that relates discrepancy to duration of sustained attention.

Although there are some exceptions, most studies suggest that the effect of a discrepancy does not seriously affect fixation time during the first two months of life. This change in quality of cognitive functioning is paralleled by other changes in the 2- to 3-month-old infant, behavioral as well as physiological. The Moro reflex begins to disappear, crying decreases sharply and babbling increases, habituation to repeated presentations of visual events becomes a reliable phenomenon (Dreyfus-Brisac, 1958; Ellingson, 1967), and three-dimensional representations (Fantz, 1966) of objects elicit longer fixations than two-dimensional representations. The latency of the visual evoked potential approaches adult form, growth of occipital neurons levels off, and alpha rhythm becomes recognizable (Ellingson, 1967). The reaction to discrepancy, however, is the most striking psychological change. Perhaps the infant's reactivity to discrepancy at this time signifies that structures in the central nervous system have matured enough to permit long-term storage of representations or retrieval of these representations.

ACTIVATION OF HYPOTHESES

As the child approaches the end of the first year, a new class of cognitive structure, called a *hypothesis,* begins to influence fixation time. A hypothesis is an interpretation of a discrepant event accomplished by mentally transforming the unusual event to a form the child is familiar with, where the familiar form is the schema. The cognitive structure used in the transformation is the hypothesis. To recognize that a particular sequence of sounds is human speech rather than a telephone requires a schema for the quality of the human voice. Interpretation of the meaning of the speech, on the other hand, requires the activation of hypotheses, which, in this case, are linguistic rules. The critical difference between a schema and a hypothesis is analogous to the difference between recognition and interpretation. It is assumed that the activation of hypotheses to explain discrepant events is accompanied by sustained attention. The more extensive the repertoire of hypotheses, the longer the child can work at interpretation and the more prolonged his attention. That is, the more hypotheses he has about a class of events, the longer he can work at this assimilative construction and the more prolonged his attention. Consider, as an analogy, a child's distribution of attention in an art museum. Moderately unusual pictures that provoke a rich set of hypotheses to aid assimilation should attract longer study than colorful or oddly shaped pictures that do not engage any hypotheses.

In summary, three factors appear to control duration of fixation in the infant. High rate of change in physical qualities dominates attention during the opening few weeks; discrepancy becomes a dominant factor at 2 to 3 months, and density of hypotheses begins to exert its influence around one year. These three factors supplement each other, and a high contrast, discrepant event that activates hypotheses should elicit longer fixation times from a 1-year old than a stimulus with only one or two of these attributes. The combined action of discrepancy and density of hypotheses is seen in a comparative study of children from two cultures. Finley (1967) showed culturally appropriate chromatic paintings of male faces to Cambridge middle class and Mayan peasant children from Yucatan, aged 1, 2, and 3 years. Figure 3-4 shows the fixation times for the three age and two cultural groups. Fixation time increased with age (following the principle of increased density of hypotheses associated with age), but the largest increase occurred to the scrambled face (a discrepant stimulus), rather than to the regular face.

We affirm Piaget's (1952) profound suggestion that the infant attends to discrepant experience in order to assimilate it and, as a result, produces changes in his existing schemata. This dynamic is regarded as one of the major forces for growth and differentiation in cognitive structures. It is important to appreciate, as indicated earlier, that any new event is not necessarily discrepant from some schema and, second, that the infant is

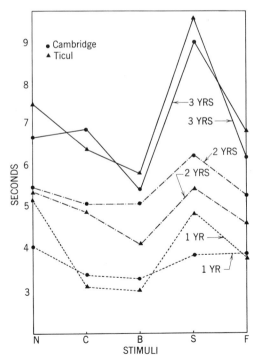

Figure 3-4   Age changes in fixation time to faces for Mayan and American children.

most likely to invest attention in events that he perceives as transformations of those that produced the original schema. "We feel neither curiosity nor wonder," wrote William James, "concerning things so far beyond us that we have no concepts to refer them to or standards by which to measure them." (James, 1890.) If the infant regards a new event as unrelated to any schema, his attention is brief and he is not excited by it. In a recent study in our laboratory, infant girls 9½ and 11½ months old were exposed for 3 successive trials to one of two different transformations following 6 repeated presentations of a 2-inch wooden orange cube. The infants exposed to the novel event saw a yellow, rippled, plastic cylinder differing in color, texture, and shape from the standard. The infants exposed to a derivative transformation saw a 1½-inch wooden orange cube, in which only the size of the stimulus was changed. Over half of the infants in the derivative group showed an increase in vocalization to the smaller cube. By contrast, only one infant exposed to the novel yellow form showed increased vocalization and most showed no change at all ($p < .05$). As we shall see in Chapter IV vocalization is a moderately good measure of stimulus excitement in young infants. It appears that the infant is more aroused by an event that is a partial transformation of the familiar than by one that is totally novel.

THE INFLUENCE OF TEMPO

The three determinants of fixation time considered above are dependent on the nature of the stimulus, its contrast, and familiarity. A temperamental disposition to become excited or inhibited when processing information may be a fourth determinant. An inhibition-excitability dimension may be related to a tendency to activate cognitive structures appropriate to an event, in contrast to acting upon the event with an initially prepotent hypothesis. The inhibited infant behaves as if he were scanning a variety of existing structures for the schema appropriate to the event, and his attention is maintained during this process. The excitable infant seems less thoughtful, and the duration of his attentional involvement is shorter. Moss and Robson (1970) have recently found some support for the idea that early signs of a temperamental irritability were predictive of short attention spans. Firstborn infants were observed at home at the end of their first and third months, and in the laboratory between 3 and 4 months when they were shown visual stimuli representing faces and achromatic checkerboards. The boys who were awake and quiet for the longest times at 1 month of age and were least irritable at 3 months displayed the longest attentional epochs to the visual stimuli.

It is difficult to invent an appropriate name for this temperamental dimension that captures its essential quality while not invoking misleading connotations. We shall refer to it as conceptual tempo. It is suggested that the slow tempo child is more likely to quiet to new events and invest attention in them. The fast tempo infant is more likely to become excited, often motorically, and maintain shorter periods of attention. The fast tempo child shows more rapid rates of habituation to repetitions of visual stimuli and reacts more directly to discrepancy than the slow tempo child. In independent studies, infants between 4 and 6 months of age were repeatedly shown a meaningless stimulus for a series of trials and then presented with a transformation of that standard. The fast habituating infants showed a larger increase in fixation time to the transformation than the slow habituating infants (McCall & Melson, 1969). Moreover, shallow habituating infants showed more frequent smiling to meaningless achromatic shapes (as shown in Figure 3-5) than rapid habituating infants. The association between a slow rate of habituation and high frequency of smiling was also found with an independent group of 4-month-old boys who viewed a three-dimensional stimulus arranged in a triangle composed of three toys

Figure 3-5   Achromatic design shown to 4-month infants.

(e.g., a red and silver Christmas bow, a black dog, a red bulb with a stem topped with a clown's face, or a blue and green flower). Each of these 3-element stimuli was presented for 30 seconds with a 15-second inter-stimulus interval. Some of the children showed a rapid decrease in fixation time over the first 5 presentations (dropped from 20 to 4 seconds); others showed no change in fixation time. The slow habituating group smiled more frequently to the stimuli than the fast habituating infants (McCall & Kagan, 1970). The association between smiling and a shallow rate of habituation to meaningless visual events suggests a biological basis for the fixation time patterns. Both Freedman (1965) and Reppucci (1968) have reported that monozygotic twins are more similar than dizygotic twins with respect to frequency of smiling to human faces during the first 4 months. The link between a slow rate of habituation, long fixation times, and smiling, together with the evidence suggesting the heritability of smiling in early infancy, implies that habituation rate and, by inference, tempo of processing, may have biological foundations.

The concept of tempo will be discussed in greater detail in Chapter VI, where its public form is the duration of sustained involvement with toys. Some children pick up a block and bang it three times on the floor before turning to another activity. Others bang the block 30 times before turning to a new object. The second child studies visual stimuli longer, lending generality to the tempo idea. In summary, duration of a fixation may have at least 4 determinants:

1. The degree of contrast and movement possessed by the stimulus; this vector is independent of the acquired cognitive structures of the viewer.

2. The degree to which a perceived event matches or is discrepant from an acquired schema.

3. The density of hypotheses activated to assimilate a discrepant event.

4. The child's preferred tempo of information processing.

LONGITUDINAL DATA

We shall consider first age, sex, stimulus, and social class differences in fixation time at each of four ages (4, 8, 13, and 27 months), and follow with a summary of the stability of fixation times across these ages. Since the battery at 27 months was different from the one used at the three earlier ages, we will consider the 4-8-13 month data as a unit. (See Appendix Table 5 for the first and total fixation time scores to visual episodes at 4-8-13 and 27 months for the sexes separately.)

Habituation. There are three generalizations contained in the fixation time scores. First, habituation occurred at every age. During the first year the children's interest in the stimuli waned considerably by the eighth or ninth trial. At 27 months interest to the forms and faces had waned by the fourth or fifth trial. This consistent habituation persuaded us to consider fixation time to the first two presentations of each stimulus at the early ages and to the first presentation at 27 months as primary variables in the longitudinal analysis. The exception to this generalization was the slide series at 27 months to which there was no change in fixation time over the 23 scenes. Each stimulus in the series was different, and the absence of habituation suggests that decreasing attention on the other series was not a function of fatigue, but of the construction of schemata for repeated events.

Age Differences. There was a U-shaped function between chronological age and fixation time. Fixation times to the faces decreased across the period 4 to 13 months but increased to the faces and forms between 13 and 27 months. These data support the earlier interpretation of the changing determinants of fixation time. The comparatively long fixations at 4 months correspond with the hypothesis that these faces were discrepant from the infant's acquired schemata for his parents' faces. Fixation times to the faces decreased at the two succeeding ages because the stimuli were less discrepant, but did not engage a rich set of hypotheses in the service of assimilation. Fixations rose between one and two years because the child was activating structures to aid in the interpretation of the event. The largest increase in fixation time between 13 and 27 months occurred for the scrambled face and form, suggesting the complementary action of discrepancy and density of hypotheses in controlling sustained attention. The children's spontaneous comments are consonant with this suggestion. One 2-year old said, "What happened to his nose? Who hit him in the nose?" Another said, "Who that, Mommy? A monster, Mommy?" A repeated measures analysis of variance on the first fixation time scores across the ages 4, 8, and 13 months revealed a significant age effect for each visual series. ($F = 61.8$, .1, 138 df, $p < .0001$ for achromatic faces; $F = 11.38$, 2/96 df, $p < .01$ for the clay faces). A repeated measures analysis of variance for the clay faces across all four ages yielded an F of 18.78 ($p < .001$); the analysis of variance for the Human Forms at 13 and 27 months yielded an F of 65.7 ($p < .0001$).

When the longitudinal fixation times to the faces (gathered at 4, 8, 13, and 27 months) were combined with those gathered by Finley at 12, 24, and 36 months using similar stimuli, a clear U-shaped function emerged between fixation time and age (see Figure 3-6). This function

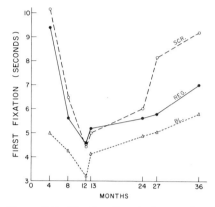

Figure 3-6 Fixation time to human faces as a function of age.

is concordant with the changing determinants of fixation time suggested earlier.[1]

Stimulus Differences. At 4 and 8 months, the two most representative faces in the achromatic series (PR and SR) and the two faces that contained eyes in the clay mask series elicited the longest fixation times. Analyses of variance at 4 and 8 months revealed a significant effect for stimuli ($p < .01$), but no effect for sex. At 13 months the three faces that contained eyes elicited longer fixations than the two without eyes ($p < .01$) and, on HF I, free form elicited shorter fixations than the other three stimuli.

There was a curvilinear relation (for HF I) between degree of discrepancy from schema and fixation time at 27 months, for head between legs and scrambled form produced significantly longer fixations than either regular or free form (see Figure 3-7). (Repeated measures analysis of variance on first fixation times to the separate stimuli yielded an F of 5.21; $p < .05$ for stimuli). Similarly, for the clay faces, a repeated measures analysis of variance yielded an F of 4.46, ($p < .05$) for stimuli; and the scrambled face elicited the longest fixation time. Since there were three different orders of presentation used at both 13 and 27 months, this

[1] Carpenter (1969) has recently reported that infants show a monotonic increase in fixation time to faces across the period 2 to 8 weeks, with the 8-week values similar to the 4-month scores. It appears, therefore, that the function describing the relation between age and fixation time from 2 weeks to 4 years has two inflection points, the first at 2 to 4 months when fixation time is maximal, and a second at 8 to 12 months when fixation time is at a minimum. Moreover, a recently completed study of Indian children in rural Guatemala also reveals a U-shaped relation between fixation time to faces and age for children 4 through 36 months.

result was not a function of order of presentation. (Neither order nor sex yielded a significant effect.)

Slide Series at 27 Months. It will be recalled that there were 23 visual stimuli in the slide series and each was exposed for a total of 15 seconds with a 4-second interstimulus interval. The first 7 seconds were silent, the next 3 to 7 seconds presented an auditory message and the final 1 to 5 seconds were silent. Six of the 23 stimuli were discrepancies from the child's experience—a man in a dress, a boy crouched in mid-air, an oversized cat, a woman holding her head in her hand, a man with 4 arms, and a girl sleeping in a bathtub. Four of the 23 scenes contained auditory discrepancies—a girl speaking nonsense, a telephone accompanied by the sound of an auto horn, a girl's face accompanied by the sound of a barking dog, and a man with the voice of a woman.

There was no significant difference in mean fixation time between the 6 visual discrepancies, on the one hand, and the 17 other scenes. However, examination of the differences in fixation time between each of the 6 visual discrepancies and the *preceding* nondiscrepant scene revealed that the oversized cat, man with 4 arms, and girl in the bathtub each elicited significantly longer first fixations than the *preceding,* nondiscrepant scene (a difference of about 2½ seconds for each of the scenes, and $p < .01$ for each of the 3 comparisons). These 3 scenes were among the 4 that produced the largest positive difference in fixation time when compared to the preceding stimulus.

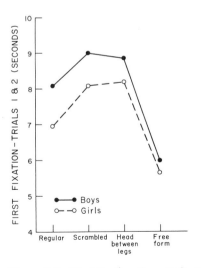

Figure 3-7   First fixation times to human forms at 27 months.

Sex Differences. Although there were no striking sex differences in mean or variance values, fixation to some of the scenes had strong correlations with fixation time across the whole series. Among boys, fixation time to the two realistic animals (cat and dog) had the largest correlations with total fixation time ($r = .53$ and $.52$), even though fixation time to these two scenes was not higher than that displayed to the other pictures. Among girls, fixation time to the man in the car, man in the dress, and girl barking had the highest item to total fixation. (correlations of $.62$, $.57$, and $.56$ respectively).

INTERCORRELATIONAL PATTERNS FOR FIXATION TIME

The pattern of intercorrelations was generally similar at the three early ages. There were high correlations within an episode, low to moderate correlations across episodes, with interepisode correlations increasing with age.

Four Months. The correlations among mean first fixation time to the four achromatic faces (trials 1 to 2) ranged from $.43$ to $.69$. Among the clay faces, the range was $.56$ to $.69$ (see Appendix Table 6). The stability across episodes was markedly lower, especially for the girls. Among boys the median correlation was $.32$; among girls it was only $.13$. (In general, a difference in correlation of 0.3 between boys and girls is significant at $p < .05$ for these sample sizes.) Boys with long fixation times to either set of faces were larger in size (linear combination of weight and height) and smiled more frequently than boys with short fixations. Among girls, fixation time was unrelated to body size but was associated with more frequent smiling.

Eight Months. Fixation time to the two-dimensional faces behaved as it did at 4 months. There was good generality within an episode for both sexes, but cross-episode generality only occurred for boys (see Appendix Table 7). The absence of interepisode consistency for girls was due, in part, to faster habituation and more frequent occurrence of fear to the clay faces among the girls.

The correlates of fixation time were more similar for the sexes at 8 than at 4 months, and resembled the pattern at the earlier age. Even though smiling was infrequent at 8 months, the cluster of long fixations, smiling, and large cardiac decelerations retained.its integrity for achromatic faces.

Thirteen Months. First and total fixation times showed excellent intra-episode consistency and good interepisode consistency for both sexes (see Appendix Table 8). The cross-episode correlations were higher than those at the two earlier ages and there were moderate relations between fixation time and both cardiac deceleration and quieting. (See Appendix Tables 9 and 10.)

ORIENTATION TO SPEAKER DURING AUDITORY EPISODE AT 8 AND 13 MONTHS

The auditory episode elicited a behavior that might share some variance with fixation time. Some infants cocked their heads about 45 degrees and fixated the source of the voice—a speaker baffle ringed with a white circle of plastic. Many children who oriented to the baffle became quiet and there was no doubt that they were attending to the strange male voice. Unlike fixation time to the faces, the child had to make an effort to orient to the speaker. There was a decrease in orientation with age (although not statistically significant), with girls showing a slightly greater decrease than boys. It was not necessary to watch the speaker during the auditory episode in order to process the information. Many children quieted motorically and showed a deceleration when the voice began, but never oriented to the speaker. The act of orientation may index a special tendency to become active when alerted by an interesting event. Orientation may be a partial indicator of general attentiveness, for it was correlated with fixation time to the forms at 13 months, although more consistently for girls than for boys.

Twenty-Seven Months. The cross-episode correlations for the three visual episodes were positive (correlations ranged from .28 to .61) and slightly higher for girls than boys (see Appendix Table 11). Fixation time was generally more independent of other variables at the two older than at the two earlier ages suggesting increased differentiation of the response indexes that accompany information processing as the child matures.

EDUCATIONAL LEVEL OF FAMILY AND FIXATION TIME

Educational level of the infant's family showed no relation to fixation time at 4 months, a suggestive relation at 8 months, and a moderate relation (.3 to .4) at 13 and 27 months. The covariation between class and fixation time increased with age, and was always a little stronger for girls than for boys (see Appendix Table 12). The sex difference in size of correlation was significant for first fixation to HF II at 13 months; to FF on HF I at 27 months, and to three-dimensional faces at 27 months.

RELATION OF SOCIAL CLASS TO CHANGES IN FIXATION TIME

If fixation time comes increasingly under the control of density of hypotheses as the child matures, children with more hypotheses should display larger increases in fixation time between 8 and 13 or 13 and 27 months than those with sparser nests of hypotheses, and educational level of the family should covary with density of hypotheses. In a first analysis the distributions of total fixation time to the clay faces at 8 and 13 months were split at the median and four groups created (above the median at both ages and below the median at both ages as well as the two odd quadrant groups). Over 80% of the infants were either above or below the median at both ages. Of the upper middle class girls, 54% were above the median at both ages, in contrast to 19% of the lower middle class girls (chi-square = 5.34, p < .05). The relation between educational level and fixation at the two ages was less striking for boys, but in the same direction. Of the upper middle class boys, 30% were above the median at both ages; 17% were above the median among the lower middle and middle class groups.

In a second analysis each subject was his own control. Each infant's average fixation time to the achromatic faces at 8 months (trials 1 to 8) was compared with his average fixation to HF I at 13 months. Similarly, the average first fixation to clay faces at 8 months was compared with the average first fixation to the faces at 13 months. Of the boys from better educated homes (above the median on educational level), 58% increased in fixation time from 8 to 13 months, whereas only 33% of the children from less well-educated homes showed increases. To the clay faces, 43% of the better educated increased in contrast to 21% from the less well educated. Although these differences are not statistically significant, they are in the expected direction. Moreover, 3 upper middle class boys and only 1 lower middle class boy increased on both comparisons, whereas 5 lower middle class and only 1 upper middle class boy decreased on both comparisons between 8 and 13 months. An identical analysis among girls revealed no relation between social class and *change* in fixation time from 8 to 13 months. Among the girls, social class was related to absolute fixation time at both ages, but not to change.

Social Class and Fixation Time at 27 Months. Among the girls, long fixations to the three visual episodes were positively correlated with educational level of the family as well as with vocabulary score (see Appendix Table 12). Moreover, these correlations were highest for the discrepant rather than the "normative" stimuli within each series. Fixation to free form displayed the highest relation to vocabulary and social class ($r = .40$) even though the mean or variance to free form was not larger than the parameters to the other three stimuli in HF I. The only significant correlation between vocabulary and fixation time to clay faces occurred for the scrambled face ($r = .36$), and for the slide series the three scenes that had significant correlations with vocabulary score were all discrepant stimuli (girl speaking nonsense, $r = .50$; woman with no head, $r = .34$; and girl barking, $r = .29$). These three scenes did not have larger means or variances than the remaining twenty stimuli. *Thus, girls with richer language resources displayed longer fixations to discrepant pictures than those with poorer language facility.* This finding is congruent with our interpretation of the meaning of long fixation times at 27 months.

Among the boys, fixation time was less clearly tied to educational level of the family or vocabulary. The only significant coefficient occurred to the slide series, and the association between verbal resources and fixation time to discrepant stimuli was more fragile among boys than girls.

Social Class and Change in Fixation Time from 13 to 27 Months. Increases in fixation time between 13 and 27 months should covary with density of hypotheses and, perhaps, with educational level of the family. Examination of each child's fixation times to each episode at the four ages suggested four types of age functions. The largest group of infants showed a U-shaped function with long fixation times at 4 months, short fixation times at 8 and 13 months, and rising fixations at 27 months. A few infants in this group began to show the increase in fixation time from 8 to 13 months and continued to rise from 13 to 27 months. A second large group showed a steady decrease in fixation time and no increase between 13 and 27 months. A third large group showed no change in fixation time across the four assessments. A fourth, very small, group, showed small fixations at 4 months and a steady logarithmic increase in fixation time with succeeding assessments.

Since most infants either increased their fixations between 13 and 27 months or showed no essential change, we computed, for each child, two change scores for first fixation between 13 and 27 months. We computed the changes in first fixation for HF I and for clay faces, and correlated each of these two change scores with educational level of the family and indexes of verbal ability (see Appendix Table 13).

There was a positive relation for girls between social class and increases in fixation time between 13 and 27 months ($r = .20$ and $.31$) but not for boys ($r = .06, - .04$). (The sex difference for faces was statistically significant.) Moreover, the girls who most often verbalized spontaneously to the visual stimuli and had the largest vocabulary scores at 27 months had the largest increases in fixation time. Figure 3-8 shows the fixation time functions for several girls, two with a U-shaped function and two with a steadily decreasing curve.

Summary. Three generalizations emerged from the contemporaneous correlational pattern for fixation time at each of the four ages. First, cross-episode consistency increased with age. Second, fixation time became increasingly independent of vocalization, smiling, and body size as the child

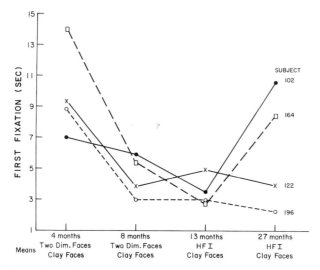

Figure 3-8 Fixation time curves for four individual girls.

matured, implying that fixation time at 4 months was more likely to be under the control of general alertness than it was at the older ages. Finally, the relation between the educational level of the infant's family and fixation time increased from 4 through 27 months. This relation emerged earlier and was slightly higher for girls than for boys, asymptoting at about 0.4. Fixations to the transformations of the face showed the strongest covariation with social class at the older ages. As we shall see later, there was no strong relation between vocalization, deceleration, or smiling and social class at any of the ages. Fixation time was the only variable in the study to covary with social class in a consistent way across the later assessments.

CONTINUITY FOR FIXATION TIME

There was moderate intraindividual stability from 8 to 13 and from 13 to 27 months, but minimal continuity from 4 to any of the three older ages. This pattern is concordant with our interpretation of the changing meaning of fixation time. Let us examine the cross-age comparisons in more detail. There was minimal continuity of fixation time to the faces from 4 months to any of the three successive ages, suggesting that the degree of articulation of schema for faces at 4 months is independent of richness of hypotheses to faces or forms at 1 or 2 years. However, there was moderate continuity from 8 to 13 and from 13 to 27 months (see Appendix Tables 14 and 15), implying that a construct we might call *richness of hypotheses surrounding representations of humans* retains some stability across these periods. When the average standard score for fixation time to all three visual episodes at 27 months was the criterion, there were significant correlations with clay faces and HF II at 1 year.

Moreover, the 8- to 13-month stability correlations were slightly higher for girls than for boys. The strongest support for a sex difference in degree of continuity was revealed in the correlation between total fixation to two-dimensional faces at 8 and clay faces at 13 ($r = .41$, $p < .01$ for girls versus .23 for boys); and total fixation to clay faces at 8 and clay faces at 13 ($r = .51$, $p < .01$ for girls versus $r = .08$ for boys) (latter difference significant at $p < .05$). There was no instance in which a stability coefficient was significantly higher for boys than for girls.

Although fixation time to each of the 13-month visual episodes predicted fixation time to the slides at 2 years, the coefficients averaged only about 0.3. It has been our continual assumption that density of hypotheses to discrepant events is a major determinant of duration of fixation after 8 to 10 months of age. The occurrence of continuity from 8 to 13 and 13 to 27 months, without comparable 8 to 27 month continuity suggests that the determinants of fixation time change between 8 and 27 months.[2]

DERIVATIVES OF FIXATION TIME AT 4 AND 8 MONTHS

Faith in the continuity of an attentiveness dimension from 8 to 13 months is supported by the relation between fixation time at 8 months and postural quiescence and alertness at 13 months (see Appendix Table 16). There was no relation between fixation time at 4 months and postural indexes of attentiveness at 1 year, in contrast to the more consistent relation between 8-month fixations and postural signs of attentiveness at 1 year. Eight-month-old infants with long fixations to the achromatic faces were less restless during the 13-month episode and were rated as more alert. As usual, the coefficients were slightly higher and more consistent for girls than they were for boys.

STABILITY FROM 8 TO 13 MONTHS FOR ORIENTATION TO SPEAKER

There was homotypic continuity for the duration of orientation to the taped sound source, and the two high inflection paragraphs were the best

---

[2] *Stability for trial by trial analyses:* Analyses were performed for first fixation times on single trials (for trials one through eight), rather than the mean fixation times across pairs of trials or all trials. This analysis allowed us to check for the possibility that continuities were specific to certain stimuli.

In general, the trial by trial correlations across the first eight trials were not markedly different from those derived from mean scores. There was minimal stability from 4 to 8 or 13 months and moderate continuity from 8 to 13 months.

criterion variables[3] (see Appendix Table 17). However, there was no relation between orientation to speaker at 8 months and deceleration at 13 months. The infant could, of course, attend to and process the speech without ever looking at the speaker. Many infants dropped their jaws, quieted in their chairs, and displayed 10-beat cardiac decelerations when the stimulus was presented, but did not necessarily orient to the speaker. To our surprise, there was no continuity between orientation to the sound source at 8 or 13 months and fixation time to any episode at 27 months, suggesting that these responses are tapping slightly different processes.

DISCUSSION

Fixation time was most stable from 8 to 13 and 13 to 27 months and slightly more stable for girls than for boys *during the last half of the first year*. Except for a few low significant correlations, there was minimal consistency for boys from 8 to 13 months. Among girls, total fixation time to the achromatic faces at 8 months predicted fixation time to each of the 5 clay faces at 13 months. When the clay faces at 8 months were the predictors, there was also better continuity for girls than boys. The only other comparable study of stability of fixation time has reported remarkably similar results. Lewis assessed fixation times to visual stimuli in 60 infants (30 boys and 30 girls) at 6, 13, and 25 months. The infants' fixation times to facial stimuli at 6 and 13 months were correlated with their fixation times to human forms at 25 months. There was no stability from 6 to 13 or 25 months, but moderate continuity from 13 to 25 months ($r = .41$). Moreover, the infants who showed the largest increases in fixation time between 6 and 13 months had the longest fixation times at 25 months ($r = .35$). These data are concordant with the longitudinal data reported in this chapter (Dodd & Lewis, 1969). The stability of fixation time reflects, in part, the stability of richness of symbolic structures sur-

---

[3] *Trial by trial analyses: total orientation to speaker 8 to 13 months:* The trial-by-trial analyses were comparable to those using mean scores and continuity occurred for both sexes. The stability was more impressive for girls than for boys and, among girls only, there were significant correlations linking a particular trial at 8 months with its exact homologue at 13 months. For example, there were significant correlations for high-low trial 3, low-high trial 3 and high-high trial 1 ($r = .38$, .33, and .28 respectively). The 8- to 13-month coefficients for orientation were as consistently high as those observed for fixation time to faces and forms across this same time interval. But the contemporaneous correlations between orientation and fixation time at 13 months were only moderate. The children who oriented to the sound source *were not the same ones* who showed long fixations to the visual events, despite the fact that there was stability for each disposition.

rounding faces and forms[4] and we have noted that girls' fixation times covaried with parental education at 13 and 27 months. The less impressive continuity for boys for the period 8 to 13 months suggests either that (a) social class is a less powerful determinant of the growth of hypotheses, (b) rate of acquisition of cognitive structures is fundamentally less stable for boys, or (c) boys are maturationally behind girls and do not establish stable structures as early as girls.[5]

The lack of predictive stability from the 4-month fixation scores is due, first, to the fact that the 4-month values are not yet influenced by the hy-

[4] A small group of children (18 girls and 12 boys) from the longitudinal sample were administered three different memory tests when they were 4 years old. In the first test of the session the child leafed through a looseleaf notebook containing 12 photographs, half of which were realistic, the other half violations of reality created by collaging two or more objects. After the child had leafed through the book at his own pace, the book was taken from him and he was asked to recall as many of the pictures as possible. The second memory test tapped recognition and was a variant of Shepard's procedure. The child looked at 50 chromatic pictures taken from magazines. The child was given the pictures one at a time and when he handed the picture back or pushed it away the examiner gave him another picture. Each child typically examined each picture 2 to 4 seconds. After he had looked at all 50 scenes he was shown a pair of pictures, one of which was in the set he examined, the other was new. He had to point to the picture he had seen. The third memory task required the child to imitate a pointing sequence demonstrated by the examiner. A slide illustrating 3, 4, 5, 6, or 7 familiar objects was presented on a screen in front of the child. The examiner pointed to the objects in a particular order and required the child to imitate the sequence.

There were no sex differences in quality of performance on the three memory tests. Correlations were run (for sexes separately) between fixation time at 13 or 27 months and memory scores. Long fixations at 13 months predicted superior memory performance at age 4 on all three memory tests. Human Forms I was the best predictor for boys ($r = .78$, $p < .01$; $r = .46$, $p < .10$; $r = .69$, $p < .05$ for the three memory tests). Human Forms II was the better predictor for girls ($r = .62$, $p < .05$; .53, $p < .05$; $r = .66$, $p < .05$ for the three memory tasks).

Since fixation times at 27 months were not as highly correlated with the memory scores, the mediating variable is not primarily richness of cognitive structures. The data suggest that a predisposition to attentiveness may mediate both sets of behaviors.

[5] McCall has analyzed the predictive relation between the Gesell Developmental Scale at 6, 12, and 18 months and Stanford-Binet IQ scores for the Fels longitudinal sample. These correlations are markedly higher for girls than for boys. For example, the Gesell score at 6 months predicts the Binet IQ at 3½ and 6 years for girls ($r = 26$, 22, $p < .05$), but not for boys ($r = -.01$, $-.06$). Similarly the Gesell score at 12 months is correlated with the Binet at 3½, 6, and 10 ($r = .57$, $p < .01$, $r = .51$, $p < .01$, $r = .37$, $p < .01$) for girls; the comparable coefficients for boys are .16, .22 ($p < .05$), and .12. Thus even the multidimensional Gesell score, which reflects many differential cognitive factors in the infant, provides a better preview of level of cognitive development for the school age girl than for the school age boy.

pothesis vector. The second reason may rest with different maturational rates among the infants. Major biological changes occurring between 3 and 4 months should affect fixation time. The occipital EEG rhythm and the photic following response do not appear in clear form until the end of the third month (Dreyfus-Brisac, 1958) and latency of the visual evoked potential does not approach adult levels until the same time (Ellingson, 1967). Finally, Conel's histological studies of the brain reveal striking development of occipital neurons between birth and 3 months (Conel, 1947). When these observations are viewed together with the more purely behavioral changes at this age—disappearance of the Moro, dramatic increases in smiling to faces and spontaneous babbling—it becomes reasonable to assume that the infant undergoes important reorganizations in psychological function between 3 and 4 months. There should be individual differences in the age at which these vital psychological changes occur (genetic influences often lead to individual differences in the time at which maturational events occur) and consequently some of the 4-month-old infants may have been functioning at the ontogenetically more primitive level. Their fixation times should be less clearly a function of articulation of schema for faces and more closely related to their position on a maturational vector of alertness. As a result, stability from 4 to 8 or 13 months would be minimal.

Since girls are generally advanced over boys in aspects of physical development, more girls than boys should have passed through the reorganization phase by 4 months and their fixation times should have been more consistently a function of their experience. We should, therefore, expect slightly better continuity for fixation time for girls during the first year and the data verify this expectation.

We cannot help noting the parallel between the data on stability of physical growth and fixation time. Both parameters are more stable over time for girls. The magnitude of predictive validity for many anthropometric dimensions is markedly better for girls, and Acheson states, "In almost every respect the physical development of the female is more stable than that of the male" (Acheson, 1966, p. 497). For example, the use of onset of ossification in any single bone to predict when ossification will begin in another center is more reliable in the female than the male (Garn, Silverman, & Rohmann, 1964). The greater stability of growth processes in the female is also reflected in the fact that debilitating environmental influences (disease, radiation, nutrition) are more likely to retard maturational milestones in boys than girls (Acheson, 1966). An improvement in environmental circumstances also has a greater effect on the male than on the female. Analogously, fixation times at 8 months are more predictive of fixation times at 13 months for girls than boys. Girls' development seems to stabilize earlier than that of boys and this stabilization probably has a biological basis. Each child has a route to follow, the direction of that route is determined by both biological factors and the rearing milieu. Once the child is established on his route his velocity and direction resist change. The data suggest either that girls find their route before boys, and/or that the girls' path is more heavily magnetized and she is held to it with greater firmness.

The biological stability of the girl would help to explain the clearer continuity of fixation time, but will not explain sex differences in the relation between fixation time and parental education. We need additional assumptions to account for this phenomenon. There are several independent affirmations of this general finding. Moss (1967) reported a similar sex difference in the degree of covariation between amount of mother-infant face-to-face contact and the 3-month old infant's fixation time to achromatic faces. The association was highly positive for girls ($r = .61$; $p < .01$), but was close to zero for boys. Hess, Shipman, Brophy, and Bear (1968) report a larger correlation between mothers' verbal ability and daughters' IQ than between mothers' verbal ability and sons' IQ among 4-year-old black children in Chicago. Moreover, Gordon has reported that the effect of experimental intervention programs intended to change the behaviors of mothers toward their infants had a stronger effect on mother-daughter pairs than on mother-son pairs (Gordon, 1969). These data agree with the present longitudinal data and suggest that the expected effect of maternal practices on cognitive functioning is realized more clearly in the girl than the boy.

One interpretation of this puzzling finding rests on the notion that girls are less variable than boys. If biological variables (e.g., irritability, apathy, activity) predispose the infant to differential attentiveness, and these dispositions display a greater range for boys than girls, they might attenuate the effect of experiential factors on attentiveness in boys, and dilute the correlation between fixation time and an index of environmental tutoring. Let us assume the following principle: the more often the mother attempts to interest her child in an event the stronger the child's tendency to develop a general sensitivity to change and the greater his capacity for sustained attention to discrepancy. This principle is likely to be less valid for infants who temperamentally have a tendency toward exaggerated apathy or hypervigilance. There are many functional relations in nature that lose their validity when one of the variables assumes an extreme value, and this may be another instance of that phenomenon.

A second interpretation of the class-fixation time relation assumes greater differences between well- and poorly educated mothers in their behaviors toward daughters than toward sons, especially maternal actions that promote attention and language acquisition. A mother is more likely to project her motives, expectations, and self-image on her daughter than on her son, and is more likely to assume that her daughter will come to resemble her. Many poorly educated mothers feel less competent intellectually than the college graduate and have greater doubts about their daughters' potential for intellectual accomplishment. Such a mother may set lower standards and be less enthusiastic as well as less consistently encouraging to her infant girl mastering new skills. The well-educated mother sets higher aspirations and acts as though she held the power to catalyze her child's development. The situation with sons is somewhat different. Most mothers, regardless of class background, believe their sons will have to learn how to support a family and achieve some degree of independence. Hence mothers of all classes may be more alike in energizing the cognitive development of sons. The restricted range of acceleration of sons, compared with daughters, would result in closer covariation for girls between social class and indexes of attention.

These ideas have some empirical support. For example, lower and middle class mothers are more similar in their acceleratory pressures toward sons than daughters. The middle class mother of a daughter actively tutors her, whereas the lower class mother is generally more apathetic with her daughter (Hess, Shipman, Brophy, & Bear, 1968). Furthermore, home observations on this sample, which will be summarized in the next chapter, reveal significant differences in the amount of distinctive face-to-face vocalization between upper middle and lower middle class mothers of daughters, but no comparable class differences for sons. Observations of a sample of 60 mother-daughter pairs at 10 months of age (Tulkin, unpublished) also indicated that middle, in contrast to lower, class mothers spend significantly more time in face-to-face contact with their daughters, vocalize more often to them, and more frequently reward their attempts to crawl and stand.

A final source of data comes from home observations on 90 mother-child pairs from this longitudinal sample made soon after the 27-month visit to the laboratory. The female observer visited each home twice for a total of about five hours of active data gathering. The observer only recorded a small segment of behavior; namely, maternal reprimands, prohibitions, commands, and anticipations of the child's behavior, as well as child-initiated requests of the mother. The observer recorded the entire sequence, as close to verbatim as possible, and these protocols were typed and scored by two independent coders who had never visited the home. There are two results of special relevance to this discussion. First, although mothers of all educational attainments were more likely to reprimand or prohibit sons than daughters, one category of reprimand reversed that trend and interacted with social class. Well-educated mothers were more likely than less-educated ones to chide the daughter for incompetence at a task, for not performing some act of mastery with sufficient talent. There was no comparable social class difference for sons. Moreover, daughters of these well-educated mothers were far more obedient to maternal commands and prohibitions than daughters of less well-educated parents. Again, there was no relation between maternal education and obedience among sons. The upper middle class mother was more concerned with her daughter's developing competence and her daughter seemed receptive to the mother's values. The ballet proceeded with least effort for this special mother-child pair, but was less neatly joined for other dyad. This interaction between maternal social class and sex of child could help to explain the closer covariation between the girls' attentiveness and maternal social class noted in this chapter. Social class differences in treatment practices toward sons and daughters could produce the pattern of results reported.

A third possible interpretation involves three assumptions—the advanced maturation of the girl, the stronger attachment of middle class infants to their caretakers, and a relation between degree of attachment and receptivity to maternal stimulation. The infant becomes attached to the person to whom he is allowed to make responses. The mother who initiates and maintains reciprocal vocalization and smiling with her infant should produce a child who is more attached to the caretaker than one who has less frequent opportunities to practice reciprocal actions with the caretaker. Since middle class mothers are more likely than lower class mothers to behave this way, middle class infants should be more strongly attached to their mothers than lower class babies. This prediction is supported by the data on incidence of crying to separation at 8 months. More middle than lower class infants cried when the mother left the room. Moreover, an independent study of 10-month-old infant girls revealed earlier crying to separation by middle than by lower class female infants (Tulkin, unpublished). The second assumption states that the stronger the attachment to the mother, the more closely the infant will attend to her, and the more receptive the infant will be to maternal rewards, smiles, and speech; the more finely attuned the infant will be to the mother's behavior. The third assumption calls again on the presumed maturational precocity of the girl. The sooner the infant passes through the early period of nonalertness (birth to 12 weeks), the earlier it will begin to establish an attachment to the mother. The girl, who is precocious, should establish her attachment earlier and become more receptive to the mother's behavior and more malleable to the distinctive stimulation she provides. As a result, there should be a closer relation between a mother's class-correlated practices and the cognitive development of girls than boys.

These three explanations of the sex difference in magnitude of the relation between class and fixation time: (a) girls are less variable and, therefore, reflect imposed experience with greater fidelity; (b) class differences in maternal reaction to daughter versus sons; and (c) girls' earlier maturation together with class differences in attachment, are not mutually exclusive. Each of these mechanisms could be valid and if all were operative several forces would be pushing for a stronger relation between social class and aspects of cognitive development in the female.

It is relevant to note that the correlation between social class and varied indexes of cognitive development (IQ, academic achievement scores) among school age children are typically higher for girls than for boys in this society. The classic interpretation of this fact has been that the girl is more concerned with parental and teacher acceptance than the boy, for this is a major motive for intellectual achievement in the girl. Since middle class girls are given acceptance for academic competence, this relation is not surprising. This dynamic is to be contrasted with the more varied motive spectrum for boys, where hostility, power, and identification with male figures who represent academic excellence each operate as incentives for intellectual mastery. However valid these psychodynamic propositions, they are not operative during the first year of life. The girl appears to be shaped by experience earlier than the boy, and in that early sculpting we may be previewing the greater predictive power of social class for females than for males.

IV

Vocalization

The production of sound by the primate infant usually accompanies a change in arousal state, and when the infant is human, we are tempted to name those states by affect words like distress, fear, anger, contentment, happiness, and excitement. Ploog, who has studied the squirrel monkey (Saimuri sciureus) in detail, writes:

Vocalizations are the most important signals in squirrel monkey communication. The first shrieks may be heard immediately after birth. Rooting and sucking are accompanied by the so-called milk purring which occurs within the first hours of life. In later life it may be heard during huddling and short interruptions of play and in connection with genital display. When a female begins smelling or touching an infant on its mother's back, the female may utter a series of purrs. The low intensity of this call suggests that it is directed towards an animal close by. In certain contexts purrs indicate a slightly aggressive motivation. Otherwise, the signal content is not yet fully understood. Peeps as well as trills are heard during the first days, and several other calls can be recorded during the first week. The total repertoire of the adult consists of about 26 distinguishable calls. Because of technical difficulties we do not yet know how many of them are present in the period immediately after birth. At least some of them occur only later—during maturation—for they are linked to behavioural stages, such as play, which appear sequentially. (Ploog, 1969, p. 290).

Ploog suggests that the neuroanatomical bases for these vocalizations lie partially in the limbic system, which contributes in a major way to a variety of emotional states. Observation of the human infant under one year confirms the belief that affective states are accompanied by specific types of vocalization. The cry of pain, the giggle of surprise, the purring of satiation are familiar to all who have spent any time with the human infant.

The controlled situation in the laboratory elicited three fundamental classes of vocalization. First, if the infant was either frightened or hungry, he would cry. We terminated the session if the cry persisted for any length of time. We shall not be concerned with this reaction in this chapter. If the infant became bored with the stimuli, he was likely to issue a mild protesting vocalization. This response was most likely to occur during the latter half of each episode. Finally, the infant could become aroused or excited by the unusual events presented to him and issue short, one or two second bursts of positive vocalization. It is this reaction that comprises the primary subject of this chapter. Although there is no difficulty distinguishing the cry or fret from this excited vocal sound, it is more difficult to distinguish it from a vocalization that reflects restlessness and boredom. The reader should keep in mind as he studies this chapter that there is an unknown amount of contamination of the sounds of beginning boredom with those of excited interest.

The basic assumption that will guide the interpretation of the vocal response is that a discrepant stimulus alerts the young infant and provokes him to assimilate it. This affect state, which we arbitrarily name *excited interest,* can produce, as an epiphenomenon, a vocalization. We do not suggest that this affect state is always accompanied by vocalization, for observation suggests that many babies were alerted by and intently studied the stimulus, but remained quiet. The working hypothesis is that some infants, as a result of either familial experience or biological temperament, are disposed to vocalize when they are aroused by an interesting event; others are not. To preview the major conclusion, infant girls are more likely than boys to display vocalization when they are in this special state.

SEX, STIMULUS, AND AGE DIFFERENCES IN VOCALIZATION DURING THE FIRST YEAR

At 4, 8, and 13 months the primary variable was duration of nonmeaningful vocalization, whereas at 27 months, when the child was speaking language, the primary variable was discrete number of stimuli to which the child verbalized or number of words in an utterance. Since the metrics were different, we shall consider, initially, the first year data as a unit, separate from the two year verbalization scores.

Appendix Table 18 contains the average vocalization scores by sex, stimulus, and episode for each of the three ages. Age differences in vocalization were dramatic. Vocalization decreased markedly from 4 to 8 months and rose slightly at 13 months of age. A repeated measures analysis of variance revealed significant age effects for two- and three-dimensional faces ($p < .01$). Vocalization to the faces was infrequent at 8 months because the facial stimuli were not very interesting and easily assimilated. Although bored, the infants did not babble. They would occasionally twist in the chair or look for something to manipulate, but did not make much noise. The auditory stimuli, which were interesting, did provoke vocalization, especially following termination of the taped voice. Typically, the child would quiet to the onset of the stimulus, and babble as soon as it ended. These vocalizations seemed to index the excitement generated by attending to and attempting to understand the recorded speech. Although vocalization at 13 months was still unintelligible, it may have served primitive labeling. It is reasonable that by one year of age some of the children's sounds of excitement were mixed with symbolic associations to the stimulus. Occasionally, a mother would tell the observer the meaning of the infant's vocal reaction to a particular stimulus. By 27 months all vocal utterances were meaningful, either private speech or verbalizations that were communicative in nature.

There were no sex differences in vocalization at any age. Moreover, differential vocalization to the visual stimuli within an episode was not impressive, in contrast to the fixation time data which revealed significant stimulus differences. In sum, vocalization behaved similarly to fixation time as far as sex and age differences were concerned, but unlike fixation time, did not covary with the discrepant quality of the stimulus or with social class during the first year.

Intercorrelations: Four Months. Vocalization times were highly intercorrelated within an episode (r ranged from .62 to .81 for achromatic faces; from .28 to .80 for the clay faces), and boys and girls showed equivalent generality across episodes. About one-half of the cross-episode correlations were significant, in contrast to the absence of interepisode consistency for fixation time at 4 months. However, unlike fixation time, vocalization at 4 months was unrelated to smiling, cardiac deceleration, or body size. There was one notable exception to this independence: fixation time and vocalization to the regular clay face were positively correlated for girls at 4 months ($r = .31$, $p < .01$ for trial 1; $r = .40$, $p < .01$ for trial 2). The corresponding correlations for boys were .11 and 00. (The sex difference in the magnitude of the trial 2 correlation was statistically significant.)[1] This is the first of a series of provocative sex differences in the correlational patterns for vocalization which we view as suggestive of a basic sex difference in the tendency to vocalize when excited by interesting events.

Eight Months. Vocalization to the faces continued to be relatively independent of the other variables and continued to display generality across episodes, despite its infrequent occurrence (see Appendix Table 19). Girls showed greater interepisode consistency of vocalization than boys, especially for the auditory episode. The average correlation between vocalization to the separate auditory stimuli and clay faces was .45 for girls and .15 for boys, and 9 of the 16 correlations between the auditory stimuli and the clay faces were significantly larger for girls than for boys.

The correlates of vocalization to the auditory episode implicate this response as a partial index of the excitement that accompanies information processing, but primarily among girls. The girls who vocalized when the voice terminated showed the largest cardiac decelerations during the presentation of the voice *on the preceding trial.* Appendix Table 20 presents the correlations between vocalization upon termination and magnitude of cardiac deceleration on the preceding trial. Significant correlations occurred primarily for girls, not for boys. The differences in correlations for the sexes were significant for LL,trial 2; HL,trial 2; and HH,trial 3. In addition to the trial by trial homologous correlations, there were also nonhomologous correlations between vocalization and deceleration. Of the total of 132 possible correlations between these two variables, 25% were significant for girls, in contrast to only 3% for boys. Since magnitude of cardiac deceleration is a partial index of the degree of quiet attentiveness to a signal, it appears that the girls who were most attentive during the auditory input—and, therefore, most likely to become aroused—vocalized most when the voice stopped. Since there were no sex differences in deceleration or vocalization, we cannot conclude that girls were more attentive than boys, but only that the covariation between attentiveness and subsequent vocalization was closer for girls.

Thirteen Months. Interepisode generality continued to be more impressive for girls than for boys (see Appendix Table 21), but the strong association between vocalization and deceleration to the auditory episode noted at 8 months, was absent at 1 year. Girls showed increased vocalization

[1] Although mean fixation and vocalization times to the regular or scrambled faces on trial 1 were equivalent for girls, the magnitude of the correlation between fixation and vocalization differentiated these two stimuli. This finding suggests that the magnitude of covariation between the two responses to a stimulus can be an index of the child's tendency to differentiate among them, when the absolute magnitudes on each variable are equivalent.

to both high meaning episodes across the period 8 to 13 months, but decreased babbling to the two low meaning episodes. Boys, by contrast, showed increased vocalization to all stimuli. This differential pattern of vocalization at the two ages affirms the trend, noted first in the 4-month data, that girls' vocalization is more closely linked to the nature of the stimulus than that of boys.

In summary, vocalization during the first year showed good inter-episode generality at every age, much better than fixation time, and the generality was more consistent for girls than boys. Vocalization to the visual episodes was generally independent of fixation time, smiling, and deceleration at every age. Finally, vocalization following termination of the auditory stimulus appeared to be related to the excitement that accompanies attentiveness in girls, but not boys. Let us now consider the intercorrelational pattern for meaningful verbalizations at 27 months.

VERBALIZATION AND VERBAL ABILITY AT 2 YEARS

There were eight independent situations in which verbal competence or spontaneous verbalization were coded: vocabulary recognition and vocabulary naming scores, spontaneous verbalization during free play, slides, human forms, clay faces, and, for a slightly smaller sample, ratings of quality and quantity of speech during seven hours of home observation. Appendix Table 22 contains the intercorrelations among all variables derived from these situations.

Among girls, a verbalization factor emerged that was consistent across episodes and related to vocabulary resources. Among boys, some consistency was present, but in attenuated form. For example, vocabulary score and verbalization during the play episode were significantly related to all other variables for girls; this was not true for the boys. Spontaneous verbalization to the slides, forms, and faces showed the best generality, for over 80% of the correlations were significant. Spontaneous verbalization during the slides was associated with smiling because it usually was part of an affective communication to the mother. The child would note an interesting stimulus, and smile and verbalize as he looked toward his mother, as if to announce that he recognized the strange event. Verbalization in the 2-year old seemed to be communicative, whereas, during the first year of life, it indexed a diffuse excitement.

SOCIAL CLASS AND VERBALIZATION

Appendix Table 23 contains the correlations between parental educational level and the major verbalization and vocalization variables from

4 through 27 months. Social class was more clearly correlated with richness of vocabulary than with amount of spontaneous verbalization among 27-month-old girls, although there was a suggestive correlation between social class and spontaneous verbalization during the initial part of the free play. Among boys, there was no significant correlation between social class and either vocabulary, speech quality, or spontaneous verbalization during the laboratory episodes. (Sex differences in magnitude of correlation were significant for vocabulary and verbalization to forms and faces.) One must differentiate between quality of vocabulary, which reflects linguistic competence, and the temperamental disposition to talk a lot. The usefulness of this differentiation is supported by the fact that vocabulary score, but not spontaneous verbalization, predicted long fixation times and long periods of uninterrupted play. In short, the verbalization data contain two vectors; one measures richness of language resources, the other is a generalized, tendency to speak when affectively aroused.

As at the earlier ages, spontaneous verbalization was relatively independent of other major variables. Spontaneous verbalization during the free play was significantly associated with smiling on the Embedded Figures Test for boys, but with more accurate performance on the Embedded Figures Test for girls. There was a general tendency for spontaneous verbalization to be more closely related to indexes of attentiveness and quality of problem solving among the girls; more closely linked with other signs of affect among the boys. Verbalization to the forms or faces at 27 months was accompanied by long fixation times to these stimuli, supporting the earlier suggestion that activation of hypotheses to explain an event leads to prolonged fixations. The more the child talked to the stimulus, the longer he gazed at it.

In sum, verbalization showed the best cross-episode consistency of any variable in the 27-month battery, confirming its centrality in the psychological organization of the child. As early as 27 months a "g" factor, so apparent in school age children, had already emerged. Vocabulary level—the essence of the intelligence test—was positively related to social class, sustained attention, and accuracy on a nonverbal perceptual problem, especially among the females. This pattern replicates the many studies on older children and adults, implying that verbalization is more central to the girls' cognitive profile than it is to the boys'.

STABILITY OF VOCALIZATION

There was good stability for girls from 8 to 13 and from 13 to 27 months, but minimal stability for boys across these periods (see Appendix Table 24). For example, vocalization to the achromatic or clay faces at

8 months predicted vocalization to the clay faces at 13 months for girls ($r = .30$, $p < .05$; $r = .47$, $p < .01$), but not for boys ($r = -.02$; $r = -.15$). The sex differences between each of the pairs of correlations was statistically significant. Moreover, vocalization to HF I at 13 months predicted verbalization to HF I and clay faces at 27 months for girls ($r = .39$, $p < .05$; $r = .47$, $p < .01$). The corresponding correlations for boys were $-.09$ and $-.19$, and again the differences between the pairs of correlations were statistically significant. The sex difference in continuity of vocalization furnishes additional support for the special significance of vocalization in the infant girl. Let us consider the cross-age comparisons in more detail.

FOUR-MONTH VOCALIZATION AS A PREDICTOR

Although there was no continuity from 4 to 8 months there was a provocative relation, among girls only, between vocalization to the achromatic faces at 4 months and orientation to the speaker at 8 months. It will be recalled from Chapter III that orientation to the speaker may have reflected an active interest in the taped voice. The relation between 4-month vocalization and orientation is seen in clearer relief in an analysis in which the children who showed short fixation times at 4 months were eliminated and we examined the data for those infants whose fixation times to the regular faces (PR and SR) were above the median. Some of these infants vocalized several seconds; others rarely vocalized. The distribution of first fixation times to PR and SR for the first two trials (stimuli were considered separately) were split at the median. The group above the median on fixation time was divided again at the median value for vocalization to PR or SR for the first two trials (median splits were performed separately for the sexes). We then compared the 8-month orientation scores for high versus low vocalizing groups (see Appendix Table 25). There were no differences between the two groups in vocalization at 8 months. However, there were clear differences in orientation. High vocalizing 4-month-old girls displayed orientations of 8 to 9 seconds, whereas low vocalizing girls oriented less than 2 seconds. This difference was significant for three of the four comparisons for SR ($p < .05$). Differences between high versus low vocalizing 4-month-old boys were the reverse of those found for girls. High vocalizing boys oriented *less* frequently to the speaker than low vocalizing boys.

The same pattern emerged when vocalization to PR or SR at 8 months was the basis for dividing the children into high versus low babblers. We again selected only those infants who were above the median on first fixation time at 8 months of age (i.e., attentive children). The high attentive group was then divided into those infants with high versus low vocalization times to PR or SR (see Appendix Table 26). Girls who babbled to PR looked longer at the speaker than those who were silent, but the boys who babbled to PR stared less often at the speaker than the silent boys. Although these 8-month differences were less striking than those considered earlier, the trend was the same.

Let us assume that when a child attends to an interesting event, he assumes either a quiet, inhibitory state or an aroused, excited one. The excited state should lead to a discharge of some kind, either babbling or a motor reaction, such as orienting toward the speaker. The correlation between 4-month vocalization and 8-month orientation to the sound source may reflect the continuity of an inhibitory-excitability dimension that is revealed when an infant is attending to an interesting event. This disposition seems to be preferentially expressed through vocalization in the girl, but not the boy. We shall see further evidence for this hypothesis later, but wish to note here that girls who vocalized to PR at 4 months waved their arms excitedly as they watched the human forms at 13 months ($r = .51, p < .01$); there was no comparable relation for boys.

STABILITY FROM 8 TO 13 MONTHS

Vocalization to the faces was so infrequent at 8 months that we shall only report coefficients for the average vocalization time across the whole series for each of the two visual episodes. Vocalization following termination of the auditory sequence was more common and separate correlations by stimulus are reported for that episode. There was good stability for girls, but only suggestive continuity for boys. Among girls, vocalization to the two-dimensional faces or the auditory events predicted vocalization to all three visual episodes at one year (r in the high 30's and 40's) (see Appendix Table 24). In fact, vocalization to the auditory event at 8 months was more highly correlated with vocalization to faces than with the auditory episode at one year. The 8-month-old infants who vocalized when the voice terminated were usually attentive during its presentation. They oriented toward the speaker and often showed decelerations of 8 to 10 beats. Occasionally their babbling sounded like an imitation of a word they had heard (e.g., mommy or daddy), and several infants smiled when the voice requested, "smile for me."[2]

---

[2] *Stability for trial by trial analyses:* The preferential stability of vocalization among girls was also evident in a trial by trial analysis, for which the correlations were between homologous trials (e.g., trial 2 at 4 months with trial 2 at 8 months). The data were based on the first 4 trials of two-dimensional faces at 4 months

HETEROTYPIC DERIVATIVES OF 8-MONTH VOCALIZATION

There were few theoretically meaningful derivatives of vocalization at one year for either sex. The vocalizing boys twisted restlessly during the auditory episode, suggesting that boys' vocalizations reflect a general motor excitability. The relation between 8-month vocalization to the auditory episode and indexes of attentiveness at one year was clearer for girls than for boys, as was the case at 8 months. For example, there was a positive relation, for girls only, between vocalization to the first auditory stimulus (low meaning-low inflection) at 8 months, and deceleration to the first stimulus (again low meaning-low inflection) at 13 months ($r = .36$, $p < .01$ for girls; $r = -.06$ for boys). And vocalization at 8 months predicted duration of orientation to the speaker at one year for the girls, but not for the boys.

Since vocalization at 8 months predicted vocalization, deceleration, and orientation to the speaker at one year with greater consistency for girls than boys, it appears that *the tendency to babble a few seconds after listening to a 20-second speech sample is a sensitive index of an attentive-excitability dimension in the 8-month-old girl that is stable during the second half of the first year.*

Girls' vocalizations seem to reflect the excitement that accompanies the attempt to assimilate discrepant information. This hypothesis is supported by an examination of the descriptive comments written by the observers on those girls who were frequent or infrequent vocalizers at both 8 and 13 months. The 10 girls with the highest vocalization scores to the auditory episode at both ages were compared with 10 girls who had the

---

with HF I at 13 months; clay faces at 4 or 8 months with clay faces at 13 months. As in the original analysis there was no continuity from 4 to 8 months for either set of faces.

The trial by trial analyses for 4 to 13 months were congruent with the results based on mean scores. There was no continuity for boys but, among girls, vocalization to the achromatic faces predicted vocalization to HF I; vocalization to the clay faces on the early trials predicted vocalization to the clay faces at 13 months. Stability of vocalization among the girls is supported by both analyses.

The 8- to 13-month coefficients revealed no continuity for boys, but excellent continuity for girls. The magnitudes of the coefficients were higher for the trial by trial analyses than those based on the means. The highest coefficients involved the first three trials supporting the suggestion that the stability of babbling in girls reflected excitability created by processing the stimulus, rather than boredom (e.g., trial 1 correlations for the clay faces was .51 for girls but $-.07$ for boys). Among girls, vocalization displayed a stability that was not only superior to boys', but also superior to the stability of fixation or deceleration. The favored interpretation is that when a girl is excited by an event that has meaning there is a prepotent tendency to vocalize, and this tendency remains stable during the first year.

lowest vocalization scores at both ages (1.5 seconds versus 0.5 seconds). The high vocalizing girls were more often described as alert and interested: the low vocalizing girls were more often described as apathetic and uninterested in the episodes.

PREDICTION OF 27-MONTH VERBALIZATIONS

The pattern of correlations with the 27-month variables as criteria was similar to that noted for fixation time. There was no strong continuity from 4 to 27 months for either sex, whether the criterion was spontaneous verbalization or vocabulary score. Although the correlations between vocalization at 4 and 27 months were close to zero for the entire group, it is possible that we might learn something about the forces that contribute to continuity or discontinuity by looking at a small group of girls who differed in vocalization to the first episode at 4 months (achromatic faces) and verbalization to the first episode at 27 months (free play). When each of these two distributions was divided into thirds, there were 9 girls in the top third of both distributions. Eight of these were from better educated families (top two social class categories), and only one was from the bottom two social class categories. By contrast, of the 8 girls in the bottom third of both distributions, 4 were from better and 4 from less well-educated parents ($p = .10$, by exact test). The two girls with the highest vocalization scores at both 4 and 27 months were the daughters of our most verbal mothers.

There was minimal continuity from 8 to 27 months and vocalization scores at 4 or 8 months were unrelated to either vocabulary or quality of speech in the home. These results *do not replicate* those of Moore (1967) or Cameron, Livson, and Bayley (1967), who found that babbling in the first year predicted vocabulary score and IQ at later ages.

The 13- to 27-month correlations were moderate but, as with earlier data, a bit stronger for girls than for boys (see Appendix Table 24). Vocalization to the first human forms episode predicted verbalization to three of the four episodes among the 2-year-old girls, but not among boys. Moreover, the correlations were as high for the first stimulus at 13 months (regardless of what it was) as they were for the entire series. That is, vocalization to the first stimulus of HF I at 13 months (and it could have been one of three different forms) predicted spontaneous verbalization to the free play and clay faces, suggesting that some girls retained a disposition to express—or not express—excitement to an interesting event with a vocal response. Most of the girls oriented to and showed interest in the first stimulus on HF I. Some girls quieted as they studied the forms, others talked, and the predisposition appears to be moderately stable. Similar relations emerged when clay faces was the one year predictor. Girls who vocalized to the first clay face were more likely to talk during the free play period, especially during the *initial* 5-minute adaptation period. This tendency was unrelated to social class or quality of vocabulary; *it was a disposition to express excitement through talking.* These relations were present in attenuated form for the boys. To our surprise, vocalization to the auditory episodes at 8 or 13 months was a poorer predictor of verbalization at 27 months than vocalization to the visual events. Spontaneous verbalization during the adaptation period of the free play was the best criterion variable, supporting the claim that these coefficients are tapping the stability of a tendency to talk upon encountering a new situation.

In order to learn more about the type of girl who displayed continuity from 1 to 2 years we examined groups of girls who were high or low vocalizers across several ages. In the first analysis, we looked at the distributions at 8 and 13 months. It will be recalled that there was good stability for vocalization to visual stimuli between 8 and 13 months for girls, but not for boys. We therefore divided each of the distributions of vocalization to the first episodes at 8 and 13 months (achromatic faces at 8 and Human Forms I at 13) into thirds and compared the 14 girls who were in the top third of both distributions with the 11 girls who were in the bottom third of both distributions. (Thirds were chosen because the distribution of scores suggested this division.) As might be expected, the high vocalizing girls, in contrast to their low vocalizing counterparts, vocalized more to the faces at 4 and 8 months and to the faces and free play at 27 months. But important support for the excitability interpretation is in the finding that the high vocalizing girls were more restless and more mobile in the free play at 1 year and displayed faster decision times on the conflict task at 27 months. *Each of these differences was statistically significant.* There was no difference in social class or vocabulary competence between these two groups. We then matched five pairs of girls, all from better educated families, so that one member of the pair was low vocalizing to both faces at 8 months and HF I at 13 months (bottom third of distribution); and the other member was in the top third of those two distributions. As can be seen from Figure 4-1, the high vocalizing girls showed faster tempo of play at both 8 and 27 months, had faster response times to the embedded figures and conflict tasks, and made more errors on the Embedded Figures Test.

We also examined the distribution of vocalization to the *first episode at each of the four ages:* achromatic faces at 4 months, achromatic faces at 8 months, HF I at 13 months, and the free play at 27 months. Each distribution was again divided into thirds and each child's score for all four distributions was examined. Some patterns were rare; for example,

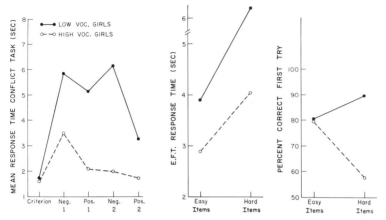

Figure 4-1 Decision time and inhibition for high versus low vocalizing girls.

very few children showed a linear increase or a linear decrease in vocalization over the four ages. The most common pattern was maintenance of one's relative rank across the four ages. We then compared groups of girls who were high or low on vocalization-verbalization at all four ages, but made these comparisons *within social class*. The "high vocalizing" group was in the top third of the distribution for all four ages; the "low vocalizing" group was in the bottom third of all four distributions. We then compared high versus low vocalizing girls within the top or the bottom half of each social class distribution. There were five girls in each social class-vocalization group. The association between high vocalization and independent indexes of excitability held mainly for the high versus low vocalizers *within the better educated families*. That is, the consistently high vocalizing middle class girls, when compared with low vocalizing middle class girls, had both faster response times ($p < .10$) and higher error scores ($p < .10$) to the Embedded Figures Test, and *shorter* fixation times at 8 and 13 months ($p < .05$). These differences between high and low vocalizing middle class girls did not occur for lower middle class girls, which suggests a different functional interpretation of vocalization and verbalization, depending on the social class of the girls' family.

CHANGE IN VOCALIZATION FROM 8 TO 13 MONTHS

Although absolute amount of vocalization at either 8 or 13 months was not related to parental education, amount of *increase* in vocalization from 8 to 13 months did covary with social class. There is some reason to suspect that vocalization at one year is under the dual control of the excitability factor, as well as a tendency to issue simple morphemes, for girls high in vocalization to the visual episodes at *both* 8 and 13 months were more likely to come from upper middle class families where language tutoring was more consistent. In a first analysis, a ratio was computed to evaluate the proportion change in vocalization from achromatic faces at 8 months to Human Forms I at 13 months (the first episodes administered at these ages). The highest ratio possible was 2.0; a ratio of zero signified no change and a negative value signified a decrease in vocalization.

Girls' Data. There was an approximately monotonic relation between degree of increase in vocalization from 8 to 13 months and parental education. The average ratios for the four educational levels were .07, .64, .60, and .96 ($p < .01$). The lower middle class girls showed essentially no increase in vocalization; the upper middle class girls showed a 50% increase.

The data were also examined nonparametrically. The number of trials (for trials 1 through 8) with a vocalization lasting one or more seconds was called a vocalization positive trial. Each lower middle class girl was matched with an upper middle class girl for number of vocalization positive trials at 8 months. Change scores were then computed for these matched pairs. The second order difference between the two classes was significant. The lower middle class girl showed a mean increase of 0.2 positive trials; the upper middle class girls a mean increase of 2.3 trials. Moreover, 8 out of 9 middle class girls increased in vocalization positive trials ($t = 2.2$; 7/df $p < .05$).

Increases in vocalization positive trials were then plotted against changes in fixation time to these same episodes across the same two ages. Most of the girls (41%) increased in both fixation time and vocalization time from 8 to 13 months; only 6% showed decreases on both variables. But there was no relation between social class and increases in fixation time, only between class and increase in vocalization. Two upper middle class girls who increased on both vocalization and fixation time were among the most verbally proficient children seen at 27 months. These two girls had the highest ratings on quality of speech in the home (6.5 on a 7-point scale), and vocabulary recognition scores of 21 and 17 out of a maximum of 22 correct.

Boys' Data. Identical analyses of the boys' scores were unrevealing. Social class was unrelated to changes in vocalization from 8 to 13 months. It will be recalled that many girls showed absolute increases in both vocalization and fixation time from 8 to 13 months (41%) and few (6%) decreased on both dimensions. Among boys equal numbers fell into each of the change cells—28% increased on both variables; 22% decreased on both variables. A chi-square test of the sex difference in increase versus decrease on both dimensions yielded a value of 7.4 ($p < .01$). This sex difference did not result from regression to the mean for there were no sex differences in mean vocalization or mean fixation time to either the faces at 8 or the forms at 13 months. In a related analysis we selected the 5 upper middle class girls and the 5 upper middle class boys who showed the largest increases in fixation time from 8 to 13 months (achromatic faces at 8 and Human Forms I at 13) in order to control for general attentiveness. We then compared changes in vocalization between the 5 boys and 5 girls. Four of the 5 girls increased in vocalization; only 2 of the 5 boys did.

Thus, increases in vocalization for the first visual episode from 8 to 13 months were more frequent among the upper middle class than among the lower middle class girls. Moreover, among middle class children the degree of covariation between *increases* in vocalization and *increases* in fixation time from 8 to 13 months was a bit clearer for girls than for boys, strengthening the hypothesis that vocalization during the first year is preferentially linked to the excitement that accompanies information processing in the girl.

THE JOINT EFFECT OF CLASS AND TEMPERAMENT

The large increases in vocalization from 8 to 13 months for the upper middle class girls should be a result of parental encouragement of vocalization and long periods of reciprocal communication between parent and infant. However, it is also reasonable that the mother is more likely to be responsive to a babbling infant than to a silent one. Hence, we might expect an interaction between the young infant's tendency to vocalize and his experiences at home, with respect to vocalization and verbalization at 1 and 2 years. We are assuming, first, that high vocalization scores at 4 months partially reflect a temperamental tendency to express excitement through a vocal response and, second, that a babbling girl born to a better educated mother will show larger increases in vocalization than one born to a less well-educated parent. The data tentatively support this pair of assumptions. We divided the distribution of 4-month vocalizations to the first episode (achromatic faces) into thirds (about 24 children in each tertile). We then compared children from better educated versus less well-educated parents, within each vocalization tertile, at 8, 13, and 27 months. That is, we inquired of the future behavior of infants from families above or below the median on the educational variable, all of whom were in the bottom third of the vocalization distribution at 4 months, the middle third of the vocalization distribution, or the top third of that distribution.

There was generally a linear relation, for girls only, between an initial tendency to vocalize at 4 months and (a) vocalization to Human Forms I and auditory at 13 months; (b) free play at 27 months, and (c) vocabulary score at 27 months. This relation was better for middle and upper middle class girls than it was for lower middle class girls. To paraphrase the above, an upper middle class girl who was a frequent vocalizer at 4 months was more likely to be a high vocalizing and highly verbal girl at 1 and 2 years than was a high vocalizing infant who came from parents who did not attend college (see Appendix Table 27). This relation did not emerge for the boys. Social class had a more critical influence on the verbalization and vocalization performance of girls than boys. (The interaction among sex, educational level, and initial 4-month vocalization was significant for auditory vocalization of 13 months ($F = 3.22$, $p < .05$).

One of the best examples of this generalization is seen in the vocalization scores to HF I at one year (see Figure 4-2). The difference between the top and bottom half of the social class distributions was greater for the two discrepant forms (head between legs and scrambled), and these were the forms that elicited the longest fixation times. The tendency to vocalize to the discrepant forms at one year was a joint function of the girl's social class and her initial tendency to be a babbling or silent infant.

Our interpretation, which was implied earlier, is that well-educated mothers of girls respond to their young vocalizing daughters by entering into frequent interactive episodes with them. These experiences increase the girls' disposition to vocalize and talk. Better educated mothers are less likely to behave this way with their sons and, therefore, the effect is at-

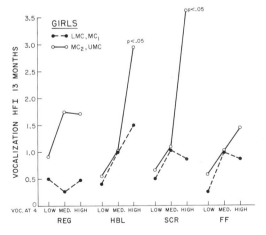

Figure 4-2 Vocalization to HF I at 13 months as a function of social class and initial vocalization scores at 4 months.

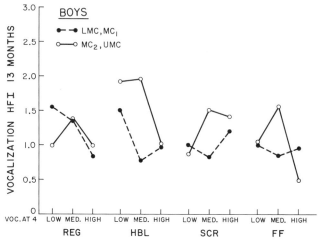

Figure 4-2 (Continued)

tenuated. If this explanation has validity, these data are a persuasive demonstration of the principle that infant and mother each make a contribution to the final behavioral outcome. A child has an initial disposition to be a high or a low babbler, but the probability that this tendency will lead to a spontaneously verbal child depends on the reactions of the caretaker to this characteristic.

DISCUSSION

Vocalization was most stable from 8 to 13 and from 13 to 27 months and minimally stable across the other four age comparisons, a pattern similar to that found for fixation time. However, the forces controlling vocalization are probably different from those governing fixation time. First, unlike fixation time there was no significant relation between absolute amount of vocalization and educational level of the parents at 8, 13, or 27 months. Class was correlated with *increases* in vocalization during the first year. Second, vocalization showed greater interepisode consistency than fixation time, but was far less differentiating among the stimuli within an episode. Most important, vocalization showed strong evidence of a sex difference that did not occur for fixation time. Vocalization seemed to be in the service of the excitement that accompanies active assimilation among girls, but not among boys. This suggestion is based on many facts, but especially sex differences in (a) the relation between 4-month vocalization and orientation to the speaker, (b) relation between vocalization following the auditory stimulus and deceleration during its presentation, (c) the stability of vocalization, (d) covariation between social class and increases in vocalization during the first year, and (e) the suggestive interaction of class, sex, and initial disposition to babble at 4 months on vocal behavior at 1 and 2 years. All of these phenomena implicate girls' vocalization as a reflection of the special excitement that accompanies attentiveness. The remainder of this chapter is devoted to this theme. Let us first examine other corpuses of data congruent with this hypothesis.

The reader may recall from Chapter III the experiment in which 4-month-old infants were first exposed to a standard mobile and then assigned to 6 different groups, each group viewing a different mobile at home for 21 days. Each infant was then shown the standard stimulus again, which was now of varying discrepancy from one viewed at home. The girls were more likely than boys to show increased vocalization on the second visit, suggesting that the excitement generated by encounter with a discrepant event was preferentially expressed through vocalization, but only in the female. In a recent study, also described in Chapter III, girls and boys $9\frac{1}{2}$ and $11\frac{1}{2}$ months old, were shown the same 2-inch wooden orange cube for 8 trials, followed by either a smaller version of the same cube or a completely novel yellow form. The smaller cube, but not the novel form, produced an increase in vocalization among the girls, but not among the boys, affirming again the idea that the special affect state engendered by encounter with discrepancy is preferentially tied to babbling in the infant girl.

Six-month-old infants (16 boys and 16 girls), Caucasian, and mostly firstborn, were shown a series of 6 stimuli (3 photographs of human faces and 3 geometric forms) in random order in a procedure similar to the one used at 4 and 8 months in this study. The girls vocalized more to the faces—which were discrepant from their schema for the parents' faces—than to the geometric forms ($p < .10$), whereas the boys showed equivalent vocalization to both classes of stimuli.

In a similar study, an unresponsive adult (one of 5 men or 5 women) stood 2 feet from each of 20 infants, but maintained eye-to-eye contact over two 6-minute trials. Infant females vocalized significantly more to male adults than to females; male infants did not vocalize differentially (Zelazo, 1969b). Thus, in several separate studies, infant girls showed greater differential vocalization than boys to visual and auditory stimuli that were discrepant from an established schema. One might conclude either that the boys did not have the schema for the original events or that the boys were less disposed to vocalize when they encountered the relevant discrepancy. We favor the second hypothesis because the fixation time data, summarized in Chapter III, did not reveal comparable sex differences.

It is also relevant to note that the predictive validity of vocalization in girls is affirmed by others. Bayley and her colleagues (Cameron, Livson, & Bayley, 1967) have reported that high scores on a vocalization factor on the Bayley Intelligence Scale from 6 to 12 months of age predicted Stanford-Binet IQ scores for older girls during childhood and adulthood (r ranged from .40 to .60), but the vocalization factor was unrelated to later IQ among males. McCall has analyzed comparable data available for the Fels longitudinal sample and finds similar results. Vocalization scores on the Gesell scale at 12 months predicted Stanford-Binet IQ scores at $3\frac{1}{2}$ years for girls, ($r = .3$), but not for boys ($r = .1$). However, Gesell indexes of cognitive development that did not involve vocalization also predicted Binet IQ at $3\frac{1}{2}$, 6, and 10 years, but only for girls. The 6-month Gesell scores had no predictive power for either sex. We did not find a strong relation between early vocalization and vocabulary score, but girls who increased in vocalization were from better educated families and high babbling infant girls raised by well-educated parents had the highest vocabulary scores at 27 months.

A final source of evidence comes from a longitudinal study in London conducted by Terrence Moore (1967). Moore studied 41 boys and 35 girls at 6 and 18 months as well as 2, 3, 4, 5, and 8 years of age. At 6 and 18 months each child was assigned a speech quotient from the Griffiths' Infant Scale. High scores are based on frequency of babbling to people, making different sounds, listening to conversation, babbling to music. High scores at 18 months reflect spontaneous verbalization. There was a positive relation between the speech quotient at 6 and 18 months for girls ($r = .52$, $p < .01$) but not for boys ($r = -.01$). And the correlation between the child's social class and speech quotient at 18 months was $+.39$ ($p < .05$) for girls and $-.31$ for boys.

The entire corpus of data is persuasive in suggesting that vocalization to representations of human faces, speech, or discrepant visual stimuli reflects cognitive excitement with greater fidelity among girls than boys. There are at least two possible interpretations of this inductive generalization. A learning or environmental position argues that mothers who are motivated to accelerate their daughter's mental development are likely to spend much time in face-to-face vocalization with them; more time than they would with a son, and more time than mothers who are not overly concerned with their daughter's rate of development. The mother's face-to-face vocalization should lead to increased babbling in the girl and better articulated schemata for human speech. This "accelerating" mother should continue to stimulate her daughter by teaching her words and encouraging the development of other cognitive skills. The predictive link between early babbling and quality of cognitive performance in the future would be a function of the continuity of the mother's acceleration of her daughter's development. The absence of this predictive link between infant vocalization and cognitive development in the boy requires the additional assumption that accelerating mothers do not preferentially engage in as much reciprocal vocalization with their sons. Preliminary data support this assumption.

Observations of the mother-infant interaction in the home, for half of the sample at 4 months, revealed that well-educated mothers engaged in more distinctive face-to-face vocalization with their daughters than less well-educated mothers, whereas there was no comparable difference among the mothers of sons. The female observer asked the mother to attend to her daily routine and to act naturally with the child. A selected set of mother and child variables was coded every 5 seconds. The observer wore a small, inconspicuous, battery powered device in her ear which produced a brief auditory signal every 5 seconds. Some of the variables included: mother vocalize to infant, mother touch infant, mother vigorously manipulate infant, mother pick up infant, child vocalize, child extend limbs, child smile. Each mother-child pair was observed for about four hours. There were no class differences for most of the variables, except for distinctive vocalization from mother to child (i.e., the mother was vocalizing to the infant in a face-to-face orientation and was *not providing any other stimulation;* she was neither tickling, nor feeding, nor holding the infant). The upper middle class mothers displayed this action toward their daughters significantly more often than lower middle class mothers (10.5% of the time observed versus 5.0%, $t = 2.75$, $p < .05$). However, there was no comparable class difference for mothers of sons (5.2 versus 6.0%).

The class difference for daughters was only significant for *distinctive vocalization,* not for a more general maternal vocalization variable, which disregarded other activities the mother might be engaging in while she was vocalizing (17.0% for upper middle class mothers versus 10.8% for lower middle class mothers). Moreover, the upper middle class mother was more likely to respond in some way to her daughter's vocalization within 10 seconds of its occurrence (39% versus 22%, $p < .05$). There was no comparable class difference for mothers of sons (29% versus 36%). The class difference for daughters is not a function of differential vocalization rates among the infants, which was 14% for each group.

Moss (1967) has observed the mother-child interaction at 3 months of age under similar conditions and found that middle class mothers of daughters were more likely to imitate the vocalizations of their infants than mothers of sons. Moreover, intelligent, animated, and verbose mothers, as determined by an interview prior to the birth of the child, were predisposed to be physically affectionate toward their 3-month-old sons, but stimulating of auditory and visual modalities with their daughters (Moss, Robson, & Pedersen, 1969). That is, the same kind of mother issued different behaviors depending on the child's sex (Moss, Robson, & Pedersen, 1969). Comparisons of Japanese and American mother-infant interactions furnish strong support for the shaping role of maternal behavior on an infant's vocalization. Caudill and Weinstein (1969) observed both Japanese and American mothers and their 12- to 16-week old infants. The Japanese families were residing in Tokyo or Kyoto; the Americans, near Washington, D.C. The observations followed a time sampling procedure for four hours a day on each of two days. American mothers directed more stimulating vocalization to the infant than Japanese mothers through talking, singing in a lively fashion, or playing word games. The Japanese mother, by contrast, softly hummed or rocked the infant in order to quiet or soothe him. As might be expected, the American infant was much more vocal than the Japanese baby, and much more active.[3]

The authors concluded:

The Japanese baby seems passive and he lies quietly with occasional unhappy vocalizations while his mother, in her care, does more lulling, carrying and rocking of her baby. She seems to try to soothe and quiet the child, and to communicate with him physically rather than verbally. On the other hand, the American infant is more active, happily vocal and exploring of his environment and his mother, in her care, does more looking at and chatting to her baby. She seems to stimulate the baby to activity and to vocal response. It is as if the American mother wanted to have a vocal, active baby and the Japanese mother wanted to have a quiet, contented baby. (Caudill & Weinstein, 1969, p. 31.)

Persuasive support for class differences in mother-daughter interaction comes from observations of 30 middle class and 30 lower class white mothers and their firstborn, 10-month-old daughters (Tulkin, unpublished). Time sampled observations of the mother-daughter interactions

---

[3] Dr. Freda Rebelsky has reported informally that scores on the Cattell Infant Intelligence Scale obtained on a sample of Dutch infants at 3 and 6 months of age are considerably behind American norms; the average scores being in the low eighties. The infants in this sample reside in a town in the eastern section of the Netherlands where it is common practice for a mother to place her infant in a covered cradle in a room removed from the main parts of the house and to come to the infant only when it is time for feeding or diapering. These infants receive minimal maternal stimulation of all kinds, including verbal and vocal interaction between mother and infant.

were made in the home on two occasions. The better educated mothers engaged in significantly more face-to-face vocalization with their infant, as well as more reciprocal and distinctive vocalization than the poorly educated mothers ($p < .001$ for most comparisons). However, there were no class differences in amount of physical manipulation, in the form of holding or kissing. These 10-month-old infants were subsequently seen in the laboratory. One of the episodes was the set of auditory stimuli used at 8 and 13 months, but with a female voice reading the material. The middle class girls showed significantly greater differentiation between high meaning-high inflection and the preceding stimulus (low meaning-high inflection) than the lower class girls, by displaying motor and vocal quieting *during* the presentation of high meaning-high inflection. On a subsequent episode they listened alternately to taped recordings of their mother's voice or a strange woman's voice speaking the same sentences. The middle class infants showed a *larger increase in vocalization following termination of the mother's voice than the stranger's voice.* The lower class infants *did not* make this differentiation. (The second order difference between the classes was statistically significant.) The middle class girls showed both increased vocal excitement following exposure to a familiar sound (i.e., mother's voice), as well as differentiation of meaningful from meaningless speech. And these cognitive accomplishments were accompanied by theoretically relevant differences in experience in the home. Thus, the sex differences in the correlational pattern for vocalization could be solely the result of *differential* interaction patterns with the mother.

A second, more speculative, interpretation has a biological flavor, and hypothesizes an initial sex difference in neurological organization of the central nervous system mechanisms serving vocalization. Vocalization in the infant female may be a more prepotent reaction to the arousal occasioned by the processing of interesting events. This speculation finds some support in varied classes of observations. Among the langur of northern India, for example, squeals and screams are observed more frequently among females than among males. Furthermore, infant girls appear to be more aroused by auditory stimulation than boys, for a soft 1000 cps tone behaves like a reinforcement for 10- and 14-week-old girls, but not for boys (Watson, 1969). In this study, the infant lay supine with two white circles located one foot above his eyes. The infants were "reinforced" for fixating one of the two circles and the infant received either a visual reinforcement (a red circle with two eyes and mouth) or an auditory reinforcement (1000 cps soft tone). The girls' fixations were influenced by the auditory but not by the visual reinforcement. The 14-week-old boys were influenced by the visual, but not by the auditory reinforcement; the 10-week-old boys were not influenced by either class of reinforcements. These data suggest that auditory input has a more excitatory effect on the girl than the boy (Watson, 1969).

It is possible that the typical dominance of the left cerebral hemisphere over the right may emerge earlier ontogenetically and be more clear-cut in the female than in the male. If the two cerebral hemispheres were less equipotential for females there might be a closer functional relation between information processing and expressive vocal sounds among girls than boys.

Support for this hypothesis comes from a developmental study of dichotic listening (Kimura, 1967). A series of independent studies has affirmed that when pairs of different digits are presented simultaneously to the two ears through earphones, more digits are accurately reported from the right ear than from the left ear. Since the auditory receiving area of the temporal cortex receives a greater number of fibres from the contralateral than from the ipsilateral ear, the right ear advantage indicates that the left hemisphere, typically the speech hemisphere, is preferentially processing the information (Kimura, 1967; Broadbent, 1954; Rosenzweig, 1951). The dichotic digits task was administered to boys and girls 5, 6, 7, and 8 years of age. Both sexes showed left hemisphere (right ear) dominance at the three older ages, *but at age 5, only the girls showed a significant superiority of right over left ear* ($t = 3.29$; $p < .01$). The boys' scores indicated no clear dominance at age 5 (Kimura, 1967). Kimura writes:

The data do suggest that boys may lag behind girls in the development of left hemisphere dominance for speech. This finding has a parallel in Ghent's (1961) demonstration of a lag in the development of somesthetic asymmetry in boys. Ghent has pointed out that slower development of functional asymmetry of the two hemispheres in boys would be in accord with their slower development of speech. (Kimura, 1967, p. 169.)

Moreover, the left hemisphere advantage only holds true for language (digits, words, or nonsense syllables); it does not hold true for nonlinguistic sounds, such as melodies, or familiar environmental sounds. If two different melodies are presented dichotically and the subject subsequently has to select the melody he heard from a group of four melodies (two of which he did not hear), adults show a left ear (right hemisphere) superiority (Kimura, 1967). The preferential processing of nonlinguistic information by right hemisphere is present by age 5. Children (age 5 to 8) were presented with 12 pairs of sounds (e.g., dishwashing-phone dialing; rooster-horse) and asked to state the one they heard. All children showed right hemisphere dominance (i.e., left ear superior to right ear, Knox & Kimura, 1970) but boys' performance was superior to that of girls. The authors argued that this sex difference might be mediated by a difference in functioning in the central nervous system. They reviewed evidence indicating that boys' performance on visio-spatial tests, which also seems to be dependent on right hemisphere functioning, is superior to that of girls. They concluded, "the superior performance of boys on non-verbal tasks may be best explained in terms of sex differences in neural functioning" (Knox and Kimura, 1970, p. 236).

Additional support for the notion that language competences are more elaborated in the left hemisphere for females than for males comes from a study in which right or left temporal cortex was removed from male and female adult epileptic patients. The patients were tested one year after surgery on the adult Wechsler-Bellevue Intelligence Test (Lansdell, 1968). Removal of left temporal cortex had a more serious detrimental effect on verbal functioning among female than among male patients. Removal of right cortex had a more detrimental effect on quality of functioning on the nonverbal tasks for males than for females. The data suggest that left hemisphere dominance and accompanying language elaboration are less equivocal for females than for males, and, consequently, verbal functioning is more clearly elaborated in the left hemisphere for female than for male. This suggestion corresponds with the finding that, among dyslexic children, girls show the typical left hemisphere dominance in dichotic listening tasks; dyslexic boys do not (Taylor, 1961).[4]

Although the data base is thin and the hypothesis a little too bold, it is not completely bizarre to suggest that the sex differences in the significance of vocalization during the first year reflect subtle differences in cerebral dominance.[5] The data are consistent, statistically reliable, and invite theoretical attention. The hardiness of the data makes it likely that we are dealing with an important psychological phenomenon. Comparative psychologists routinely discover that behavioral reactions to varied states of arousal or experimental intervention differ among closely related strains or between sexes within strains. Excited vocalization in the infant male and female may be just one more instance of this common phenomenon.

[4] An analysis of 8 brains of 4-year-old children (taken from Conel's [1963] series) revealed that 4 of the 5 female brains showed greater myelination in the left FAγ hand area than in the corresponding area in the right hemisphere. This difference was *reversed* in the three male brains (Lansdell, 1964).

[5] It is possible that myelination of the medial surface of the temporal lobe proceeds precociously in the infant female. If centers in the limbic area of nonhuman primates are destroyed, vocalizations disappear. These vocalizations are typically reflections of emotional states. These limbic areas are anatomically connected to the medial surface of the temporal lobe, which is not completely myelinated at birth (Lancaster, 1968). If myelination of this area were advanced in infant girls, this precocity might lead the female to express stimulus excitement through vocal reactivity (see Jurgens, Maurus, Ploog, & Winter, 1967; Ploog, 1969).

V

Cardiac Deceleration

The use of cardiac deceleration in the assessment of attentional processes is of recent but, nonetheless, impressive history (Graham & Clifton, 1966). One of the reasons for the tardy development of this variable rests with the prejudices born of arousal theory. The arousal hypothesis, stated in simplest form, implied that an organism that was tensed as a result of any experience, be it fear, sexual passion, joy, or intense attention, would show a pattern of autonomic activity concordant with increased arousal. In the case of the heart, this would mean an increased heart rate. Investigators did not search for decreases in heart rate to laboratory exercises that involved attentional processes, nor did they know how to interpret them when they were so salient that they could not be ignored. In the mid-1950's R. C. Davis (1955) was studying autonomic reactions to various arousing manipulations, one of which was a set of photographs of attractive seminude women. Davis expected these pictures to arouse his late-adolescent male subjects and to produce an unequivocal cardiac acceleration. Instead, he noted consistent decreases in heart rate when the men studied the pictures. He wrote of his puzzlement honestly and gave to this phenomenon the simple descriptive name, "P" reaction, or picture reaction. Several years later, the Laceys (1967), who were not closely wedded to the catechism of arousal theory, hypothesized that cardiac deceleration was a biologically adaptive reaction when an organism was processing external stimuli, and produced consistent decelerations in adult subjects requested to watch lights or listen to monologues. Once the relation between attention to external events and cardiac deceleration had been established in adults it was obvious that this variable might be a useful index with children and infants. In a series of studies Kagan and his colleagues (Kagan & Rosman, 1964; Lewis, Kagan Campbell, & Kalafat, 1966; McCall & Kagan, 1967) found support for the general proposition that the probability of a cardiac deceleration increased when an infant or child was watching a visual event or listening to an auditory stimulus. The relation is far from perfect, since a deceleration does not always occur when the child looks as though he is attending to the external event. Investigations have been initiated in an attempt to determine the constraints on this rule. The work with infants suggests that, other things being equal, a deceleration is most likely to occur when the infant is surprised and shows an orientation reaction. Two different classes of events can surprise the infant. A totally unexpected stimulus, as occurs in the beginning of each new series, surprises the infant and, typically, decelerations were largest to the first stimulus in every series. Second, an event that is a moderate discrepancy from a schema is likely to surprise the infant. But in both cases, the child is likely to quiet motorically, adopt an attentive posture, and display a deceleration of 6 to 10 beats over a 4- to 6-second interval.

There is some support for the notion that moderately discrepant stimuli elicit the largest decelerations. In one investigation, 5½-month-old male infants were shown a simple stimulus consisting of 5 green three-dimensional elements vertically arranged on a white background. The order of stimulus presentation was SSSSSSSSTSSTSSTS in which S was the standard and T was one of three transformations of that standard. Each infant was shown only one of the three transformations. Magnitude of cardiac deceleration was larger to the moderate transformation of the standard than to the two more serious transformations (McCall & Melson, 1969). This result is congruent with an earlier study that used the same stimuli with slightly younger infants and established the schema over a 4-week period in the home (McCall & Kagan, 1967). In a related study (McCall & Melson, 1969) 27, 5½-month-old infants listened to a sequence of 8 notes on a piano (either an ascending series or a random series) for either 4, 8, or 12 repetitions. On the 5th, 8th, or 13th presentation a discrepant stimulus was presented (a random sequence for children who heard the ascending series; and ascending sequence for infants who heard the random series). After this discrepancy the children heard two more repetitions of the standard, then a discrepancy, two more standards and another discrepancy, and finally one more standard. The discrepant events produced larger cardiac decelerations than the preceding standards (regardless of whether the discrepant event was in the ascending or the random series) and the longer the initial familiarization with the standard, the greater the deceleration to the discrepant stimulus.

Lewis and Goldberg (1969), in a similar design, presented 3½-year olds with 6 repetitions of a stimulus (meaningful as well as meaningless) followed on the 7th presentation with transformation of the previously repeated visual standard. Magnitude of deceleration decreased over the 6 repetitions but increased by 50% when the transformation was presented. Finally, Fischer (1969) administered to each of 18 adults mental tasks, some of which required a sudden insight for solution, and others did not. The former problems produced larger decelerations at the moment of solution—at the time of surprise—than the control tasks.

THE BASIS FOR THE CARDIAC RESPONSE

There are two interpretations of the cardiac deceleration reaction. Lacey (1967) has suggested that the cardiac deceleration is the organism's way of increasing its receptivity to the external events. Lacey views the deceleration as a quasi-instrumental response, and bases this provocative hypothesis on the fact that a change in rate of sensory afferents from the heart stimulates the carotid sinus to discharge. These signals are passed to the reticular formation and thence to the cortex. It is assumed that this bombardment of cortex decreases the organism's sensitivity to inputs from eye, ear, and skin. A low and steady heart rate minimizes these noisy signals from the carotid sinus and leads to increased sensitivity.

Obrist offers the alternative hypothesis that a decrease in heart rate is a result of vagal excitation and is accompanied by a decrease in somato-motor activity. Obrist argues that heart rate decreases as the organism becomes quiet and that both cardiac and somatic effects are different biological manifestations of the same process. He notes, "The heart may provide in one muscle a picture of the total somatic involvement at any given time." (Obrist, Sutterer, & Howard, 1969.) Obrist also comments:

If cardiac and somato-motor events are significantly coupled as proposed, then a decrease in one aspect of the response would be associated with a decrease in the other aspect of the response. There is both neurophysiological and psychophysiological evidence which suggests just such a possibility. Areas in and around the cingulate gyrus and related subcortical pathways appear to be involved in both somatic and cardiovascular inhibitory effects. Vagatonic effects on the heart have been observed under stressful conditions where somatic motor activity also decreases. Finally, the likelihood that such inhibitory mechanisms are involved during aversive conditioning in humans has been confirmed in work now in progress where both the inhibition of spontaneous bursts of striate activity and of respiratory events have been found to be concomitant with the anticipatory deceleration of heart rate. Such evidence surely suggests that cardiac and somatic motor processes are coupled. Furthermore, such coupling may be relevant to an understanding of attention processes and the modification of certain behaviors which some investigators have recently proposed are associated with cardiac effects. (Obrist & Webb, 1967, 29–30.)

Obrist's suggestion has to be partially correct for the large decelerations are typically accompanied by obvious decreases in motor activity. The infants suddenly stopped moving and their heads became fixed. The best phrase to describe this concatenation of events is the term "double take." The infant looked surprised by the event and the surprise was often accompanied by a sudden quieting and cardiac deceleration. The Obrist hypothesis implies that cardiac acceleration is not on a continuum with deceleration, for events that cause motor quieting in the service of attention are not theoretically similar to the events that lead to increased somatomotor activity and acceleration. The organism may become diffusely active when he is frightened or bored; he quiets when he is surprised. These states are qualitatively different and respiratory changes are more likely to covary with acceleration than with deceleration. We only coded cardiac decelerations, for our major interest was in the attentional processes of the infant.

The cardiac deceleration variable was made a central part of the assessment procedure in the hope that it would add extra information to the fixation time data. Deceleration values were quantified for all episodes at 4, 8, and 13 months and for the chromatic slides and Embedded Figures Test at 27 months. The other episodes at 27 months produced very few decelerations and the data were not reduced.

SEX, AGE, AND STIMULUS DIFFERENCES IN DECELERATION PATTERNS

Figure 5-1 contains the trial-by-trial deceleration values for the episodes at 4, 8, and 13 months. Figure 5-2 presents cardiac deceleration to the slides, but in slightly different form; namely, the proportion of subjects showing decelerations equal to or greater than 6 beats.

There are several salient trends in the data. First, there were no sex differences in mean deceleration or variance to any stimulus episode at any of the ages. However, as with fixation and vocalization, the patterns

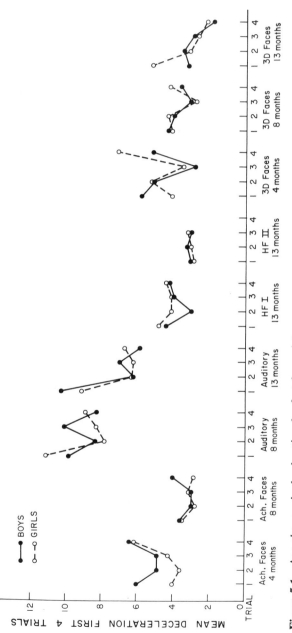

Figure 5-1 Age changes in deceleration for first four trials.

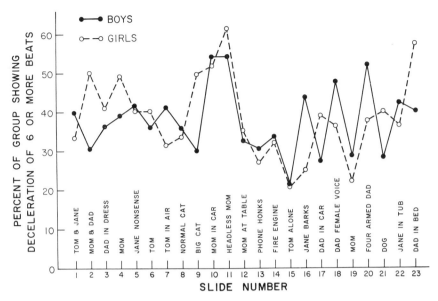

Figure 5-2 Proportion of children showing decelerations of $\geqq 6$ beats per minute to each of 23 slides for fixation component.

of correlations were different for the sexes. Second, magnitude of deceleration decreased markedly after the first four trials. Age changes in cardiac deceleration across the first year also matched those found for fixation time. The two sets of faces elicited smaller decelerations at 8 than at 4 months, suggesting that as a schema for a face becomes established, the surprise value of that stimulus wanes. Repeated measures analyses of variance for the two-dimensional faces at 4 and 8 months and the clay faces at 4, 8, and 13 months yielded highly significant F ratios for age ($F = 23.1$, $p < .01$ for the achromatic faces; $F = 43.9$, $p < .01$ for clay faces). The small decelerations at 8 months were specific to the faces, for the auditory stimuli elicited larger declerations than the faces at 8 months. Magnitude of deceleration to the auditory episode, however, was smaller at 13 than at 8 months ($F = 28.3$, $p < .01$) corroborating the earlier statement that as stimuli become familiar, they elicit smaller decelerations.

Stimulus Differences at 4, 8 and 13 Months. Stimulus differences at 4 months matched those found for fixation time, for the two regular faces (PR and SR) elicited larger decelerations than the irregular faces ($p < .01$), and regular, scrambled, and no eyes each elicited larger decelerations than the blank face. Stimulus differences were minimal at 8 months, but at 1 year free form elicited smaller decelerations than the other

3 stimuli in HF I. Since free form probably had a minimal relation to any existing schema, there was little cognitive surprise and, therefore, minimal deceleration. Novelty alone—apart from a sudden, unexpected input—is not a sufficient basis for deceleration. There must be some psychological relation between the stimulus and the relevant schema if the organism is to become surprised.

Twenty-seven months: Slides. The 2-year-old children were not surprised by the human forms or the clay faces and decelerations to these episodes were small and not included in the analyses. Decelerations to the slide series and during the first fixation of each Embedded Figures Test item were of sufficient magnitude to be analyzed. As at the earlier ages about a third of the children showed no change in heart rate during fixation of the slides. Since the distribution was skewed toward low values, we scaled the decelerations to each stimulus and assigned a score of 1 to a deceleration of 0, a score of 2 to decelerations of 1 to 5 beats, a score of 3 to decelerations equal to or greater than 6 beats. Figure 5-2 shows the proportion of boys or girls showing decelerations of 6 or more beats (i.e., scale scores of 3) to each of the slides for the visual fixation component of each stimulus. As with fixation time there was neither marked habituation of deceleration nor striking sex differences. However, a few of the discrepant scenes elicited larger decelerations than the preceding nondiscrepant scene. The mean deceleration to discrepant scenes was higher than the mean to the nondiscrepant scenes, but this difference was not statistically significant. Among boys the 5 scenes to which the largest number of children showed scale 3 decelerations were (1) woman with no head, (2) woman in car, (3) man with four arms, (4) man with female voice, and (5) girl with a dog's bark. Among the girls the top five scenes were (1) woman with no head, (2) man in bed, (3) woman in car, (4) oversized cat, and (5) man and woman standing.

The scene of the woman holding her head in her hand (number 11 in the series) elicited large decelerations from most of the children (57% of the total sample). Intuitively, this scene is one of the two most blatant discrepancies in the series. Cardiac deceleration differentiated this particular scene from the other stimuli, whereas fixation time was not noticeably higher to that stimulus.

The pattern of decelerations to the auditory component of the slides was suggestive.[1] The largest decelerations occurred to the nonspeech sounds (car horn, dog's bark). Since 16 of the 23 scenes were accompanied by a human voice speaking, one can argue that each of the 7 non-

---

[1] Decelerations during auditory were computed by subtracting the three lowest decelerations during the auditory period from the three lowest beats prior to the onset of the stimulus.

vocal sounds was a discrepant event that should have produced large decelerations. It is possible that we could have produced the opposite effect by having 16 nonhuman and 7 human sounds, supporting the view that large decelerations are most likely to occur to a violation of an expectancy. (Appendix Table 28 ranks the scenes with respect to magnitude of deceleration to the silent and narrative components of the stimulus.)

Embedded Figures Test at 27 Months. Magnitude of deceleration during the first fixation of each embedded figures item was related to item difficulty, especially for boys; on 4 of the 6 series deceleration was larger to test items 2 or 3 than to the first and easiest item. Response times were longer to the more difficult items and therefore decelerations should be larger, since the child was usually quiet while searching the figure prior to his first solution hypothesis.

SOCIAL CLASS DIFFERENCES

Social class was moderately related to cardiac deceleration at 4 months but relatively independent of class at 8, 13, or 27 months, a pattern that reversed the one found for fixation, where the relation to class increased with age. Four-month lower middle class children showed smaller average decelerations to the faces than upper middle class children and the strongest class difference occurred among girls to the regular clay face. Since the distribution of decelerations contained many zero scores, a more conservative nonparametric analysis was performed. The distribution of decelerations was divided, by trial, into low (0 to 2 beats), moderate (3 to 5 beats) and large decelerations (6 or more beats). We examined the proportion of infants in each social class group falling into each of these three magnitude levels (a 4 × 3 contingency table). Appendix Table 29 presents the proportion of infants in each of the four social class groups who displayed large decelerations to each stimulus to each of the first 3 trials (chi-square based on a 4 × 3 table with 6 df; that is, 4 social class levels by 3 levels of deceleration (for each stimulus trial). Fewer lower middle class subjects displayed large decelerations. In 6 instances, out of a possible 48, not one lower middle class infant showed a deceleration of 6 beats or more. By chance alone, the lower middle class infants should have had the largest proportion in 12 of the 48 instances; whereas, they were only the highest in 3 instances. The social class effect occurred for both sexes to the scrambled and regular faces in the three-dimensional faces, each of which contained eyes. If we assume that a large deceleration is most likely to occur when the infant is surprised by a moderately discrepant event, these data suggest that the lower middle class child either has a poorer or a better schema for a human face than a middle class infant. He either saw no relation between his schema for a face and the clay masks, or he assimilated them at once.

In contrast to the 4-month data, there were minimal class difference in deceleration to the faces at 8 and 13 months. The absence of class differences in deceleration to the visual episodes at 13 months may seem puzzling, for HF I and HF II were interesting and fixation times did covary with social class. But the class differences in fixation time to these forms were interpreted as reflecting differences in density of hypotheses activated to assimilate the event, *not surprise*. Magnitude of deceleration at 1 year did not vary with social class because all the 1-year-old children had a good schema for the distinctive elements of a human form and few were surprised by what they saw. Class differences among the 1-year-old infants involved density of hypotheses relevant to the stimuli. This conclusion matches data on Mayan and American children (1, 2, and 3 years old) shown various human faces and forms. Differences between the two cultural groups are best explained as a function of activation of hypotheses, rather than differences in schema articulation. The absence of class differences in deceleration to the slides at 27 months is viewed in a similar way.

INTERCORRELATION OF DECELERATION SCORES

Four Months. Magnitude of deceleration was consistent within an episode, generalized across episodes (see Appendix Table 30), with cross-episode correlations slightly higher for boys than for girls. The trial-by-trial correlations between deceleration, on the one hand, and fixation, vocalization, and smiling on the other, revealed that magnitude of deceleration was moderately correlated with fixation time and smiling, but was independent of vocalization.

Eight Months. The disposition to display large cardiac decelerations generalized across all three episodes for both sexes (see Appendix Table 31), and was superior to the cross-episode consistency noted for fixation time. Moreover, boys with large decelerations to achromatic faces looked longer at these faces and at the sound source, suggesting an attentiveness cluster. Among girls, deceleration to auditory was also part of an attentiveness factor for large decelerations were linked with long orientations to the speaker, and long fixations to the achromatic faces.

Thirteen Months. Magnitude of cardiac deceleration showed excellent generality across episodes (see Appendix Table 32), much better than fixation time, and was relatively independent of vocalization. Deceleration was associated with length of first fixation, and the magnitude of this association became larger with each succeeding episode. There are varied interpretations of this trend. It is possible, first, that the infants were more vigilant and apprehensive during the first series (HF I) than they were during the last series, and this initial vigilance could have attenuated the relation between fixation time and deceleration. It is also possible that viewing the forms in HF I created a schema or an expectancy that was violated when the transformations of HF II were presented. The children were surprised by these different forms and the conditions were optimal for a positive relation between deceleration and fixation time.

Twenty-seven Months. Magnitude of cardiac deceleration showed poor consistency within the 23 scene slide series or the 18-item Embedded Figures Test. Moreover, there was no relation between the two episodes in contrast to the good cross-episode generality at the earlier ages. The absence of cross-episode generality seems to result from the fact that the Embedded Figures Test generated a state different from the one that accompanied watching or listening to interesting events. But this would not explain the lack of consistency within the test. It is possible that by 2 years of age the deceleration response has become much more stimulus specific than it was at the earlier ages.

CONTINUITY OF DECELERATION

There was moderate continuity from 4 to 8, 8 to 13, and 13 to 27 months, and, unlike fixation time or vocalization, stability was slightly better for boys than for girls. Appendix Table 33 contains the stability coefficients for cardiac deceleration from 4 to 8 months, by stimulus, and for the mean of the maximal deceleration to each of the four stimuli. There was no stability for girls, but moderate stability for boys, especially for achromatic faces. The correlations for the mean maximal values were in the high fifties for boys, significantly higher than those obtained for girls, and among the highest coefficients encountered.

One interpretation of the sex difference in stability of deceleration from 4 to 8 months rests with an assumption concerning the determinants of deceleration. We have suggested that one determinant is an encounter with a moderately discrepant stimulus; a second is a more general disposition to quiet motorically to any new event. This suggestion is supported by empirical studies of animals implicating two components to an orienting reaction. "One component seems to be an indicator of searching and sampling while the other component is manifest when novelty is registered." (Pribram, 1967). Any tendency to quiet and to adopt a postural orientation of receptivity to an event is likely to produce cardiac deceleration. Boys may be more likely than girls to display these postural changes in the service of information processing. At one year, boys were more likely than girls to quiet motorically to the onset of the stimulus for all three visual episodes. Yet, boys were not more active during the inter-trial periods. Hence, this propensity to quiet is not a regressive artifact because the boys were more active than the girls prior to stimulus presentation.

Stability from 4 or 8 to 13 Months. There was suggestive stability from 4 to 13 months, in contrast to the lack of continuity for fixation and vocalization time over the same 9-month period. The stability for 8 to 13 months was also reliable. The highest correlations were between the auditory episodes at 8 and 13 months, with deceleration to high meaning-high inflection as the best predictor of 13 month deceleration values (see Appendix Table 34).

Patterns of Predictive Stability to 27 Months. There was moderate stability from 13 to 27 months, only suggestive stability from 8 to 27 months, and no stability from 4 to 27 months (see Appendix Table 35).

Thus, there was suggestive stability from 4 to 8, 8 to 13, and 13 to 27 months for both sexes, although the size of the coefficients favored the boys. If we interpret the deceleration as an epiphenomenon to somato-motor quieting to a new event, it would appear that such quieting is a more stable characteristic for boys than for girls. The state of attentiveness, we argue, occurs equally for both sexes, but this state may be preferentially linked to somato-motor quieting in the boy and to vocalization in the girl. In short, it is suggested that each sex preferentially displays different reactions when each is aroused by a discrepant event. The differential significance of deceleration for boys and vocalization for girls was revealed in an analysis in which only the reactions to the *first stimulus* of each episode were correlated. Most infants were maximally alert for the first stimulus, showed long fixations, and were in the state of excited interest to which we have often referred. If individual differences in this basic state are stable, but manifested in different response modalities, we should see differential continuity for vocalization and deceleration. As anticipated, the stability correlations for vocalization were higher across age for girls than for boys (see Appendix Table 36 for the first trial correlations for the episodes at 4, 8 and 13 months). Vocalization to the first trial of each of the three episodes at 8 months predicted vocalization to the first trial of clay faces at 1 year for girls ($r = .48, .51, .45$). The corresponding coefficients for boys were .03, $-.07$, and .06, and the differences in the magnitudes of those correlations were statistically significant. By contrast, deceleration to clay faces and auditory at 8 months each predicted deceleration to HF II at 13 months for boys ($r = .35$ and $.43$). The corresponding coefficients for girls were $-.04$ and .08; and the sex differences in the magnitude of these two pairs of correlations were also significant. If these first trial reactions sensitively reflect the state of "excited attention," and this disposition is stable over time, it appears that the continuity of this tendency is reflected through vocalization in girls and through deceleration in boys.

This speculative suggestion finds additional support in the sex differences between consistently high versus low decelerators at 8, 13, and 27 months. The boys who displayed large decelerations to the auditory episode at 8 and 13 months and Human Forms I at 27 months were more attentive in their play at 2 years than boys who were consistently low decelerators. This difference did not occur for girls.[2] High decelerating boys seemed capable of long periods of involvement with the toys and longer response times to conditions of uncertainty. This pattern is consonant with the suggestion that deceleration among boys reflects a disposition toward inhibition of action and a tendency to quiet in the service of dealing with a novel encounter. High decelerating girls do not have these characteristics. It is possible that, like vocalization, deceleration has a slightly different significance for girls than it has for boys.

[2] In order to determine if there were any special sets of characteristics for those children who were consistently small versus large decelerators we compared high versus low infants on maximal deceleration values. Since the auditory episode elicited the largest decelerations and displayed stability from 8 to 13 months, the first comparison was based on this episode. The infants above the median on mean maximal deceleration at both 8 and 13 months (a mean of about 17 beats per minute) were compared with infants below the median at both ages (mean of 7 beats per minute).

As might be anticipated, the differences were not similar for the sexes. Large decelerating boys were endomorphic in physique, likely to scan the room during the initial adaptation period in the free play and displayed longer response times to the Embedded Figures Test. The high decelerating boys were generally more attentive and inhibited than those with small decelerations, despite no differences in social class or language competence. High decelerating girls, by contrast, were most likely to have a fast tempo of play at 27 months, and showed no signs of inhibition.

A second analysis involved high versus low deceleration at 13 and 27 months. High decelerating children were above the median on the maximal deceleration to HF I and HF II at 13 months and on the scaled deceleration to the chromatic slides at 27 months. The low decelerating children were below the median on all three variables. High decelerating boys displayed a slow tempo in play at 27 months; high decelerating girls were more likely to be fast tempo. Again, the high decelerating boys seemed more inhibited; the high decelerating girls more excitable.

In a third analysis we included the deceleration patterns to the Embedded Figures Test. High decelerating children were above the median on maximal deceleration to the clay faces at 13 months and scaled deceleration to the cat-car-flower items on the Embedded Figures Test. Low decelerating children had the opposite profile. High decelerating boys showed a slower tempo of play than the low decelerating boys; whereas, the high decelerating girls had a faster tempo, shorter decision times, and more errors on the Embedded Figures Test—an impulsive performance.

Fixation Time and Deceleration Combined. We suggested earlier that fixation times at 1 year covaried with density of hypotheses to a discrepant event, while deceleration presumably indexed surprise. Since the child can have a rich nest of hypotheses for a stimulus, but not be surprised by it, we would not expect a high correlation between these two reactions. And indeed deceleration and fixation were unrelated to HF I and correlated only +.50 to HF II. These variables seem to reflect different processes. We created, therefore, four groups of children by dividing the distribution of mean first fixation time and mean maximal deceleration to HF I or HF II (at 13 months) to determine if the combination of fixation and deceleration was a better predictor of 27-month behavior than either variable alone (see Appendix Table 37).

Children below the median on both fixation and deceleration to HF I and HF II came from less well-educated families and had poorer vocabulary scores than those who were high on both fixation and deceleration. It should be noted that the combination of fixation and deceleration differentiated the social classes better for girls than for boys. The girls who showed long fixations with low decelerations at one year seemed to have the richest set of hypotheses. They had the best vocabulary scores, showed the longest fixation times to HF II and slides, especially to the discrepant scenes, and verbalized most often to the slides. Perhaps these girls, with a dense set of hypotheses, had such a well-articulated schema for human forms that none of the stimuli surprised them and, hence, decelerations were minimal.

SUMMARY

The deceleration data were the most difficult to interpret for the determinants of a cardiac deceleration are more enigmatic than those for fixation or vocalization. We have assumed that a surprising stimulus elicits a larger deceleration than one that is not surprising, and very familiar events are not surprising. Unlike fixation time, deceleration showed no relation to social class at one or two years, and there was a steady decrease in magnitude of deceleration with age, rather than the U-shaped function characteristic of fixation time and vocalization. But deceleration, unlike fixation and vocalization, displayed slightly greater stability for boys than girls, suggesting that boys are more likely than girls to show motor quieting to discrepant events. This decrease in motoricity, perhaps accompanied by vagal excitation to the heart, is correlated with cardiac deceleration. The better stability of deceleration for boys probably does not indicate greater attentiveness or more stable attentiveness for boys. Instead, it suggests that boys are more likely to display a change in postural quiescence when they are attentive. Psychologists study the continuity of specific response variables but are always concerned with the more elusive internal processes surrounding attentional dynamics. It is possible that the response variables may not map on the hypothetical processes in the same way for the sexes. This is a problem common in personality study. Study of the stability of power motives in men and women requires selection of different contexts, for men and women do not seek to gratify this motive in the same halls. Since the theory that ties overt behavior to hypothetical construct is inadequate, we must work both inductively and deductively, inching up on a solution to the problem.

VI

Tempo of Play

A child of 8 months picks up a block and bangs it on the floor once, twice, three times, stops, and turns to another object. A second child bangs a block 15 times before stopping. One child picks up a toy lawnmower and rolls it back and forth four times before turning away; another repeats this simple act two dozen times. How can we understand these differences in duration of involvement with an object? This question raises a prior and more general issue: why does a child terminate any activity it has begun when it can be shown that no other external stimulus elicited a competitive response or was a rival for the child's attention? Termination of an overt action is not unlike the phenomenon of habituation, for an infant or child will turn away from a stimulus after a given number of presentations. What is responsible for the habituation? One interpretation starts with the axiom that the organism continually seeks variability in sensory feedback. The 8-month-old infant banging the block on the floor provides himself with auditory, visual, tactile, and kinesthetic stimulation that is discrepant from the mosaic of sensations he experienced prior to initiating this act. The "banging" disturbs his adaptation level, and he continues this action until the new mosaic of stimulation creates a new adaptation level. The gradual reduction in perceived discrepancy from the earlier adaptation level elicits termination of the act. Termination occurs when a new adaptation level has been established. This interpretation is reasonable since the central nervous system is typically most responsive to changes in rate of stimulation, and actions are released or inhibited by such changes. Hence differences among children in speed of satiation could result from either (a) differences in the rate at which the child established a new adaptation level, or (b) differences in the fineness, or degree of articulation, of perceptual experience. A child who was perceptually analytic in his experience would perceive subtle differences in feedback that a child with a coarser perceptual screen would not notice and the former would require more time to establish a new adaptation level. Thus one interpretation emphasizes differences in rate of establishing an adaptation level, and assumes equivalent perceptual experience. A second assumes equal rates of establishing new adaptation levels but posits different perceptual experiences to the same input. One strategy that might test the validity of each explanation involves observing children with predetermined thresholds for satiation with objects of increasing variability of input, from minimally to maximally variable. If differences in "rate of reaching adaptation level" were critical, then "time before termination" should increase equally for both groups. If articulation of experience were critical, time to termination for the two hypothetical groups of children should be very similar for the simple object (which provides minimal difference in feedback), but as the objects increased in variety and quality of feedback, the curves should diverge in proportion to that variety.

A second, quite different, theoretical orientation to the behavioral phenomenon of satiation relies not on differences in establishing adaptation level but on the exploitation of existing responses. Assume that each child has a finite set of potential manipulative responses; the child continues to play with the object until the repertoire is exhausted, and the activity is then terminated. Individual differences in satiation would be a function of (a) differences in the richness of the reservoir of responses, (b) their rate of emission, or (c) the tendency to activate all the responses in the repertoire.

The differential validity of these hypotheses might be tested experimentally by teaching the same set of new responses to a novel object to subjects known to be fast or slow satiators. If they satiated at different rates, despite the presumed equivalence of their repertoires, rate of emission or the disposition to activate the hypotheses would be likely explanatory candidates. If not, the hypothesis of repertoires of different size would

Table 6-1

Interpretation of Fast versus Slow Satiation in Manipulation of Objects

Adaptation Level		versus	Response Repertoire		
(1)	(2)		(1)	versus	(2)
Faster rate of establishing adaptation level	Global perceptual experience		Faster rate of emission of schemata		Fewer schemata in the repertoire
			(3) Differences in tendency to activate existing schemata		

be supported. A subsequent test of the latter hypothesis would involve teaching different size repertoires to groups of fast versus slow satiation subjects. If richness of repertoire were critical, the fast and slow satiating children should show similar termination times when taught equally rich repertoires.

Differences in rate of satiation can be viewed, therefore, as a function of either afferent or efferent processes. These two interpretations are not as independent as they seem, for the child does not reinitiate the same set of responses after he has exhausted the reservoir the first time. A corollary about adaptation level and change in feedback must be invoked in order to explain why the child does not rerun the response routine until fatigue sets in. A rat receiving intracranial stimulation in the "pleasure" area of the hypothalamus will continue to perform a simple bar press response until he is physically exhausted if it is instrumental in obtaining the brain stimulation. Table 6.1 summarizes the two different interpretations and the four possible explanations of individual differences in satiation rates.

The Empirical Reality. The free play situation presented to our children at 8, 13, and 27 months unfortunately was not structured to allow sensitive assessment of each of these processes. It could only permit indirect evaluation of these varied explanations of satiation. Each child had many toys available to him, and it was possible for termination of an act to be occasioned by distraction. Second, the mother was present and any tendency to approach her or play with her might occasion termination. The index of satiation at 8 and 13 months was the number of act changes (for successive 4-minute periods, as well as across the whole episode). Since the time period was fixed, the child with many act changes typically played continually and displayed relatively short attentional epochs with each toy. However, the child with few act changes could have achieved this score by spending a long time with a few objects or a long time not involved with any activity because of fear, long periods of visual exploration of the room, or clinging to his mother.

At 27 months the primary index was based on the duration of attentional involvement with each object and, therefore, was much closer to the semantic definition of the construct. It will be recalled that free play was the first episode of the morning for all 27-month-old children. The first 5-minutes were an adaptation period during which no toys were present; this was followed by a 30-minute play period. The major variable coded was the duration of each *sustained directed activity,* henceforth called an SDA. We derived several variables from the SDA values, including the 75th percentile value (Q_3), the number of short SDA's (less than 20 seconds in duration), number of long SDA's (longer than 2 minutes), mean of three longest SDA's, etc.

The results are provocative and shall be discussed in some detail because we made specific *a priori* predictions about this dimension. Earlier investigations at the Fels Institute suggested that frequent act changes were characteristic of children with short fixations to visual stimuli. This association was interpreted as reflecting a generalized tendency for rapid satiation; a tendency to reach adaptation level quickly. We have called this dimension *conceptual tempo.* It is relatively independent of the level of gross motor activity, but we shall present, simultaneously, the data for mobility during the play session so that the reader can compare the patterns of correlations for each of these variables. Appendix Tables 38 and 39 present age and sex differences in mobility (number of squares traversed) and tempo for all three ages.

MOBILITY

There was a large increase (by a factor of 8) in locomotor activity from 8 to 13 months but only a small increase from 13 to 27 months. The 8-month olds were generally immobile and most stayed within a radius of 5 feet of where they were placed initially. A few rolled over, but most infants neither crawled nor crept for very long. By contrast, all infants crawled or walked a great deal at 13 months and ran at 27 months. At 8 months mobility was greatest during the second 4 minutes; whereas, at 13 months, it was greatest during the first 4 minutes. The 8-month-old child seemed initially inhibited, requiring a few minutes to warm up to the situation.

Mobility at 8 months was consistent through each of the four shorter time periods of the episode. There is no reason to expect mobility to be related to indexes of cognitive development and the pattern of coefficients with mobility at 8 months reveals no strong link to attentiveness or educational level. The highly mobile boys vocalized more frequently at 4 and 13 months, but this relation did not occur for girls. Mobility at 13 months was more goal directed, and served many motives. The child moved because he was chasing a toy, pulling the bug or running back to his mother to give her a toy or to maintain contact. There was no consistent set of 4-month variables that predicted mobility at 13 months for either sex. The contemporaneous correlations suggested that the most mobile boys were least attentive during the visual episodes.

TEMPO OF PLAY

Despite the large increase in mobility from 8 to 13 months the number of act changes increased only moderately (about 30%), and the greatest number of act changes occurred during the initial 4 minutes. Appendix Table 39 contains the Q_2 and Q_3 values and number of acts during the 27-month play session. Number of acts decreased in a linear fashion as time progressed, because of either boredom or intense involvement with one particular toy. The variable of major interest was the duration of individual SDA's. Figure 6-1 illustrates a cumulative percentage curve for each child's longest SDA at 27 months. The slope is steepest for durations that

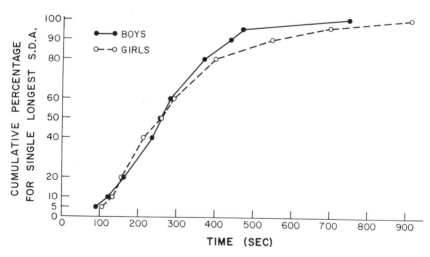

Figure 6-1 Cumulative percentage curve for single largest SDA in 30-minute play session.

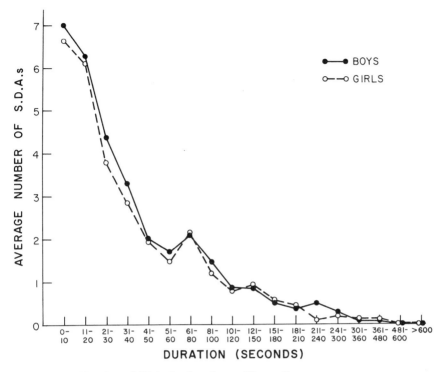

Figure 6-2 Number of SDAs by duration at 27 months.

lasted from 2 to 6 minutes. The single longest uninterrupted activity was less than 6 minutes for 80% of the children and less than 3% of all SDA's lasted longer than 4 minutes (96 out of a total of 4410 SDA's). Figure 6-2 illustrates the mean number of SDA's by duration. The average child displayed about 30 sustained actions during the half-hour session and played about 24 of the 30 available minutes. The median duration for a single uninterrupted activity was a half minute, and the majority of SDA's were less than 1 minute long. It is interesting to note that at both 8 and 13 months the number of acts also remained constant at about 7 to 8 acts every 4 minutes, or an act change every 30 seconds. The play of the typical 27-month-old child contained a large number of short attentional involvements, punctuated by 2 or 3 involvements that lasted several minutes.

Contact with and Proximity to the Mother. Time in physical contact with the mother was higher for girls than for boys during all periods, including the adaptation period. The children were close to their mothers during the first 5 minutes of adaptation and during the last 15 minutes when some became bored. But the rise in contact with mother during the last half of the session was greater for girls than for boys. Total amount of time in close proximity to the mother (within 3 feet) was also greater for girls, but these differences were not as significant as the means for physical contact.

Play with Specific Toys. We examined the total time the children played with each of the 10 toys. The blocks, train, and large plastic box were most often used by boys; the plastic ball and doll least often. The blocks, wagon and play dough were most often used by girls; the gun and the ball least often. Although sex differences were not dramatic, girls were more likely to play the role of mother using the doll as the baby and the play dough as food. The boys were likely to ride the train, shoot the gun, or try to get their whole body into the plastic box. These differences correspond with other data indicating that girls are more imitative of adult actions while boys' play contains more aggression (Pedersen & Bell, 1970). Interviews with the mothers revealed that more girls had dolls at home (99%) than boys (65%) and more boys had guns than girls (59% versus 19%). However, there were no sex differences in availability of the other eight toys. Although there was no strong relation between mobility and tempo of play at any age, the direction of the association was in the expected direction, with the more mobile children displaying more SDA's less than 20 seconds in duration.

Relation of Tempo to Social Class. The upper middle class boys showed the largest increase in act changes from 8 to 13 months; the lower middle class boys showed the smallest increase (see Appendix Table 40). This effect was even more dramatic among girls. Not only was there a class difference at 13 months, with lower middle class girls showing the smallest number of act changes ($F = 2.97$, $p < .05$), but the lower middle class girls *decreased* in number of acts from 8 to 13 months, while all other groups increased. This pattern suggests that number of act changes at 1 year may reflect processes somewhat different from those mirrored at 8 months. The absence of continuity of "act changes" from 8 to 13 months is in accord with this idea.

There was a curvilinear relation at 27 months between social class and act changes, especially for boys, with the lower middle class and the upper middle class children showing the fewest number of act changes and the middle class children the most. (See Appendix Table 40.) As we shall see, the smaller number of act changes among the upper middle class children was a result of very long involvements with one or two toys, while the small number of acts for lower middle class children seemed to result from a sparser repertoire of hypotheses.

PATTERNS OF STABILITY: MOBILITY AND ACT CHANGES

Appendix Table 41 contains the stability coefficients for number of squares traversed from 8 to 13 and 13 to 27 months. There was moderate stability from 8 to 13 months for girls, but only suggestive stability for boys. Also, there was minimal continuity from either 8 or 13 to 27 months. *A general activity factor did not emerge.* Since most of our other major variables showed good stability from 8 to 13 or 13 to 27 months, it seems fair to conclude that a tendency to "run around," independent of the context of the activity is not a stable disposition in young children.

There was no stability for number of act changes among boys for any age comparison and only suggestive stability from 8 to 13 or 13 to 27 months among girls ($r = .3$ for each comparison, $p < .05$). However, the number of times a child changes activity at 27 months is not regarded as the most sensitive index of our tempo variable. Rather, the duration of each sustained involvement with toys and the number of especially long involvements are assumed to be more sensitive signs of tempo. A 2-year old could display 3 or 4 act changes within a single sustained activity, for he might use the blocks to build a tower on the floor, then knock down the tower, bring the blocks over to a table and remake the tower on the table top. This sequence would be scored as 3 act changes but as 1 sustained directed activity. Appendix Table 42 contains the correlations between number of act changes at 8 and 13 months and measures of sustained involvement. Among boys, many act changes at 8 months predicted a low Q_3 value at 27 months ($r = -.26, p < .05$).

A REFINED INDEX OF TEMPO AT 27 MONTHS

Faith in the importance and continuity of a tempo dimension is increased when a more complex definition of tempo is constructed from the 27-month data. The semantic definition of slow tempo implies that the child will not only have a high Q_3 value but that he will also have a few, long uninterrupted acts. There was a positive relation between length of the Q_3 and number of SDA's longer than 2 minutes (r in high 50's). We combined these two variables to create fast and slow tempo groups on the rationale that it was possible to have a high Q_3 value and no long acts, or a low Q_3 value but several long acts. About one-third of the children had low Q_3 values, and less than 3 long acts. These were the *fast tempo children.* A second group had the opposite profile and were called *slow tempo children.* Specifically, a slow tempo child had a Q_3 value over 75 seconds and 3 or more acts that lasted longer than 2 minutes. A fast tempo child had a Q_3 less than 75 seconds and fewer than 3 long acts (for the girls the distribution of long acts made it necessary to define a fast tempo girl as one whose Q_3 value was less than 75 seconds and less than 2 long acts). There were 5 boys and 3 girls in the fast tempo group who had no act that lasted as long as 2 minutes. This classification yielded 14 fast tempo and 14 slow tempo girls; 27 fast and 18 slow tempo boys. There was no relation between tempo and either social class or vocabulary score for girls; but a slight positive relation between class and vocabulary and a slow tempo among the boys.

Initially, we asked how these children differed at 27 months, the age at which the free play data were gathered. The central hypothesis was that a slow tempo child would show greater capacity for inhibition and involvement, longer epochs of sustained attention and longer decision times in a conflict situation. Let us first summarize the data derived from the embedded figures and conflict tests at 27 months, for performance on these instruments was expected to relate to tempo of play. We shall then turn to aspects of the infant data that might be predictive of 2-year-old tempo.

Response Time to the Embedded Figures Test. Response time was the total duration of visual scanning of the disguised array prior to the child's first solution hypothesis. Figure 6-3 shows the response times to the 3 items on each of the 6 series. Response times generally increased with increasing item difficulty, and hard items elicited response times of 7 or 8 seconds. These delays indicate that a 2-year old is clearly capable of inhibiting decisions in uncertain problem situations and is not a creature of unregulated impulse. A few children scanned a test item for a half minute before making their decision. Errors also increased with item difficulty. Only 25% of the children made one or more errors on easy items, while 65% made one or more errors on difficult items. As with response time, there were no consistent sex differences in error rates. There was good interitem con-

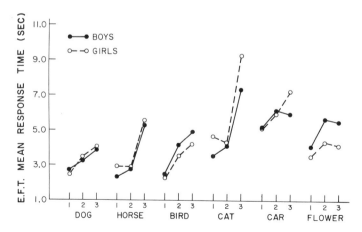

Figure 6-3 Response time to EFT items.

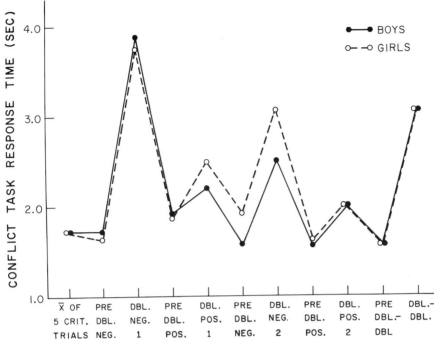

Figure 6-4 Response time to conflict and immediately preceding trials.

sistency for response time and errors across all items, although slightly better for girls than for boys. Unfortunately, errors and response time were unrelated. Long response times, therefore, were not just indexing consideration of alternative hypotheses. Some children must have delayed because they were not sure how to solve the task; others because they were considering alternative solution hypotheses.

Reaction to Conflict. Each child had to master a simple discrimination by learning to touch a yellow light but inhibit touching a red light. After the child reached criterion (5 consecutive correct trials) he was given 5 conflict trials (2 red lights, 2 yellow, 2 red, 2 yellow, and finally all 4 lights). These 5 conflict trials alternated with regular trials in which both a yellow and red light appeared. As might be expected, some children did not learn the initial discrimination within a reasonable time. Of the 75 boys and 66 girls who were administered the task, 44 boys and 48 girls reached criterion (58% of the boys and 73% of the girls). The average child required about 20 paired presentations to reach criterion. We shall only consider the data for these 92 children. As Figure 6-4 indicates, response time during the last 5 criterion trials, prior to the first conflict, averaged about 1.5 seconds. Each child knew what he was doing and was responding quickly. Response time to the first conflict trial (2 red lights, called negative 1) was 3.6 seconds, over twice as long as the decision time to the immediately preceding trial (and statistically significant). None of the remaining conflict trials elicited response times as long as negative 1, but each succeeding conflict trial elicited a longer response time than the preceding nonconflict trial.

Relation of Performance on Embedded Figures Test to the Conflict Task. Girls with long response times on the Embedded Figures Test also showed slightly longer delays to the second presentation of the pair of correct lights (positive 2), and girls who were most accurate on the Embedded Figures Test showed longer response times to three of the four conflict trials. There was, therefore, some generality of an inhibition vector among the girls. This generality was less apparent among the boys, although the correlations were in the same direction.

Relation of Tempo of Play at 27 Months to Embedded Figures, Conflict Tasks, and Fixation Time. It will be recalled that the refined classification of fast versus slow tempo children at 27 months was based on both the Q_3 value, as well as the *number of acts lasting longer than two minutes*. The slow tempo girls had significantly longer decision times and markedly fewer errors on the Embedded Figures Test than the fast tempo girls. The results for boys were in the same direction but were not significant (see Figure 6-6). Similarly, slow tempo girls showed significantly longer re

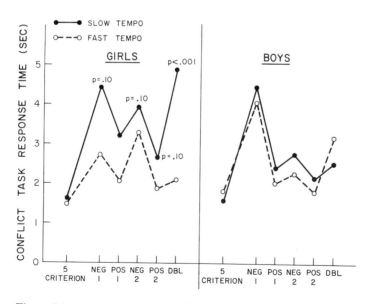

Figure 6-5 Response time to conflict trials for fast and slow tempo children.

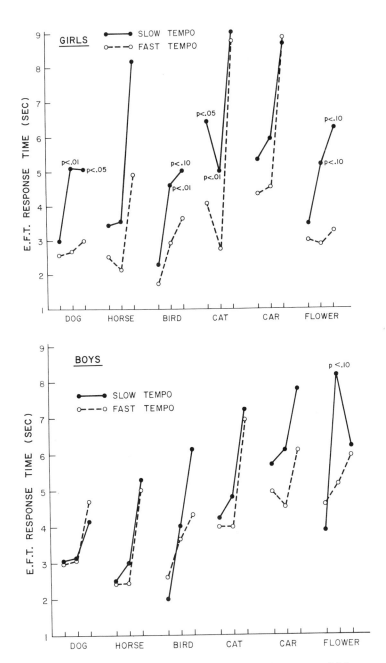

Figure 6-6 Response time to EFT for fast and slow tempo children.

sponse times to each of the conflict trials, especially the first conflict trial, and the final conflict trial when all 4 lights appeared. The results for boys, as in the Embedded Figures Test, were in the same direction but attenuated. (See Figure 6-5.) Finally, the slow tempo boys and girls also displayed longer fixation times to the 3 different sets of visual stimuli at 27 months (human forms, clay faces, and chromatic slides). (See Appendix Table 43 for mean values.)

In sum, slow tempo children showed longer decision times, longer epochs of sustained attention to visual events, and were more accurate on perceptual problems. It should be remembered that these differences are not the result of differences in language ability, for there was no difference in social class or verbal competence between the fast and the slow tempo girls, and only a slight positive relation between social class and a slow tempo for the boys.

RELATION OF TEMPO TO INFANT BEHAVIOR

The homotypic continuity of the tempo variable is revealed in the relation between act changes at 8 months and tempo of play at 27 months. The slow tempo children had significantly fewer act changes at 8 months than the fast tempo children (see Figure 6-7). The difference was significant for boys for the whole session ($p < .10$) and for girls for minutes 5 through 8 ($p < .05$). For both sexes, however, slow tempo of play at 27 months was related to fewer act changes at 8 months of age. This result is more persuasive if one examines the extremes. For example, 4 of the fast tempo 27-month boys had more than 30 acts at 8 months, in contrast to only 1 of the slow tempo boys. As might be expected from the absence of stability for act changes between 8 and 13 months, there was no relation between act changes at 13 and indexes of tempo at 27 months. We believe that the toys, which were the same at both 8 and 13 months, were too simple for the 1-year-old children and did not engage active involvement. As a result, the children were prone to shift their interest rapidly.

Robert McCall of the Fels Research Institute has reported a similar result. He noted that the difference between fast and slow tempo infants is greater for interesting and complicated toys than for simple ones. A disposition like tempo only has meaning with respect to a particular set of objects. The tempo disposition is most apparent when the stimuli permit sustained interest and manipulative involvement. An 8-month old likes to bang or throw, and a block, a pail, or a mallet is appropriate for this simple action. A 13-month old is bored with these activities and likes to build or relate objects. Unfortunately, there were not enough toys available at 1 year to permit constructions or sensorimotor schemes that involved relations between objects.

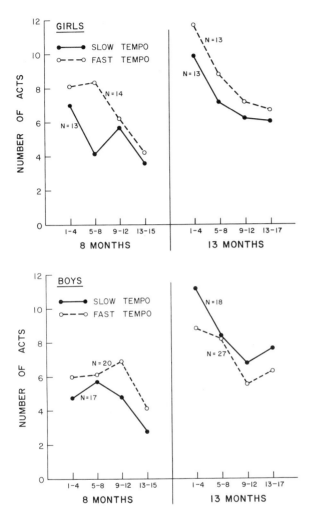

Figure 6-7 Number of acts at 8 and 13 months for fast and slow tempo children.

Relation to Motor Excitement at 1 Year. Film records of the children's behavior during the visual and auditory episodes at 1 year were reliably scored by an observer who had no knowledge of the child's early or later behavior in any situation, nor his social class. Two indexes of motor excitability were twisting of the trunk while sitting in the highchair, and waving of arms while fixating the stimulus. Fast tempo boys engaged in more twisting and arm waving than the slow tempo boys, the differences being most significant for the first two episodes. This difference did not occur for the girls, but we have noted many times that motor discharge is more closely related to the excitement generated by information processing among boys than girls.

Relation to Early Smiling. The smile during the first year of life, especially the smile that peaks at 4 months of age, is an intriguing response that reflects, among other things, an assimilatory recognition. Children do not display this smile with equal frequency and this tendency is not related to any index of social class or ability. Instead, it seems to be a temperamental attribute. Gewirtz (1965) studied children in 4 different home-rearing environments and found that the smiling peaked at 4 months for all of them. Frequency of smiling during the latter third of the first year, however, was related to quality of social interaction. Both D. G. Freedman (1965) and C. M. Reppucci (1968) have found that the 4-month smile displays heritability. Reppucci (1968) studied 16 pairs of monozygotic and 14 pairs of dizygotic twins at 4 and 8 months of age. The 4-month-old boys were too irritable to provide reliable data but 5 monozygotic and 5 dizygotic girl pairs were shown a set of 4 achromatic faces and a set of 4 clay faces at 4 months of age. Frequency of smiling to the faces showed heritability for this sample ($H' = .93$, $F = 14.67$, $p < .005$ for the achromatic faces; $H' = .87$; $F = 7.50$, $p < .05$ for the clay faces). Fixation time did not display heritability. Moreover, it will be recalled from Chapter III that in two separate studies in which 4-month-old infants were exposed to either nonsense achromatic designs or a 3-element chromatic mobile, shallow habituation of fixation time, in contrast to rapid habituation, over the first 5 trials was associated with more frequent smiling (McCall & Kagan, 1970).

In light of these data, it is interesting to report that the slow tempo 27-month children smiled significantly more often than the fast tempo children, when they were 4 months of age, to the same representations of the human faces used by Reppucci with the twins ($p < .05$, by t-test). Although smiling is less frequent at 8 and 13 months, this difference also held true at the two older ages. Throughout the first year, slow tempo children smiled more often than fast tempo children (see Figure 6-8). We suggest that smiling is most likely to occur when assimilation follows mental effort, and is not likely to occur if the answer to a problem or assimilation to a schema is immediate. The hypothesis has been affirmed in a study of children's laughter to cartoons (Zigler, Levine, & Gould, 1966). We found a linear relation between spontaneous smiling and item difficulty on the Embedded Figures Test. The harder the item, the longer the child worked at it and the greater the probability of smiling upon success before the examiner reinforced the child (see Figure 7-1). A smile is most likely to occur following the gradual buildup and release of the tension that is

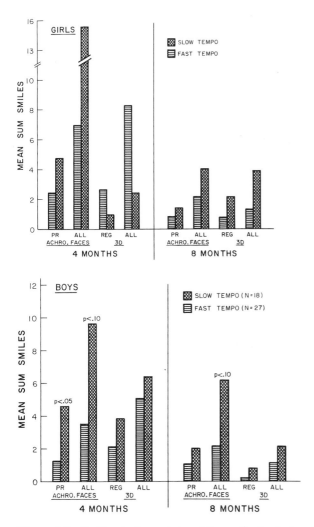

Figure 6-8 Smiling to faces at 4 and 8 months for fast and slow tempo children.

involved in mental effort. If assimilation is immediate, no tension builds up and no smile occurs. If some children work at solution or assimilation with greater effort, they are more likely to smile when assimilation occurs. Slow tempo infants may be capable of greater attentional involvement in an event. Perhaps that is why they play longer, smile more upon assimilation, and show more conflict in time of uncertainty.

Relation of Habituation of Fixation Time to Tempo. The final set of data is closest to the original *a priori* conceptions behind the work. We argued in Chapter III that fixation time comes under the control of different factors during the first year. The major determinant of fixation time after 8 or 9 months is the richness of cognitive structures activated by the event, while earlier, fixation time is more closely controlled by degree of discrepancy between schema and stimulus. Fixation times are prolonged because the infant is trying to assimilate the event to a relevant schema. Infants with characteristically long fixation times at 4 months may be predisposed to invest more effort in the assimilation process. If the tendency to "invest effort in assimilation" is stable, we might expect these infants to be slow tempo at 27 months. Thus we hypothesized that slow habituating infants would be slow tempo 2-year olds.

The major index of habituation was a ratio that summarized the proportion change in first fixation time from the first 4 trials to the last 4 trials. [Average first fixation trials (1-4) minus (13-16)]. The larger the ratio the faster the habituation. *There was a positive association between rapid habituation to the two-dimensional achromatic faces at 4 months and number of act changes at 8 months for boys* ($p < .01$). Among girls there was no significant association between habituation rate and act changes at 8 months. And rate of habituation at 4 months predicted a slow tempo of play at 27 months for the boys, but not for the girls (see Figure 6-9 and Appendix Table 44).

It is important to note that the pattern of differences between fast and slow tempo 2-year olds was obtained even when social class was controlled. In a special analysis we created fast versus slow tempo children (based on the 27-month free play data) within the two major educational groups. That is, we compared fast tempo middle class with slow tempo middle class children; fast tempo lower middle with slow tempo lower middle class children. The same profile of differences emerged within both class groups. Shallow habituation and frequent smiling at 4 months, as well as fewer act changes at 8 months, were predictive of slow tempo of play at 27 months.[1]

Tempo of play was also stable for a small group of boys across the period 27 to 36 months. Twelve boys who were clearly fast or slow tempo at 27 months were observed in 2 free play sessions with 2 different sets of toys when they were 3 years old. During the first session (20 minutes)

---

[1] In an attempt to determine if these differences for extreme children held true for children less extreme, we created 2 additional tempo groups based on the free play at 27 months. The moderately slow tempo children had Q_3 values between 58 and 75 seconds and 3, 4, or 5 long acts. The moderately fast tempo children had Q_3 values under 57 seconds and exactly 3 long acts. The differences were in the same direction as noted for the extremes, with habituation, smiling, and act changes at 8 months differentiating the two groups.

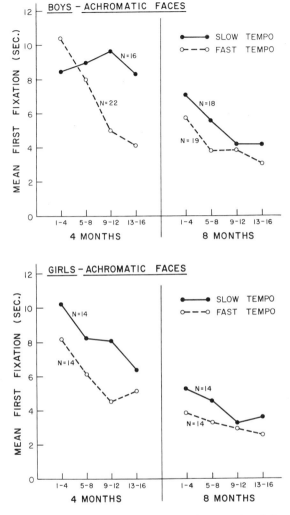

Figure 6-9 Rate of habituation to faces at 4 and 8 months for fast and slow tempo children.

the toys were erector set building materials, a board with marbles, and some clay. During the second play session (15 minutes) the toys were small blocks, a set of small magnets, and 3 plastic bottles. The duration of each sustained directed activity was coded and a median value computed for each session. The rank order correlation between the median SDA at 27 and 36 months was .81 ($p < .01$). The raw scores convey the continuity even more dramatically. The three boys with the fastest tempo of play at 27 months (median SDA values of 16, 18, and 19 seconds) had median values of 27, 39, and 55 seconds at 3 years. The 3 boys with the slowest tempo at 27 months (medians of 69, 73 and 193) had median values of 99, 176, 790 when they were 3 years of age. Finally, the rank order correlations between tempo of play at 8 months (indexed by number of acts) and the median SDA at 3 years was .54 ($p < .05$). *This small group of boys,* who were admittedly extreme, showed impressive continuity of the tempo dimension over a 28-month period.

REPLICATION ON OTHER SAMPLES

Independent investigations lend support to the findings. In one study, the subjects (*S*s) were 24 lower middle class infants (half boys and half girls); most of the parents of the children had not completed high school (22 of the 24 fathers and 19 of the 24 mothers met this criterion), and none had entered college. Thus these children are comparable to the lower middle class group in the longitudinal investigation. The occupations of the fathers were unskilled and semiskilled.

Each infant was brought to the laboratory and shown 6 achromatic stimuli in random order for a total of 18 presentations. The stimuli were 3 human faces (photograph of a man's face, photograph of a woman's face, and a schematic drawing of a man's face), and 3 nonfacial stimuli (a bull's eye, a checkerboard, and a nursing bottle). The photograph of the man's face and the schematic drawing of the man's face were identical with those used in the two-dimensional faces episode at 4 and 8 months of age (PR and SR). The stimuli were relatively simple and not very interesting to the subjects. Each stimulus was presented for 12 seconds and followed by a 12-second rest interval during which the visual field was blank. Following the visual episode the mother and baby were brought to the same playroom described earlier. The mother was seated in the corner of the room and the child was allowed to play with the same set of toys used in the longitudinal study. The child's behavior was observed for 15 minutes and the major variable coded was the number of act changes that occurred during this period.

Since the sample sizes were small and the fixation times generally short it was difficult to construct 2 discrete habituation groups with a reasonable sample in each. It was decided, therefore to use the percent change in first fixation time from the first 6 to the last 6 trials as the index of habituation. This index was derived by subtracting total length of the first fixation for the last 6 trials (trials 13–18) from the total length of the first fixation for the first 6 trials, and dividing this difference by the latter value.

This ratio was correlated with the number of act changes displayed during the free play session for each sex separately. There was a positive correlation between number of act changes and a fast rate of habituation for the 12 boys ($r = .61$, $p < .05$), but a negative correlation for girls ($r = -.81$, $p < .01$). A parallel, but as yet unpublished, study conducted by Michael Lewis and the author at the Fels Research Institute with 24 middle class, 13-month-old infants produced similar results. There was a positive correlation between rate of habituation to the achromatic stimuli and number of acts for boys ($r = .59$, $p < .05$, but a low negative relation for girls ($r = -.15$).

The data indicate that boys with rapid rates of habituation to moderately interesting visual events have frequent but short attentional epochs with play objects. This was true at 8 months for the achromatic faces in the longitudinal study, and at 13 months for the achromatic faces for the two cross-sectional samples. When one examines the least interesting episode at 13 months for the longitudinal sample (i.e., the three-dimensional faces) there is the suggestion of a negative relation between fixation time and number of acts among the boys. The correlation between number of act changes during the first 4 minutes and total fixation time to the three-dimensional faces was negative for all the faces and statistically significant for regular ($r = -.32$, $p < .01$); for scrambled ($r = -27$, $p < .05$); and for the average fixation across all the faces ($r = -.22$, $p < .05$). This negative relation did not occur for the girls. Thus, short fixation time and rapid habituation to moderately interesting stimuli are linked with a fast tempo of play among boys at 8 and 13 months for several independent samples.

There appears to be heterotypic continuity of a psychological construct dealing with the capacity to become involved in interesting stimuli. We have called this dimension conceptual tempo, and it is reflected in shallow habituation to faces at 4 months, and long periods of involvement in play at 8 and 27 months. It is suggested that long fixation times at 4 months or long epochs of play could result from the tendency to activate cognitive structures appropriate to the stimulus, to refer the event to what is known about it. If the child were older we would say he was thinking about the event. When children were selected on an index of tempo at 27 months, a set of theoretically reasonable variables was predictive of this dimension. Rate of habituation and smiling at 4 months, tempo of play at 8 months, and restless activity at 13 months each predicted the 27-month classification. Although the manifest behaviors are different at 4 and 27 months, there is tentative support for the heterotypic continuity of a tempo disposition—the caterpillar-butterfly problem revisited.

PREDICTION OF REFLECTION-IMPULSIVITY AT 27 MONTHS

One of the tantalizing hypotheses of the study was that indexes of tempo during the first year would be predictive of an impulsive or reflective conceptual attitude at 27 months. The standard classification of a child as reflective or impulsive is based on both his errors and response time on problems with response uncertainty, like the Embedded Figures Test. Unfortunately, the relation between response time and errors on this test was low. However, we adopted the same strategy we used with older children and classified children as reflective if they showed both long response times and high accuracy scores; we classified them as impulsive if they showed the reverse profile (median splits were used for each distribution). We then examined the relation between this impulsive versus reflective classification and early behaviors. There were 19 impulsive and 21 reflective boys; 22 impulsive and 16 reflective girls.

Boys' Data. As infants, impulsive boys displayed slightly shorter fixation times and much restless twisting, in comparison with reflectives (see Appendix Table 45). At 27 months impulsive boys also spent less time playing close to or in contact with their mothers during the last half of the play session. Investigations of reflection-impulsivity in school age children suggest that low anxiety over error is one determinant of an impulsive attitude. Anxiety over error is presumably a derivative of concern over maternal reactions toward the child. The child who is disposed to stay close to his mother is probably more vulnerable to this anxiety, and the fact that reflective boys played in closer proximity to the mother is congruent with the general interpretation of a reflective attitude.

Girls' Data. The impulsive girls also had shorter fixation times to the faces at 4 months, and at 27 months displayed shorter involvements with toys and stayed further from the mother during the adaptation period. Despite equivalent social class profiles, reflective children had slightly better verbal resources than impulsives. As early as 2 years of age the pattern of correlates of reflection-impulsivity resembles the one seen at age 10.[2]

Since shallow habituation of fixation time at 4 months and slow tempo of play at 8 months were positively related for boys, and predictive of

---

[2] It is appropriate to note that performance on the Embedded Figures Test at 27 months predicted performance on a different index of reflection-impulsivity at 4 years of age. A group of 18 girls and 12 boys from the sample were administered a preschool version of the Matching Familiar Figures Test when they were 4 years old. Among girls, errors and response time on the Embedded Figures Test was correlated with errors and response time on the Matching Familiar Figures items ($r = 54$, $p < .05$; $r = .57$, $p < .05$ for errors and response time respectively). The corresponding correlations for boys were .00 and .13.

tempo of play at 27 months, we combined these 2 infant variables to create 2 groups of infants. In order to avoid inventing a new pair of terms, we shall use the descriptive words fast and slow tempo to designate these infant groups, but the reader should remember that the bases for this classification are derived from habituation and play at 8 months. Fast tempo *infants* showed a rapid habituation of fixation time at 4 months (using a median split) and many acts at 8 months (again using median split). Slow tempo infants showed the reverse profile. This manipulation created 21 fast tempo and 24 slow tempo boys. Four fast tempo and 4 slow tempo boys were not seen at 27 months, leaving 17 fast and 20 slow tempo children. Appendix Table 46 shows the number of boys in each group that were fast versus slow tempo in play at 27 months, reflective or impulsive on the Embedded Figures Test, and finally, the number that were both fast tempo and impulsive versus slow tempo and reflective. The fast tempo infants were more likely, at 27 months, to be fast tempo in play and impulsive on the Embedded Figures Test. And 6 of the 7 2-year olds who were both fast tempo in play and impulsive had been fast tempo infants; whereas, 6 of the 7 2-year olds who were both slow tempo in play and reflective had been slow tempo infants ($p < .05$ by exact test). The results for girls were equivocal. Too few girls fell into the original groups (10 fast and 9 slow tempo girls) and of these, only 7 fast and 8 slow tempo girls were seen at 27 months. Nonetheless, of the 7 fast tempo infant girls, 4 were impulsive on the Embedded Figures Test, and only 1 was reflective.[3]

SUMMARY

The search for early anlage of the reflection-impulsivity attitude was one of the three major aims of this limited longitudinal study. As with all behaviors, the tendency to delay in the face of uncertainty has multiple determinants, some of which derive from contemporaneous situational factors. Moreover, the dominant accompaniment of a reflective attitude is probably anxiety over error, and there is no obvious response in infancy that previews this dynamic. Therefore, it is not reasonable to expect that

[3] The *a priori* hope was that tempo of play at 8 months might be an anlage of an impulsive or reflective conceptual attitude at 2 years. Boys with many acts at 8 months had faster response times to the conflict trials (especially Neg. 2 and Pos. 2). The results were in the same direction for girls, but not significant. Furthermore, boys with many acts during the first 4 minutes of the play session at 8 months made more errors on the Embedded Figures Test ($r = .27$, $p < .05$). Therefore, there was a group of fast tempo 8-month boys who showed fast tempo of play at 27 months, fast decision times to conflict trials, and high error scores on the Embedded Figures Test. This pattern was present for girls but in less striking form.

the infant's attributes will be highly correlated with the 2-year old's position on this dimension. Nonetheless, the disposition to be reflective or impulsive seems to share some variance with a more fundamental characteristic. As early as 4 or 8 months one can detect some infants who seem to activate a dense set of cognitive structures in the service of assimilating a new event; others seem to act on a new event with the hypothesis or action that is most readily available, and then pass on to another. There is a strong—and perhaps dangerous—temptation to see the first group as "thinking" about the event and its relation to their existing cognitive repertoire. The reflective 3-year old appears to be a thoughtful child, checking the validity of each solution hypothesis before responding. The impulsive child, by sharp contrast, acts on his first hypothesis and then turns his attention from the problem to other affairs.

The play behavior of the infant and young child may provide an index of this characteristic. One child breaks a ball of clay into 15 small pieces, then feeds them to a doll as if they were cookies. A second breaks the ball into 3 pieces, drops the clay, and pounces on the blocks. The first child seems to have a "plan" of action, a representation of some goal state. Once having generated this idea he tends to maintain active involvement with the toy until that goal is reached. The activation of a cognitive structure that represents the goal state to be reached and maintaining involvement until it is reached—which is what slow tempo infants seem to be doing—is very close to a definition of thinking used with older children.[4]

---

[4] We observed one group of 4 girls, and a separate group of 4 boys in a play situation. Although behavior with same sex peers is governed by incentives different from those present in solitary play, these observations were provocative. The children were selected so that 2 had been consistently slow tempo and 2 fast tempo in play at 8, 13, and 27 months. The children were between 4 and 4½ years of age when they were invited to play in a large room with a small set of age and sex appropriate toys and their mothers available. The 4 children were complete strangers to each other prior to the session, and we recorded the entire 60 minutes on video tape. The limitations of anecdotal data of this kind are obvious, but a brief descriptive summary may be of interest.

The most introverted and most extroverted child in each of the two sex groups had been slow tempo infants. The boy (A) who had been most extreme on indexes of slow tempo was unusually shy and inhibited. Although the other 3 boys began to play at once, A stayed close to his mother for the first 45 minutes and only entered the center of the room to play for the last quarter-hour. A made several abortive approaches toward the children but each time ran back to his mother. A showed an extreme degree of social anxiety for a 4-year old. His parents were residents in a small house where 12 undergraduate college students lived and, therefore, A was continually exposed to many strangers and to a great deal of variability in his social environment. The author visited him once in his home environment and noted that he was not as shy or anxious as he was in this laboratory

Some infants and children seem predisposed to refer events to existing structures with more completeness than others. An example from a recent study is illustrative (Dryman, Birch, & Korn, 1969). Young school age children were given a test tube partially filled with water, with a bead floating on the surface. They were also given a tray full of gadgets and told that their task was to get the bead out of the tube without turning the tube upside down. The only way to solve the problem was to use an available container of water to fill the tube and float the bead to the top. Only a small proportion of the children solved the problem, despite the fact that every child must have witnessed this class of events many times in his own experience. The children had this "rule" in their repertoire, but only some activated it in this problem situation.

---

situation. The parents noted that this behavior was not atypical whenever A was taken to a strange environment.

The girl who had been the slowest tempo as an infant (B) was not afraid to leave her mother, but was the quietest of the 4 girls. B played alone with one toy during most of the hour and rarely spoke. One episode reflects her thoughtful quality. Late in the session one of the fast tempo girls (C) became upset because she was unable to remove a peg from a block. C began to stamp her feet and whine and brought the block to her mother for help. C's mother was unable to remove the peg and C became increasingly distressed. B rose from where she was playing, walked across the room, picked up a small wooden pliers that was used to remove pegs, walked to C's mother, gave her the pliers and then returned to her play. All of this occurred without a word spoken. The pliers worked and the room was quiet again. The slow tempo extroversive girl (D) was also very talkative and showed off frequently. However, like B, D showed much longer periods of involvement with toys than the two fast tempo girls.

The two children who were most affective, verbal, and dominant had been slow tempo infants. The boy (E) often barked orders at others, yelled, and ran around the room laughing. Despite his apparent freedom and security when he first met the other children and adults, he became anxious when all the mothers left the room after about 20 minutes of play. E began to bang at the door and eventually began to weep. The mothers returned to the room at this point. Although E seemed secure when his mother was present, he became anxious when she left. The two fast tempo boys (F and G) showed no signs of anxiety throughout the hour, even when their mothers were out of the room.

The fast tempo boys were generally more active than the two slow tempo subjects. They were the first to begin running around the room, the first to initiate wrestling and the first to begin to kick around a large rubber beach ball. One of the boys (G) was usually agressive and spent the last 20 minutes taking toys away from E and initiating rough-and-tumble play with him. F, the other fast tempo boy, was quiet and played alone during the first half-hour, but engaged in lots of active games during the last half of the session. The fast tempo girls (C and H) showed shorter attentional involvements in play than B or D. Although an extroversion-introversion dimension did not covary with tempo, the two children who displayed the most extreme social inhibition had been slow tempo infants.

We believe that this tendency to invest effort in retrieving stored knowledge captures the essence of the slow versus the fast tempo child. The correlates of tempo of play were intuitively reasonable. The slow tempo children smiled more as infants, showed shallow habituation to faces at 4 months and displayed long decision times at 2 years. The infant variables accounted for 10% of the variance in the tempo dimension at 27 months. Although this is not very dramatic from an absolute perspective, one must appreciate the complexity of the behaviors, the substantial error in these classifications, and the fact that the predictions are based on behaviors observed under 1 year of age. The fairest inference to draw from the entire corpus of empirical material is that the infant's attributes obviously do not determine the reflection-impulsivity dimension, but they do exert a subtle influence on it.

VII

Smiling, Irritability, and Activity

THE SMILE

The smile that is selectively elicited by representations of human faces, which displays a peak at 4 months, is reliable, yet enigmatic. Let us be clear about the reaction under discussion, for the "turning up of the mouth and separation of the lips"—which are the distinctive features of the smile—occur at all ages, and in the service of an incredible variety of internal and external conditions. Newborns will smile while sleeping, 3-month-old babies will smile to a human voice, 12-month-old babies will smile to a clown, 27-month-old infants will smile when they solve a problem correctly, and 48-month olds will smile when they see another child laugh.

The earliest smiling in the newborn is rightly called reflex smiling. It is brief, apparently unrelated to external stimulation, and presumably occasioned by a complex mosaic of internal stimulation. A second phase of smiling, between 2 and 8 weeks, finds the response more selectively associated with particular external stimuli, primarily visual, although sounds can release the smile. Since human faces and voices are the most likely incentives for the response it has gained the name *social smiling* (see Ambrose, 1961; Jones, 1926; Buhler, 1933; Gesell & Thompson, 1934; Soderling, 1959; Gewirtz, 1965).

In the third phase, from 9 to 20 weeks, the smile becomes both more frequent and more selective, and most often elicited by a human face. The face can be static or moving, silent or speaking. The primary requirement is that there be two eyes symmetrically placed on an oval background. The presence of nose, mouth, movement, or voice each increases the probability of the occurrence of the smile, but it can be elicited without them (Ambrose, 1961; Laroche & Tcheng, 1963). This face specific smile tends to peak at 4 months, followed by a decline to a low level at 6 to 7 months. (This discussion is restricted to the smile that is occasioned by the human face. There are, of course, many other conditions that can elicit the smile, including tickling and visual surprise.) Gewirtz (1965) has studied smiling in several different environments in Israel and found provocative differences in the proportion of children who continued to smile after the 4-month peak, but the peak age tended to be similar for all groups, despite the differential conditions of child rearing. The children raised with their families in apartments or homes continued to smile at the highest level after 4 months, followed by kibbutz-reared children, and then by children raised in a residential institution. The infants who smiled the least after 4 months experienced the least face-to-face contact with other people. Laroche and Tcheng (1963) have also found that the peak of smiling to a female face occurs at 4 months, with the combination of voice and face most likely to elicit the smile response.

Appendix Table 47 presents age differences in smiling to the major stimulus episodes. Smiling was frequent at 4 months, infrequent at 8 and 13 months, and rose slightly at 27 months, paralleling the fixation and vocalization data. There were no sex differences at any age. Although 4-month smiling was much more frequent to the regular than to the distorted faces, these stimulus differences were minimal at 13 and 27 months. Interpretation of the decline in the smile between 4 and 8 months is controversial. Some investigators have compared the smile to imprinting. A precocial bird will follow the imprinting decoy for the first 13 hours, but stops following when fear and subsequent avoidance responses appear to become prepotent. It is possible that the temporary cessation of smiling results, in part, from the interfering action of fear to a strange face. The attractiveness of this hypothesis is enhanced by the fact that stranger anxiety becomes dramatic between 7 and 9 months of age, the period when social smiling is at its nadir.

An alternative interpretation—and the one to which we are more friendly—is that the 4-month smile to the face is a recognition response. The child's schema for a human face has become sufficiently articulated so that he "recognizes" the resemblance between any human face and the schema he has developed. The smile follows the process of matching his schema to the stimulus (see Piaget, 1952). The smile declines because his schema for a face becomes so well articulated that all faces or representations of faces are immediately recognized as such. There is no tension; no effort is required for assimilation, and hence, no smile. Some learning must occur if the smile of recognition is to appear.

The smile of assimilation is not restricted to human faces. Three different auditory stimuli were presented in 2 trial blocks to 13-week-old infants on each of 2 successive days. Smiling was lowest on the first block of trials on the first day, when the sounds were novel, on the second block of the second day after the stimuli had become very familiar, and highest on the two intermediate blocks, when the infant presumably was able to assimilate them following some effort. (Zelazo and Komer, unpublished).

Another illustration comes from a study in our laboratory in which 60 children, 5½ to 11½ months old, watched a hand slowly move an orange rod clockwise in an arc until it contacted a set of 3 different colored light bulbs. As the rod touched the lights, all 3 turned on. This same sequence was repeated 8 to 10 times (depending on the age of the child) during which most children remained extremely attentive. Each child then saw 1 of 4 transformations for 5 successive trials: (a) the bulbs did not light when the rod touched them, (b) the hand did not appear, (c) the rod did not move, or (d) neither hand appeared nor bulbs lit, but rod moved. Following the fifth transformation, the original standard was repeated 3 times. Incidence of smiling increased during the repetition of the standard to a maximal frequency of occurrence on the sixth trial, suggesting that it took some time for the average infant to establish a schema for this dynamic sequence. The peak smiling on trial 6 was followed by a drop in smiling on trials 7 through 10 because this event was now assimilated more quickly. Smiling dropped even further when the first transformation trial appeared, and reached a peak on the third transformation, implying increased assimilation of the transformed event. An anecdotal observation captures the dynamic process of assimilation that the smile can reflect. A 3½-month-old girl watched a small car roll down a wooden incline and, at the bottom, hit a doll and topple it over. The child watched each repetition of this event with a rapt, sober face. On the ninth repetition she smiled broadly for the first time as the car toppled the doll, and she continued to smile on the tenth, eleventh, and twelfth repetitions. On the thirteenth trial, we altered the sequence and had the doll fall before the car struck it. Her mouth began to part, as if to smile, but she never completed the action. She just stared intently at this new event. We interpret the smile on the ninth repetition as an indication that she was able to match the event to a constructed schema: She was not puzzled any more; she understood what was happening.

This interpretation of the 4-month smile to faces implies that it should not be as vulnerable to operant shaping procedures as earlier experiments have suggested (Brackbill, 1958). The 3- or 4-month infant smiles to a face because he recognizes it, not because he has been reinforced by an external agent for issuing this behavior. A recent study affirms this suggestion and questions the conclusions of earlier experiments (Brackbill, 1958; Etzel & Gewirtz, 1967). Three-month-old infants were tested by either a male or female adult over a 3- to 4-day period. Each time the infant smiled an adult smiled and talked to the infant and rubbed his abdomen. One block of base rate trials was followed by 5 blocks of conditioning trials. There was a general decline in smiling from block 1 to block 6. Within each day, the decrease in smiling over trials was even more dramatic. However, if one only examined smiling on the *first* trial of each day, there was a slight increase in smiling over the base rate (Zelazo, 1967). In a second experiment, 3-month-old infants were assigned to 1 of 3 groups; all were tested in their own homes. Base rate information on smiling was gathered on day 1 by having an adult stand 2 feet from the infant, maintain eye-to-eye contact with him, but with an unresponsive facial expression. For the *unresponsive group,* the adult maintained the same unresponsive expression for days 2 and 3. For the *contingent stimulation group,* the adult rewarded each infant's smile by smiling, talking, and touching the infant. For the *noncontingent stimulation group,* the adult issued the same reactions on a random schedule, unrelated to the infant's smiling.

There was a significant decline in smiling over trials for all 3 groups, although the contingent stimulation attenuated the decline of smiling, on the second day only. By the third day all group differences had vanished, and most infants were not smiling at all. That is, by trial 3 of day 3 the mean number of smiles to all 3 groups was less than 1.0; whereas, it was over 7 on the first trial of the first day. (Zelazo, 1969). The smiling to faces characteristic of the 3- to 4-month-old infant is not easily placed under operant control. This fact corresponds with the view that this early smile indexes a recognitory reaction to a human face and is not necessarily an instrumental response.

Scott and Fuller (1965) have suggested that a puppy's "tail wagging" may be analogous to the human smile. Tail wagging is not present at birth, and the puppy is most likely to wag his tail when he is in a state of mild excitement. One of the critical incentives for this special state of excitement is exposure to a familiar event—a handler, the bowl from which the puppy is fed, or the family automobile. The response is occasioned by recognition of a familiar context or object. But there are individual differences that seem to be genetic in origin. Age of onset of tail wagging is earlier in cocker spaniels than in basenjis, terriers, and shelties. Analogously, Freedman has reported dramatic differences among premature infants in the frequency of smiling to kinesthetic stimulation (personal communication).

What might be the cause of these individual differences in the display of the smile at 4 months, assuming that prior exposure to a face is held relatively constant? Consider the following hypothesis. The smile that accompanies recognition of a face requires, first, a build-up of tension during the brief period of uncertainty that the infant must experience before matching external event to schema; that is, the period during which the stimulus engages a part of the schema, but in which the assimilation is not yet complete. The smile can reflect the assimilation and the accompanying drop in that tension. Hence, one interpretation of individual differences in smiling assumes that the infant who smiles may have a capacity to build up a tension while matching stimulus to schema, and to be relieved of it. There is lability in the system. The nonsmiling infant either does not experience a reduced tension upon recognition (he remains vigilant), or does not build up the tension in the first place.

The pattern of smiling at 27 months lends support to this idea. Less than one-third of the 27-month-old children smiled frequently to the chromatic slide series. However, the proportion of subjects smiling to the cat, dog, telephone, and girl barking was much higher than the proportion smiling to the immediately preceding picture. These 4 scenes illustrated *familiar objects or sounds*. The 4 scenes that elicited the least smiling were: woman standing at the table, man in a car, man standing alone, and man with 4 arms. Let us assume that the 2-year-old child has a more finely articulated schema for men and women than he has for animals or telephones. He knows his father, mother, aunt, or grandmother, but none of the faces or voices of the people in the scenes resembled those of his parents or relatives. Each was a stranger. The child could not easily assimilate these scenes because his category for humans rested on more refined structures. By contrast, his categories for dogs and cats were not as finely differentiated. Every cat is a cat, and is more readily assimilated than a picture of a strange woman. Perhaps smiling to the cat or dog at 27 months reflects the same state of recognitory assimilation that smiling to the faces does at 4 months. Observations of the children match this interpretation. During the first 7 scenes, all of which were humans, many children appeared increasingly worried; their faces reflecting uncertainty as to who these people were. The smiling decreased linearly across these first 7 scenes. The cat, which appeared on the eighth slide, made the faces of many children light up. They smiled, often looked at their mother, and many uttered their first words, "Cat, Mommy, look at the cat, Mommy!" *They had finally seen something they knew.*

The pattern of orientation to the mother matched that observed for smiling. About 30% of the children looked at their mother on most scenes; but the proportion rose to over 50% for 5 scenes. Three of these 5 were of nonhumans (cat, dog, and telephone). The remaining 2 were the girl barking and the man in a woman's dress.

These 2-year olds were likely to smile, look at their mother, and verbalize when the nonhuman scenes or sounds occurred—the ones that allowed recognitory assimilation. It is assumed that smiles would have been *less* frequent if the cat and dog had been the first stimuli presented. The high proportion of smiles to the animals probably occurred because of the prior viewing of scenes that were not easily assimilated. The tension nurtured by uncertainty had to build to a certain level before assimilation of the familiar would release the smile. The occasion for the smile of recognition is a function of the child's adaptation level. The release of the smile requires a gradual growth of uncertainty followed by its reduction. Smiling to the Embedded Figures Test provides additional evidence for this rule.

The child's emotional response to successful solution of a test item was scored by assigning a value of 1 for no affect, a score of 2 for a smile, and a score of 3 for a smile accompanied by a laugh or a joyful exclamation *prior to the examiner's reaction to the child's answer.* Positive affect generally increased with increasing item difficulty (see Figure 7-1). The children showed more affect when they succeeded on the most difficult item than when they succeeded on the easiest item in the horse-bird-car-flower series. The relation of joyful affect to difficulty was linear; the harder the item the more likely the child was to smile or laugh when he solved it. Moreover, among boys, response times to successful items where affect was displayed were two seconds longer than response times to items to which no affect occurred. Smiling was more likely to accompany success that involved exertion of effort, for the reduction of uncertainty releases the smile and it takes some time for that uncertainty to grow.

The power of a discrepant event to release a smile is documented further in a study in which 3½-year-old children were shown a colored picture of randomly arranged lines for 6 repeated trials. On the seventh trial the child saw either an achromatic version of the set of lines, a set in which each line was half the length of the standard, a set with half the number of original lines, or the original stimulus rotated 180 degrees. Frequency of smiling decreased linearly over the 6 repetitions, but increased to the transformation, with the largest increase occurring to the achromatic set of lines (least subtle change) and the smallest increase to the change in

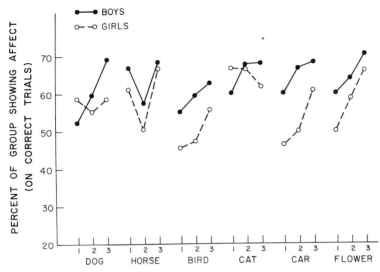

Figure 7-1 Percent of group displaying positive affect to EFT items as a function of difficulty level.

spatial orientation (most subtle change). Differential increases in fixation time to the transformations matched those for smiling (Lewis and Harwitz, 1969).

These data on frequency of smiling to the slides and embedded figure items are concordant with the earlier interpretation of the 4-month smile to the face. The smile signifies a cognitive success following some doubt over that success. The assimilation of an event that is initially discrepant from a schema, the recognition of a familiar event following exposure to an unfamiliar one, or arriving at a solution following mental effort share a common state; namely, a feeling of uncertainty followed by resolution. The smile is a sign of that dynamic process.

Intercorrelational Data. At 4 months, smiling generalized across the 2 visual episodes for boys ($r = .39$, $p < .01$ for PR with Reg), but not for girls. Moreover, among boys, smiling to PR was related to a larger body size, long fixation times, and large decelerations to the achromatic faces. For girls, smiling was only associated with long fixation times. At 8 months, smiling to the achromatic regular face (PR) was associated with longer fixations to all the achromatic faces but the coefficients were low ($r = .26$; $p < .05$). Smiling at 13 months showed good interepisode generality, but was independent of fixation time. We expected a strong relation between smiling and educational level of the parents, since "seeing the joke" in a distorted face or form should be related to richness of cognitive schema. But, to our surprise, social class was independent of smiling.

Measures of smiling and positive affect were obtained during 5 episodes at 27 months of age (human forms, clay faces, slides, embedded figures, and free play). About half the children smiled to the first presentation of each of the stimuli for human forms and clay faces, but there was no differential smiling among the 5 faces or 4 forms. With the exception of the Embedded Figures Test, smiling showed good cross-episode consistency, although slightly better for boys than for girls, as occurred at 4 months. Despite interepisode consistency, frequency of smiling was relatively independent of fixation time, social class, verbalization, or accuracy on the Embedded Figures Test.

Stability of Smiling. Since smiling only occurred with any frequency to 3 of the faces at 4 months (PR, SR, and Reg), we shall only consider the predictive correlates of smiling for these 3 faces at the early ages. In general, there was no stability, for either sex, from 4 to 8 months, suggestive stability from 4 or 8 to 13 months, and good stability, for girls only, between 13 and 27 months (see Appendix Table 48). The 4- to 27-month continuity, although low, was more impressive than that displayed by any other variable. Smiling to the regular achromatic face at 4 months predicted post-solution smiling to the Embedded Figures Test for both sexes ($r = .3$). Our favored interpretation rests on the earlier assumption that one of the occasions for the smile is the state of resolution following assimilation of a discrepant event or solution of a difficult problem. The absence of stability when faces or free play was the 27-month criterion supports this interpretation. The faces, forms, or toys did not elicit uncertainty, but the Embedded Figures Test did. Much of the smiling to the faces or during the free play was directed at the mother or emitted as an accompaniment to the general excitement of play. The 13- to 27-month correlations, which were only significant for girls, involved the Embedded Figures Test as well as forms, faces, and free play. As indicated above, the 1- and 2-year olds often smiled as they turned toward their mothers following presentation of a visual stimulus. This smile seemed to be the child's way of saying, "Isn't that funny!" This communicative smile differs from the smile that followed a correct solution to an embedded figures item. And smiling to the forms or faces was independent of smiling on the Embedded Figures Test.

In an attempt to determine if there were different correlates of the two patterns of stability we examined the psychological profiles for infants who were consistently high or low smilers to (a) faces at 4 and the Embedded Figures Test at 27 months and (b) human forms at 13 and 27 months (using median splits). The children who were high smilers to both the faces at 4 and the Embedded Figures Test at 27 months, in contrast to those who were low smilers at both ages, displayed a disposition toward slow tempo. The high smiling girls showed shallower habituation to the faces at 4 months ($p < .05$) and longer response times to the Embedded Figures Test ($p < .05$); the high smiling boys showed a slow tempo of play at 8 months ($p < .10$).

A similar analysis on those children who were consistently high versus low smilers across the period 13 to 27 months—rather than 4 to 27 months—revealed a different pattern. The high smiling girls were more spontaneously verbal than the low smilers to Human Forms I (at both 13 and 27 months) and to the clay faces at 27 months ($p < .01$ for each comparison). By contrast, talkativeness did not characterize the girls who were high smilers to faces at 4 and the Embedded Figures Test at 27 months.

Finally, the high smiling infant girls were most likely to be endomorphic in body build at 27 months, suggesting that both tempo of play and early smiling may derive from biological factors. Appendix Table 49 contains the correlations between an index of linearity of build (called ponderance index and defined by height/$\sqrt[3]{\text{weight}}$) at 27 months, and smiling at each of the ages. The 27-month-old girls who were short and fat in body build (endomorphs) were high smilers at 4 and 8 months of age. This result did not hold true for boys. Among boys, physique during the first year, rather than at 2 years, predicted smiling to the Embedded Figures Test, with tall and heavy infant boys showing the most affect to the Embedded Figures Test (see Appendix Table 50). The possibility that large male infants display more positive affect on a problem than smaller boys is supported by independent data from the Fels Research Institute. Chest girth and height in infancy predicted IQ scores in children and adolescents among boys, but not among girls. Why should large infant males become brighter or more gleeful when they solve problems? One possibility is that these larger boys have been more successful in the environment and, consequently, are more confident in problem situations.

Summary. The smile showed a unique pattern of stability during the first year for it was the only variable to show any continuity from 4 or 8 to 13 months. The 4-month smile may reflect a temperamental attribute involving the capacity to build and resolve the tension born of uncertainty. This tendency is associated with a slow tempo of play and an endomorphic physique in the 2-year-old girl. Smiling to the visual stimuli at 2 years seems to be communicative, and is correlated, appropriately, with spontaneous verbalization in 2-year-old girls. Except for the suggestive relation between early smiling and a slow tempo of play, there were no other meaningful derivatives of early smiling. The infants who smiled frequently did not have different fixation, deceleration, or vocalization patterns at 8, 13, or 27 months. The stability of smiling from 13 to 27 months among girls is one of the hardiest evidences of continuity in the entire study. Absence of continuity over this period for boys supports the repeated proposition that responses tapping cognitive and communicative functions are more stable for girls than for boys.

IRRITABILITY

The distribution of fretting or crying over the three ages was decidedly J-curved, for fretting was common among the 4-month-old subjects, but relatively rare among the older infants. A 4-month-old infant might cry because he was tired, hungry, or wet; because he did not like lying on his back; because he was bored with the pictures; or because he recognized, in some primitive sense, the strangeness of the crib in which he lay and the unusual events imposed on him.

Fretting at 4 months usually began after the first 8 or 9 stimulus presentations and trial 9 was the first trial at which 50% of the infants fretted or cried one or more seconds for two-dimensional and three-dimensional faces. About one-third of the 4-month-old infants never fretted or cried to any stimulus on either of the two visual episodes.

We attempted to minimize the occasions for somatic discomfort by bringing the infant to the laboratory following a nap and feeding, and never tested a child unless mother and staff thought he was alert, and neither tired nor hungry. If an infant began to cry during the series we stopped the presentations and tried food or a nap as the first solution to the problem. The initiation of fretting as a consequence of satiation or reluctance to lying in a supine posture (at 4 months) tended to occur during the later episodes in the series, rather than during the first episode. We might expect, therefore, different correlational patterns for irritability to the first or second episodes. In general, crying at 4 months was not elicited by a specific stimulus but by the entire situation. Fretting or crying at 4 months reflects satiation, postural discomfort, or a primitive anxiety reaction to the "strangeness" of the situation.

A very small group of 4-month-old infants only fretted when a stimulus was presented and never during the interstimulus interval when the field was blank. On some occasions the crying was so intense the session had to be terminated. These infants are not included in the correlational data and they will be discussed separately. At 8 and 13 months, fretting and crying are most likely to reflect boredom or fear, and rarely physical or postural discomfort. Crying to a particular stimulus, although uncommon, occurred most often at 8 months. A few 8-month-old infants were happy as they were placed in the highchair. They studied the first stimulus intently, but when the scrambled face appeared on the next trial they suddenly became quiet as they stared at the mask; their face gradually tightened into the characteristic signs of fear and after a few seconds they began to cry. A total of 14 girls and 10 boys showed this specific reaction (out of 158 children) and we shall discuss them later. Typically the infant was placated and we continued the episode without further incident.

There was also an opportunity for the 8-month-old child to display fretting or crying to a brief experimental separation from his mother. Following the 15-minute free play session, the mother was instructed to leave the room when the child seemed happy and involved in his play. The mother closed the door behind her and all infants noticed the mother leave. The mother was gone for a maximum of 2 minutes. Observers noted if the child began to fret or cry, and the latency to either reaction. About 50% of the children did not become upset during the 2 minutes and continued to play happily. Crying was least frequent at 13 months and was most often the result of boredom toward the end of the series. However, 13 girls showed fear to a stimulus, and 5 to the general testing situation.

If we assume that discrepancy from schema can occasion crying in the service of fear, the discrepant context at 4 months was the entire situation rather than a specific stimulus. At 8 months the fear was usually specific to the clay faces, suggesting that the child could assimilate the context of the laboratory but his schema for faces was too narrow to accommodate the unusual clay forms. At 13 months, fear was usually elicited by the experimenters or the testing situation. There was essentially no crying at 27 months.

Most of the data to be considered involve those children who never fretted or those who fretted a little (typically from 1 to 10 seconds) during an entire episode. These infants were generally placated easily and the episode was continued.

Age Differences in Irritability. Each child's fret or cry score at 4, 8, or 13 was the ratio of time fretting or crying to the total time in the episode—the proportion of time during which he was irritable. This index was chosen over the absolute time fretting or crying in order to control for those instances in which the infant became so upset that we had to stop the episode. It was assumed that had we continued to the end of the series the child would have cried most of the time. *Proportion time fretting* seemed to be a reasonable index of the child's irritability. The mean values for irritability approximated 5% of the time at 4 months, and 1% of the time at 8 and 13 months. Since boredom was a major cause of irritability at 8 and 13 months, fretting was most frequent to the episodes administered later in the session.

SOCIAL CLASS AND FEAR TO FACES

There was no strong relation between social class and irritability at 4 months, but there was a relation between social class and both specific fear to the faces and separation anxiety at 8 months (see Appendix Table 51). Each of three independent observers noted if the child showed a specific distress reaction to the faces (i.e., the child was calm prior to the presentation of the face but began to cry within 10 seconds of the presentation and stopped crying when the face was removed). Of the upper middle class infants, 39% showed a distinct fear reaction to the faces (usually the clay faces), in contrast to 17% of the lower middle class infants. This difference is not significant, but in a direction congruent with the separation anxiety data to be presented later. Four girls who showed extreme fear at both 8 and 13 months were from the top half of the social class distribution. When we examined the social class distribution for the children who showed fear to the faces at *both* 8 and 13 months, there were three times as many infants from the top half of the educational distribution as from the bottom half, although the class difference was not significant.

One interpretation rests on the assumption that the upper middle class children had developed a well-articulated schema for their parents' faces but for no other; while the lower middle class infants, who may have been exposed to a greater variety of faces in their homes (the home visit data corroborate this assumption) had a more generalized schema. Hence, the mask was a more discrepant stimulus for the upper middle than for the lower middle class children. Their inability to assimilate this discrepancy produced fear and crying. This interpretation rests on the following three assumptions:

1. The less variable and more frequent the exposure to a specific event, the firmer the schema for that event.

2. Exposure to an event discrepant from the schema alerts the infant.

3. The state of being alerted by a discrepant event that one can neither act on nor interpret leads to distress.

The above explanation utilizes the first assumption, namely, that upper middle class infants were not exposed to a sufficient variety of faces. An alternative interpretation derives from the third assumption, namely, that all the infants perceived the mask as discrepant from their schema for a face, but the upper middle class *infants attempted to assimilate the odd event.* Because they failed, they became afraid. The lower middle class infants did not try to assimilate the discrepant stimulus and, hence, did not experience the uncomfortable tension generated by being unable to cope with an unusual event. The essence of this argument is that all infants saw the mask as discrepant, but more upper than lower class infants tried to interpret it, and their failure produced fear.

This view finds some support in other work. For example, the young infant is most likely to cry in an unusual environment *if there is no response he can make to deal with it*. If there is an action he can issue, he often remains calm. Rheingold and Eckerman (1970) placed infants in a strange room without their mother, and most began to cry. But if the infants were placed in an adjoining room with their mother, and with the door to the strange room open, the infants crawled into the strange room. The infant was then in the same location where most infants cried. These infants did not show fear; they looked around and crawled back through the open door to their mothers. The availability of a response aborted the fear. Children who are suddenly exposed to a strange object or a parent leaving them alone are less likely to cry if they are actively involved in some routine, such as playing with a toy, than if their attention is not invested in any object.

We have suggested that the middle class infants cried because they could not assimilate the discrepant mask, whereas the lower class infants did not try. One might assume, however, that the lower class infants did try to assimilate the mask, and were *successful*. The absence of fear could result from either no attempt to assimilate or successful assimilation. Although this view is reasonable, it is not favored because of independent information suggesting that lower class infants are less likely than middle class ones to activate cognitive structures in the service of understanding. Ten-month-old, first-born female infants from lower middle and upper middle class families listened to tape-recorded passages read by their mother or a strange female. The mother was seated to the infant's right and a strange female to the left. The middle class children oriented to the mother following termination of her voice and to the stranger following the stranger's voice, as if they were attempting to locate the source of the tape-recorded speech. The lower class infants showed no such search pattern. They behaved as though they were not motivated to understand this strange pattern of events. Each of these interpretations is hypothetical and requires strong empirical tests. Our preferred explanation, albeit tentative, is that the middle class infants cried to the masks, especially the disarranged one, because they were motivated to assimilate it to their schema for a face. They remained alerted during this period of mental effort and their failure to understand resulted in fear.

Although the 8-month fear was to the faces and not the examiners, the 13-month-old children showed fear either to the faces, the situation, or the strange examiner. These data agree with those of Morgan and Ricciuti (1967) who report that anxiety to a stranger in a laboratory setting was more common at 13 than at 8 months, but contradict the common report of mothers that anxiety to a stranger in the home peaks at 8 to 9 months. The capacity of a stranger to elicit anxiety may be a function of the familiarity of the context. If the context is totally familiar and the stranger is the only discrepant stimulus, as occurs at home, anxiety is more likely to occur than if the stranger is encountered in an unfamiliar context where, since everything is strange, the stranger is less of a "figure" than he would be in a completely familiar surround.

Although there were no sex differences in frequency of fear to faces or forms, there was a sex difference in quality. No boy was ever described as seriously inhibited or severely frightened, while two girls displayed an intensity of fright and inhibition not observed in any boy. The boys who became frightened were easily calmed and the session continued. This was not true of several girls for whom the testing situation had to be terminated.

CONTINUITY OF IRRITABILITY

Homotypic continuity of irritability should be minimal because of the dramatic age differences in the presumed causes of crying. Consequently, we shall devote more space to heterotypic continuities. Since the distributions of fret scores were J-curved at all ages, we converted all scores to scale values (1 to 4) and all correlations were computed for the *scaled scores*. The relation between irritability at 4 and 8 months can be summarized without the support of a table. There was no relation between fretting at 4 and 8 months (correlation ranged between $-.01$ and $+.02$), and no consistent set of derivative correlations worth discussing.

There was, with one exception, no relation between irritability at 4 and 13 months. The exception was contained in the rather high correlation of $+.56$ ($p < .01$) between fretting to the three-dimensional faces and the rating of negative affect for 13-month-old girls. The rating of negative affect was based on mild protesting and dourness of attitude, occasionally in the service of boredom. These irritable girls also had shorter fixation times to the clay faces. The 8- to 13-month coefficients also suggested homotypic stability, but only for girls. Girls who fretted to the auditory stimuli at 8 months were more likely to fret to the clay faces and to HF II, the last two episodes, at 13 months of age. This fretting was usually in the service of boredom. However, many girls who became bored did not fret. The stable disposition is *the tendency to become irritable when bored,* not the tendency to become bored.

Derivatives of Extreme Irritability. There were 9 boys and 12 girls who cried so hard during the initial presentations of the clay faces at 4 months of age that the session had to be stopped. These children had also fretted mildly to the two-dimensional faces, but we managed to administer most of the series to them. It was impossible, however, to complete the administration of the clay faces on two separate occasions. In every case, we brought these children back on a second day (typically within three days of the first meeting) but, again, they cried during the opening trials and the session had to be terminated. Each of these 21 highly irritable children was matched with a child of the same sex and social class (i.e., educational level of both parents) who never fretted or cried to the clay faces. Differences between the pairs were assessed on major variables at 8 and 13 months.

There were no differences between these groups at 8 months of age. At 13 months, however, the extremely irritable 4-month-old girls behaved as if they were cognitively precocious to the nonirritable controls. The extremely irritable girls showed longer fixation times to HF II ($t = 2.35$, df 9, $p < .05$), and we have interpreted long fixation times at 13 months to reflect a denser set of hypotheses to the human forms. Second, the irritable girls vocalized more following termination of the auditory stimuli ($t = 3.66$, df 10, $p < .01$), and showed more act changes and more nonstereotyped acts than nonirritable girls ($t = 2.68$, df 11, $p < .05$; $t = 2.44$, df 11, $p < .05$). The link between 16-week extreme irritability and nonstereotyped acts at one year also held true for the girls who fretted only a little. This association did not emerge for boys.

Six activities accounted for most of the acts scored as "nonstereotyped" and each involved adaptive sensorimotor schemes for two objects (e.g., putting quoits on a shaft; pounding a pegboard with a wooden mallet; making a tower of blocks; pulling a wooden bug by a long string; piling blocks on top of a pegboard; putting the mallet in a pail). The unique acts (acts performed by only one child) involved hitting the bottom of the pail as if it were a drum, attempting to cover the blocks with the pail by placing the latter over the former; attempting to put the blocks on the shaft, and riding the pegboard as if it were a horse. In all cases the child was accommodating a complex and mature motor action to the object. These acts are to be contrasted with the more typical play of a 1-year old, which included tossing the blocks, hitting the pail with a hand, pushing the lawnmower, knocking over the toy dogs, or rolling the quoits. In these latter instances the sensorimotor acts seem less advanced, and none involves relating two objects in an appropriate way. If we assume that nonstereotyped acts at 1 year and extreme crying to faces at 4 months each reflects precocity, we have evidence for a "rate of development" construct that shows some continuity during the first year of life.

The validity of this suggestion rests on the assumption that the 4-month crying was occasioned by the child's recognition of the strangeness of the stimuli and testing context as a result of mature schemata for these events. The possibility that 4-month-old children are mature enough to become frightened in a strange context is supported by observations of rural Indian infants in Guatemala who are with their mothers constantly for most of the day. These 4-month olds display fear and crying when they are gently taken from their mothers and placed in a crib for observational purposes. The intensity of the crying is an exaggeration of that which is observed in a sample of American babies.

SEPARATION ANXIETY

It will be recalled that the child's reaction to separation was studied following the free play session at 8 months. Some of the infants (10 boys and 10 girls) were extremely irritable at the end of the play session and we could not administer the separation episode to them. However, 67 boys and 67 girls were administered this procedure. When the child was content and involved with the toy, the mother, on a signal, rose from her chair, walked slowly to the door, opened it, left the room and closed the door behind her. The child was observed for a maximum of 2 minutes. If he cried for longer than 20 seconds the session was terminated. We were interested primarily in whether he fretted or cried and the latency to this reaction. Half of the infants neither fretted nor cried and continued to play happily with the toys, (52% of the girls and 47% of the boys). Of the remaining infants, half fretted during the mother's absence but never cried intensely. The other half cried very hard during the mother's absence.

There was a positive relation between separation distress and social class, with middle and upper middle class infants more likely to cry than lower middle class infants (see Appendix Table 52). If one compares the bottom two educational groups with the top two groups with respect to *no distress* versus *any distress,* the resulting chi-square was significant for boys (chi-square = 9.50, 1 degree of freedom, $p < .01$), and just missed significance for girls. An independent study of 30 lower class and 30 middle class, 10-month, firstborn girls confirmed this class difference. The experimental context was identical with the one used in the longitudinal study—even the room was the same. Following a play session during which the mother was present, the mother quietly left the room. About 40% of the infants cried. The middle class girls cried much earlier than the lower class girls (5.4 versus 28.5 seconds, $p = .07$). All middle class infants who cried when their mothers left did so within 10 seconds of her departure; less than one-fourth of the lower class infants who cried did so within 10 seconds ($p = .001$ Fisher's exact test). (Tulkin, unpublished.) Moreover, within the lower class sample, 7 of the 30 mothers were working and were out of the home for most of the day. None of the 7 infants with working mothers cried when the mother left the room, whereas 9 of the infants of nonworking mothers cried ($p < .05$; exact test). Furthermore, when the mother returned to the room only 1 infant with a working mother crawled toward her. By contrast, 10 infants with nonworking mothers approached their mothers ($p < .10$; exact test). We interpret these data, together with the longitudinal material, as implying that frequency and quality of interactions with the mother form the basis of an attachment, and that middle class infants are more strongly attached to their mothers than lower middle class infants.

Derivatives of Separation Anxiety. We examined the difference in major reaction patterns for those children who cried versus those who neither fretted nor cried to separation at 8 months. Each of the infants who cried to the separation was matched with a child of the same sex and social class who did not fret at all, and these two groups were compared on selected variables. If separation anxiety is a partial index of the intensity of a child's attachment to the mother, we might expect that child to have more frequent interaction with the mother, and, as a result, to develop a better articulated schema for representations of human faces and figures. Such a child should react differentially to regular versus irregular faces and forms to a greater degree than the more weakly attached children. The 17 boys who cried, in comparison with the 17 matched controls, looked longer at the regular faces (PR and SR) than at the irregular faces at 4 months (10.0 versus 5.4 for the crying boys versus 12.3 and 11.0 for the controls). The second order difference between these two means was significant ($t = 2.46$, $p < .05$) (i.e., the difference for the "crying" boys was greater than the difference for the controls). In addition, the boys who cried to separation at 8 months were more likely to become upset to the clay masks at 8 months than the nonanxious controls ($t = 1.91, p < .10$).

Among the girls, the differences between the 13 girls who cried to separation and the 13 nonanxious controls were less clear. The girls who cried to separation were more irritable to the clay faces and forms at 13 months, and fretted earlier when placed behind the barrier ($t = 2.05$, $p < .05$). Since the barrier episode involved a spatial separation of mother and child there is some indication that these girls retained a low threshold for "disruption" to separation.

THE PREDICTIVE LINK TO 27 MONTHS

The relation between irritability at 4 or fear at 8 months, and behavior at 2 years can be summarized briefly. The irritable 4-month-old boys had lower vocabulary scores and poorer speech quality ratings. The irritable girls, by contrast, were restless and active at 2 years of age. The derivatives of fear to the faces at 8 months were also different for the sexes. The 8-month-old boys who showed fear to the faces, when contrasted with non-fearful controls, spent more time near their mother during the initial 5 minutes of the free play period ($p < .05$), and were less talkative—both signs of inhibition and apprehension. The fearful girls, however, were more spontaneously verbal to all the 27-month visual episodes ($p < .05$ for each), and showed no special preference to play near their mother. (These differences are based on pairs of infants matched on social class.) (See Appendix Table 53.) Fearful infant boys grew up to be quiet, inhibited 2-year olds; fearful girls grew up to be talkative 2-year olds.

In summary, irritability and distress have different meanings at each of the three ages and—as with mobility—there was no generalized tendency to cry that was stable across episodes within an age epoch or across time. Distress to separation from mother at 8 months was related to educational level of the parents for both sexes, suggesting a stronger attachment of infant to mother in the middle class families. The girls who cried at 4 months showed signs of cognitive precocity at 1 year, for they had less stereotyped sensorimotor schemes with the toys and longer fixation times. This association did not occur for boys. However, the girls who showed fear to the masks at 8 months grew up to be verbally outgoing; the boys, inhibited and shy. These sex differences in derivatives of fear or irritability, despite equal frequency of occurrence for these responses, join other instances of sex differences in patterning of variables. It is likely that mothers react differentially to fearful boys than they do to fearful girls, and these differential treatments may produce the divergent behavioral profiles seen at 27 months.

POSTURAL AND ACTIVITY VARIABLES

Unfortunately, we were not able to code motor activity or postural changes for all infants at all ages, and we shall examine these variables only briefly, emphasizing the 13-month data, which were most complete. The reader can appreciate the sample size for each variable by examining Appendix Table 3 which lists the maximal sample size for the major variables at each age.

Sex Differences. There were no major sex differences in activity at 4, 8 or 13 months. The single significant sex difference indicated that 13 month boys were more likely than girls to *quiet* when the stimulus appeared, although the boys were not more active than girls during the interstimulus periods. This sex difference supports the earlier suggestions that boys are more likely than girls to display gross postural adjustments as part of an orientation to an interesting event.

Intercorrelational Patterns. The intercorrelations of postural variables at 13 months were similar for the sexes and suggested three relatively separate and orthogonal dimensions—twisting in the chair, leaning forward to touch the stimulus, and quieting when the stimulus appeared (see Appendix Table 54). These three responses seemed to reflect different processes. Twisting indexed boredom; quieting, a tendency to orient to a change in stimulation, and leaning forward, a special interest in the stimulus. Let us now examine the correlational patterns of these three reactions at 13 months (see Appendix Tables 55, 56, 57).

The correlates of quieting, more orderly than we typically encounter, suggest two generalizations (see Appendix Table 55). Quieting covaried with fixation time, but was independent of deceleration and vocalization, with magnitude and consistency of the coefficients more impressive for boys than girls. The correlates of twisting yielded the reverse profile, for twisting was associated with shorter fixation times and, among boys, with mobility during the free play. The correlates of leaning forward paralleled those for quieting. Infants who leaned forward while fixating the stimulus showed larger decelerations and smiled more often, but their fixation times were not dramatically longer than the other infants. Infants who quieted showed longer fixations and less smiling, but their decelerations were no different from the others. The associations among deceleration, smiling, and leaning forward imply that the "leaning" was in the service of interest and this cluster suggests an active-passive continuum of interest. Among the infants who were interested in the stimuli, some quieted and studied the stimulus, inhibiting any signs of affect or action. Other children became active or tried to touch the stimulus. A second vector, lack of interest, is indexed by short fixations and frequent twisting. Let us now examine the stabilities across the three periods (scale scores were used in all correlations).

STABILITY OF ACTIVITY-POSTURAL VARIABLES

There was no stability for boys, and suggestive stability for girls from 4 to 8 months. The girls who were most active to the faces at 4 months were most active during the two facial episodes at 8 months. It should be noted that activity level to the clay faces at 8 months, like fixation time, was inversely correlated with social class for the girls ($r = -.60$, $p < .01$). Restlessness and short fixations were characteristic of the lower middle class 8-month-old girls. There was minimal continuity of the activity variable from 4 to 13 months and no systematic derivative relation to fixation time or deceleration at 13 months. This is not surprising. At 4 months the infant was lying supine, and was usually inactive. One major incentive for action was involvement with the stimulus. Many 4-month-old infants who became attentive to the stimulus began to thrash and move their arms and trunk. The postural and activity variables coded at 4 months are in the service of processes different from those operating at 13 months. The homotypic continuity from 8 to 13 months was present for both sexes, although slightly more consistent for boys than for girls. High activity scores at 8 months predicted minimal quieting, minimal alertness, and short fixations to the 1-year episodes.

The major variables at 27 months were mobility and tempo in the free play situation, restless activity during the slide session, and an impulsive attitude on the embedded figures and conflict tests. Appendix Table 58 contains the correlations between the four activity variables at 13 months across all episodes (body twisting, waving of arms, leaning forward, and quieting) and these 27-month variables. Among boys, but not girls, restless twisting predicted high error scores on the Embedded Figures Test and a fast tempo of play at 2 years of age. This heterotypic continuity over a 14-month period lends support to the assumptions surrounding the etiology of an impulsive attitude. Earlier work on first and second grade children found an association between restless motoricity and indexes of impulsivity. These data suggest that 1-year-old boys with a low threshold for restlessness to a series of visual episodes—albeit in the service of boredom—are likely to have a fast tempo of play and behave impulsively when they are 2 years old.

In summary, as with the other variables, the 8 to 13 and 13 to 27 month comparisons displayed some continuity, suggesting that a common process is mediating the stabilities for fixation, vocalization, and activity. Attentional involvement in the stimulus appears to be that mechanism. The predicted relation between restless activity at 1 year and an impulsive attitude among 2-year-old boys adds credibility to the concluding comment of Chapter VI; namely, some of the determinants of conceptual impulsivity and tempo can be previewed during the first year of life.

VIII

Summary and Conclusions

This limited longitudinal study has provided preliminary answers to the four searching questions posed in the opening chapter. We achieved some insight into the pattern of psychological continuities during the first two years, encountered provocative sex and social class differences in attentional dynamics, and found enough modest evidence to sustain the hope that a preschool child's conceptual tempo might be previewed from his reaction patterns during the first year of life. As a dividend, we learned a little of the psychological meaning of some common reactions in the repertoire of the infant. Fixation, vocalization, deceleration, and smiling provide different views of the complicated phenomena that comprise attention. It is as if a stranger peered into a small house containing four irregularly placed tiny windows, each with a different refractory index; and covered on the inside by a special filter so that objects of different hues appeared to have the same color. The view from each window offered a slightly different picture of the complicated scene on the inside. If the stranger is to know the complete contents of the house, he must learn about the refractory characteristics of the glass, the nature of the filters, and construct ingenious hypotheses about the relations among the four different perspectives; for he only has visual access to a small proportion of all that is locked within. We face a more awesome problem in trying to understand dynamic changes in attention and affect by observing an infant's looking, babbling, smiling, or heart rate. Each of these reactions mirrors different aspects of the attentional process with varying degrees of fidelity. Despite years of serious effort the relation of each of these variables to each other and to cognitive process is still ambiguous.

Fixation time provides the clearest picture, perhaps because it has been most extensively studied. Initially, fixation time is controlled by change in the physical parameters of an event, especially movement and contour contrast. Sometime between 8 and 12 weeks of age, degree of discrepancy between event and schema supplements and begins to dominate this more basic force. Toward the end of the first year the density of hypotheses activated to assimilate a discrepant event becomes a primary determinant of fixation. The data summarized in Chapter III support these theoretical and still controversial views.

Cardiac deceleration does not accompany every epoch of attention and most of the fixations—even the lengthy ones—were not accompanied by any significant change in heart rate. One hypothesis holds that events that surprise the infant, unexpected events as well as moderate discrepancies from established schemata, are most likely to produce a deceleration. These events are typically accompanied by a noticeable motor quieting and the infant's face takes on the appearance of a "double take." Magnitude of cardiac deceleration and fixation time should be closely related during the first half-year, when discrepancy is the primary determinant of fixation time, but each should become more independent of the other around 1 year of age. The data confirm this expectation, and affirm the preliminary interpretations of the cardiac reaction.

Smiling serves many different masters during the first three years and we considered only two of the many functions of this uniquely human response. First, the smile can reflect the state that follows effortful, recognitory assimilation. When the child encounters an event that is not immediately assimilable, a special state of tension is generated by the psychological uncertainty. If the child can relate the event to available cognitive structures, the uncertainty and tension are relieved and the smile is an epiphenomenon of that process.[1] The post-solution smile to the

[1] The reflex smiling seen in newborns is accompanied by pontine discharges, for the smile is typically seen during periods of sleep when REM's (rapid eye movements) are occurring, rather than during non-REM sleep (Ende & Konig,

Embedded Figures Test appeared to have a similar dynamic and the continuity between "smiling" to faces at 4 months and following success on an embedded figures item at 27 months implies that a common and stable disposition may be mediating this reaction. The disposition to smile following recognitory assimilation may have a biological correlate, for it was most characteristic of girls with an endomorphic physique, and displayed less variability for identical than for nonidentical twins. The smile of assimilation should be independent of fixation time and cardiac deceleration, for both reactions occur to discrepant events, whether or not they are eventually assimilated. Both the regular and scrambled facial masks elicited large and equivalent decelerations and fixation times at 4 months. However, smiling occurred almost exclusively to the regular face, because it could be assimilated. The sharp decrease in magnitude of deceleration and smiling at 8 months of age, which is accompanied by a better articulated schema for faces, is congruent with the general interpretation we have imposed on these variables. The smile also has a communicative function. One-year olds smiled at their mother in order to indicate that they were aware of the unusual characteristics of the experimental stimuli. These two kinds of smiles were independent of each other at 27 months, and showed different continuity patterns, even though their muscular topographies were similar. But we must always inquire about the function of a behavior in a specific context if we wish to understand it. Man is not equipped with enough variety in his response repertoire to supply the large number of psychological demands that must be filled. Whether the behavior be a cry, a clenched fist, or a laugh, we will not be able to discern its meaning unless we know the occasion of its display and have a few clues to help us guess its intended function.

Positive vocalization (i.e., nondistress) in the young infant also carries different messages. It accompanies the excitement generated by an interesting event that engages a schema, as well as the arousal tied to beginning restlessness. Vocalization, like the galvanic skin response or activity level, seems to mirror a diffuse state change and conveys the least information about the specific stimulus that provoked the change. Vocalization was typically not differential to the varied stimuli within an episode, whereas fixation, smiling, and deceleration were, on occasion, highly differentiating (see Appendix Table 59). Magnitude values for *fixation time, smiling,* and *cardiac deceleration* at 4 months were dramatically larger to the regular face than to the blank face (which had no facial features), whereas vocal-

---

1969). This suggests that the motor component of the smile is most likely to occur during moderate states of central nervous system arousal rather than complete relaxation.

ization times were equivalent to all faces. The pattern of vocalization did not reveal the fact that the presence of eyes had an obvious behavioral effect on the infants. Similarly, the two regular achromatic faces (PR, SR) elicited longer fixations, more smiling and larger decelerations than the two irregular faces at 4 months; vocalizations were equivalent to all four faces. At 13 months, fixation times were shorter and decelerations smaller to the amorphous free form (on HF I) than to the three human forms; vocalizations were nondifferentiating. Finally, at 27 months, fixation time to the human forms was a curvilinear function of degree of discrepancy from schema; vocalizations failed to show that pattern.

Thus, each of these four responses revealed different facets of the delicate phenomena of attention. Vocalization most often indexed excitement; fixation indexed time to assimilation; deceleration indexed surprise; and smiling indexed successful assimilation of an initially discrepant event. We did not begin the study with these notions; the data permitted these inferences. If future research confirms these suggestions, it will affirm the usefulness of longitudinal data in deciphering the cryptic messages that nature asks each behavior to carry.

The major responses displayed similar patterns of continuity with moderate stability from 8 to 13 and 13 to 27 months, and minimal stability across the other age comparisons (see Appendix Table 60). The absence of convincing continuity from the 4-month data, with a few exceptions, probably is based on several factors. First, some infants may have been functioning at the more fragile stage of inattentiveness characteristic of infants under 12 weeks of age. Each of the responses probably assumes a different meaning during this ontogenetically more primitive period. Human biologists have suggested that stable physical growth dimensions do not begin to emerge until about 6 months of age (Tanner, 1963), and major changes in central nervous system functioning occur between 8 and 12 weeks. Indeed, Tanner (1970) suggests that the primary cortical areas are relatively immature until 12 weeks. Hence there is considerable lability in the psychobiological system at 4 months and, on purely biological grounds, one would not expect dramatic predictive stability for behavior displayed by a 16-week-old infant. Second, the 4-month olds' fixations to the faces are presumably governed by degree of discrepancy between external face and schema; whereas, the older child's attention is more seriously controlled by the density of hypotheses activated to assimilate discrepant events. Since the basic determinants of the response change, one would not expect much continuity. And the data indicate minimal stability between degree of articulation of a face schema at 4 months and density of hypotheses surrounding human forms or faces at 1 or 2 years.

Although it is not possible to make powerful predictions about duration of attentiveness, vocabulary level, or spontaneous verbalization at 2 years from behavior during the first half-year, such predictions are improved when the data are gathered on the 1-year old. Symbolic hypotheses and language have assumed their influential role on both fixation time and vocalization by 1 year, and predictive continuity is improved. When the child's reactions to meaningful events come under the control of more symbolic structures, signs of stability emerge. This phenomenon has an obvious parallel in the fact that IQ scores become stable after 2 years of age, the time when language competence has become a major factor in psychological performance. The moderate stability of fixation time from 13 to 27 months suggests that this sample of children retained similar rates of growth for cognitive structures surrounding representations of the human.

The suggestive stability of vocalization, deceleration, and smiling pose different problems. Spontaneous vocalization and verbalization reflect two processes—the tendency to talk when excited by an interesting event, as well as the possession of sufficiently articulated schemata so that external events engage existing schemata. The consistent independence of vocalization and fixation time at every age implies that richness of hypotheses is not an important determinant of the stability of spontaneous vocalization. However, sex differences in the stability and pattern of vocalization were noted; this finding will be considered later in the chapter.

The stability of cardiac deceleration and smiling are the most difficult to explain. Deceleration is presumably facilitated by a postural orientation marked by motor quiescence. The stability coefficients argue that some children retained the disposition to display quiet orientation across the first two years. There was even the suggestion of stability of deceleration for boys from 4 or 8 to 27 months, implying that the tendency for somatomotor quieting to a new event may be a basic individual difference dimension in male infants. The continuity between smiling to faces at 4 and positive affect to embedded figures at 27 months, when viewed with the absence of stability for smiling to the faces across the same period, suggests that the smile mirrors individual differences in the capacity to build up and/or resolve uncertainty. Some children are reluctant to invest focused attention in a problem or unusual event and do not develop the unique state of unresolved uncertainty that is a necessary condition for the smile. Other children invest attention, but remain vigilant even after assimilation has occurred. The "smilers" are presumably those children who engaged the event and experienced the resolution of uncertainty that follows successful recognition or solution. The latter tendency may have a biological basis, for the 4-month smile displayed heritability and was linked to the child's physique. The heavy 4-month boys were frequent smilers, the endomorphic 2-year-old girls were frequent smilers, and these data are concordant with classic Sheldon somatotype theory. Other studies have revealed individual differences in display of the smile to transformations of a meaningless visual form, as well as an association between smiling and a shallow rate of habituation. The willingness or capacity to invest focused and prolonged attention seems to be characteristic of smiling infants. We do not imply that the pensive child is happier, but rather that his thoughtfulness allows more frequent mental victories.

If we assume that patterns of continuity and discontinuity can provide clues to changes in stages of psychological organization, these data suggest that a change occurs in the relation of behavior to internal structure toward the end of the first year. Vocalization, deceleration, fixation, and smiling each displayed suggestive stability from 13 to 27 months, but minimal stability from 8 to 27 months. The similar patterns of continuity imply that a common maturational process is monitoring the stability. Deceleration and vocalization displayed their lowest values at 13 months, and this is the time when walking, syllabic reduplication, and comprehension of language emerge. Moreover, the correlation between the mental and motor scales of the Bayley Scale of Infant Development drops from +.78 at 6 months to only +.24 at 1 year. This concordance of events around the first birthday may signify the gradual end of one developmental stage and the beginning of another.

Since most of the stability coefficients did not rise above 0.5, the relative plasticity of individual growth patterns is also affirmed. A child's cognitive development is certainly not fixed at 2 years of age. We have been continually impressed with the changes in attentiveness, affect, and activity that occur in individual children. One hyperkinetic, restless, and inattentive infant boy was placid and quiet at 27 months. Another boy who rocked his entire body and sucked his forearm throughout the three 8-month episodes—and who worried the staff—did not appear atypical at 27 months. The significant stability coefficients were usually produced by the top and bottom 15% of the sample who retained their general rank relative to the rest of the group.

As in an earlier longitudinal study (Kagan & Moss, 1962), as well as test-retest correlations for infant scale scores during the first 3 years (Kessen, Haith, & Salapatek, 1970) where correlations of 0.5 were also modal, one can be awed by the rejection of the null hypothesis and celebrate the thread of continuity, or emphasize the modest size of the correlations and the inherent instability of the young child. We have promoted the former position for two reasons. The response variables quantified are likely to be crude indexes of the psychological dimensions about which we wish to generalize. One must add a few points to the coefficients to compensate for the frail methodology psychologists bring to this problem.

Second, parents continue to believe that each of their children retains some small island of identity, despite the empiricist's failure to supply unequivocal support for this faith. Hence, any favorable evidence is to be protected.

In spite of slight evidence of stability, our inability to make predictions of later personality from observations in the first three years of life is so much against good sense and common observation, to say nothing of the implication of all developmental theories, that the pursuit of predictively effective categories of early behavior will surely continue unabated. (Kessen, Haith & Salapatek, 1970.)

But the cold, hard data are equivocal, and either group—those who champion stabilities or those who see the child as infinitely malleable—can feel validated.

. . . . to the scientist, constancy and change in nature are not antithetical. Both are there. Accent on one or the other merely reflects which partial aspects of nature one cares to single out and spotlight—stability or flux. (Weiss, 1969, p. 287.)

THE CONCEPT OF INFANT INTELLIGENCE

The phrase infant intelligence has purposely been omitted from this discussion because of its questionable significance—theoretical or heuristic. Much of the research on infant mental development has been guided by two related—and essentially unproven—hypotheses. The first posits a hypothetical entity, called intelligence, which can be measured by noting the rate of development of those response systems that are emerging at the moment. It has been implicitly assumed by some that precocity of development in one response system was correlated with precocity in other systems—a "g" factor in infancy—and that a given level of precocity might have predictive validity for the future. (Bayley, 1949, 1956.) There are neither adequate data nor persuasive theory to support this axiom. The infant possesses varied systems of schemata, hypotheses, overt responses (communicative as well as sensorimotor), and visceral afferent patterns. There is no formal theory, or even semielegant hypothesis, that predicts close covariation in the development of these systems. Kessen, Haith, and Salapatek (1970) note that psychologists have seen the infant as either an assembly of reflexes, a set of emergent behaviors, a sensory surface, a learner, social partner, or a perceiver and thinker. This study has concentrated on the last role not because perceiving and thinking uniquely define infant intelligence, but because such functions seem theoretically significant and pose an intriguing, empirical challenge.

A second assumption guiding work with infants presumes that early cognitive structures are derivative of sensorimotor actions, a view usually attributed to Piaget. The significance of sensorimotor coordinations for adaptive functioning is readily acknowledged, but their necessary causal connections to cognitive development are, we believe, still open to debate. A conditioned association can be acquired without the occurrence of peripheral motor acts and linguistic competence is being continually acquired through listening, without any necessary overt rehearsal. Experimental study of bird song indicates that exposure to the song of one's species during a critical developmental period permits the adult bird to produce its characteristic song, although the infant may have produced no sounds when first exposed to the sounds of its species (Marler and Hamilton, 1966). Infants also seem to acquire representations of sensory experience just by looking and listening. The author has no doubt that if a child's head and limbs were prevented from moving but he heard and saw the experiences in a typical family environment, he would acquire symbolic language.

The reason for assuming that motor action instructs cognition is based, in part, on the public character of the dependent variables. Progress in psychological theory would be expedited if we could easily infer mentation from movements of the arms, hands, or fingers. Unfortunately, major transformations occur between cognitive structures and overt actions, and inference about cognitive process from a set of instrumental actions is vulnerable to error.

Consider the research devoted to finding motivational sites in the hypothalamus. Some investigators have assumed that a particular area in the lateral hypothalamus was the site of hunger motivation because rats ate food pellets when particular nuclei were stimulated. It was assumed that the stimulation made the rat hungry. That inference seemed correct, considering the data. However, stimulation of the same area in the lateral hypothalamus also leads to drinking or gnawing, depending on the available objects in the cage (Valenstein, Cox, and Kakolewski, 1968). Moreover, if the pellets of chow are ground into powder—an unusual form for the food—the hungry animal will not eat, even though the same area is stimulated. These observations make the earlier inference, which intuitively seemed so attractive, equivocal. Similarly, if a 6-month-old infant picks up a cloth after an object has been placed under it, it may be fallacious to assume that he wants the object or that he knows that it is there. He may just be examining the cloth. Infants normally pick up unusual objects.

Inferring cognitive structure from behavior is perilous for the overt act is controlled by many functions, including the accommodation of the response to the shape and movement of the object, the state of the infant, and general context. When a 3-month old grabs for an attractive rattle, observers are tempted to infer a sophisticated goal directed purposiveness to the infant's behavior. However, the response may be merely a prepotent reaction to the state of excitement created by the colorful rattle. The tendency to "grab," rather than "coo" or "kick," might be occasioned by the presence of a small object, as Valenstein's rats tended to eat when food was available, drink when water was present, and gnaw when wood chips carpeted the cage. This hypothesis could be tested by exciting the infant, using an auditory or tactile stimulus, and noting the degree to which the specific behavior elicited was a function of the context. The infant might vocalize if a face were present, reach for a small object, or kick if a large rubber ball were available. We do not deny that the 4-month infant possesses cognitive structures that direct his actions. *There is purposive behavior in infants.* But there is a facile tendency to infer sophisticated cognitive processes from ambiguous infant reactions. We have, no doubt, made this error many times in this text. The author was observing a film of a 7-month old made by an intelligent graduate student in which object permanence was being assessed. At one point in the procedure, after an object had been hidden by the examiner, the infant looked over the side of the highchair. "Do you see?" exclaimed the student, "she's looking for the lost object." I demurred, insisting that this was unlikely and suggested that the infant was either bored or saw something on the floor that attracted her attention. Several moments later the film affirmed the second hypothesis. Overt actions are seriously controlled by context, state, and motivation, and only reluctantly expose their well-kept secrets about inner structure.

Hence, one source of error in using overt action as a window to the mind resembles a Type 1 error in statistical inference, when a causal hypothesis is accepted on the basis of insufficient evidence. A second source of error results from failing to assume existence of a cognitive structure merely because the relevant behavior is absent or distorted. A 3-year old's graphic reproduction of a face or a man is a horrendous scribble of lines, but his verbal description is better, and his ability to point to a well versus a poorly formed human being is perfect. His cognitive competence outstrips his performance. A child can say exactly how one should hold a bat, throw or catch a ball, or slide into home plate without ever having played baseball. But he would probably be incompetent and clumsy on the field. The psychological child consists of a system of actions, cognitive structures and visceral afferent feedbacks. Each of these systems has parallel representations in biological structures (dualism is still necessary), provides different information to observers, and is differentially activated. The systems are joined at many places, but transformations occur at each of these junctures. Thus even when all three systems are operational, probes will give divergent perspectives, depending on the system studied. Perhaps the best strategy is to assess all three systems simultaneously. Schaffer and Parry present a nice example of what happens when two response systems are assessed. Six- and 12-month-old infants were shown nonsense objects for seven repeated presentations, followed on the eighth trial by a novel object. Fixation times for both 6- and 12-month subjects dropped over the seven repetitions, but increased on the eighth trial when the novel stimulus appeared. However, latency to grab for the object—which may have indexed a general inhibition in the situation—did not rise on the eighth trial. Moreover, although 6-month subjects showed habituation of fixation time over the seven repeated presentations, they showed no change in latency to touch the habituated object. The sensorimotor system and attentional system each presented a different picture of what was happening psychologically. The occurrence of the discrepancy, so clearly represented in fixation time scores, was not at all apparent in the latency values (Schaffer and Parry 1969).

The longitudinal data contained a similar message. Looking, smiling, vocalizing, decelerating, and posturing offered slightly different clues to cognitive processes. If we knew how to combine these fragments of information we might begin to solve part of the puzzle of infant thought.

SEX DIFFERENCES

The form of the sex differences that emerged was remarkably similar to that noted in our earlier longitudinal study. There were minimal differences in mean or variance values for all variables, but major differences in the patterning and stability of these measures. A similar conclusion was written in 1962 in the final chapter of *Birth to Maturity*, "Many of the variables showed no significant sex differences in the two parameters but yielded different patterns of intercorrelations" (Kagan & Moss, 1962, p. 275). The most dramatic sex differences involved the significance of vocalization (i.e., better continuity for girls and the link between excitement and vocalization), as well as the closer relation between parental education and fixation time. Alternative interpretations for these phenomena were discussed earlier (see pp. 104–111). The unusual stability of girls' vocalization seems to reflect continuity of a tendency to make sounds when excited by an interesting event. It is not suggested that vocalization indexes a general excitability across all situations. Instead, it is likely to be specific to events that are discrepant from acquired schemata. Put plainly, the tendency to become affectively aroused by an interesting event or context and to vocalize as an accompaniment to that arousal seems to be more stable among girls than boys, and to be more consistently associated with indexes of attentiveness. For example, the 8-month girl who babbled following the termination of the auditory stimulus was more attentive at both 8 and 13 months, and vocalization to the first trial of a particular episode displayed much better continuity for girls than boys. Girls' vocalization to faces and human forms seemed yoked to the excitement generated by unusual events. It is probably not a coincidence that upper middle class girls showed the largest increase in vocalization from 8 to 13 months; lower middle class girls showed the smallest change. Changes in boys' vocalization scores across this 5-month period were independent of parental education. This sex difference in functional significance of vocalization could be the result of either different patterns of maternal treatment toward daughters and sons, structural differences in the central nervous system, or both. Let us consider these alternative explanations.

Two of the major dimensions on which mothers can be distributed are a desire to accelerate the cognitive development of their children and positive feelings about them. Interviews and observations suggest that most of the mothers in our sample felt affection toward their infants, but they differed in concern with and encouragement of the child's psychological development. The mothers had different conceptions of the ideal boy or girl, and engaged in different practices in order to attain these idealized goals. Many mothers valued verbal proficiency and language skills in the girl, perhaps because these are traditionally female accomplishments. Girls are typically superior to boys on language skills, but not on other intellectual talents. And mothers seem to have an implicit theory of tutoring that states that verbal stimulation of the infant and exposure to speech facilitate language development. By contrast, many mothers believe that boys should be strong and proficient at gross motor talents, and the mother's implicit theory of tutoring dictates that rough-and-tumble play facilitates attainment of this goal.

We suggest that an accelerating mother treats her infant in ways that are consonant with her idealized goals and her theory of appropriate instrumental procedures. Hence, she should engage in reciprocal vocal and verbal stimulation more frequently with her daughter than with her son; in more motor play with her son than with her daughter. Observations of the mother-infant interaction at 3 and 4 months give partial support to this idea. One possible consequence of this difference in maternal behavior is the girls' stronger tendency to vocalize when excited by an interesting event. This conclusion follows from the assumption that the mothers' continued reciprocal vocalization leads to a conditioning of the vocal response to representations of human faces and to states of excitement. The boys' vocalization would be less strongly conditioned to either because the mother is less likely to respond to the boys' vocal behavior with an excited vocal reactions. The major fault in this argument is that it predicts more frequent vocalization to our stimuli by girls; this sex difference *did not occur at any age*. Our *post hoc* interpretation is that some of the boys' vocalizations were in the service of restlessness rather than excitement. Perhaps a more careful analysis of the acoustic quality of the vocalizations would have produced sex differences in quality of babbling.

DIFFERENCES IN CENTRAL NERVOUS SYSTEM ORGANIZATION

Although differential maternal responsivity to daughters versus sons is the most likely interpretation of the sex difference in vocalization patterns, it is possible, albeit speculatively, that differences in central nervous system structure are influential. Experiments cited earlier suggest that dominance of left over right cerebral hemisphere may be less equivocal in the young female than in the young male (Kimura, 1967; Knox and Kimura, 1970). Since anatomical and physiological systems mature earlier in the girl than in the boy, perhaps the normal dominance relation of left over right hemisphere becomes established earlier in girls than in boys. As a result, language functions might mature earlier and the association between information processing and vocal responsivity emerge earlier in the girl. The emergence of a more unified language-verbal factor among 27-month girls than boys is certainly concordant with this idea.

This hypothesis generates some provocative corollaries, some of which are consonant with general experience and existing data. If the language functions of the left temporal cortex elaborate earlier in the female, experience is more likely to be transformed into linguistic structures early in development, at the expense of other categories of representation. If "language" is given primary responsibility for representation of the environment, the girl's language skills should be superior to other classes of intellectual competence. The equipotentiality of the hemispheres among young boys should lead to a more even development of mental talents and less obvious superiority of language over nonlanguage talents during early childhood (Knox and Kimura, 1970). Spatial skills, which are nonlinguistic and preferentially elaborated in the right hemisphere, should develop to higher levels in boys than girls. The empirical data affirm this prediction. Boys, from various cultural groups, are superior to girls on spatial problems; girls are superior to boys on verbal tasks. Moreover, dichotic recognition of nonlinguistic sounds, which seems to be mediated more by right than by left hemisphere, is better for 8-year-old boys than 8-year-old girls; while there is no sex difference for dichotic recognition of numbers (Knox and Kimura, 1970). These data fragments seem reliable enough to invite additional empirical inquiry. Although they do not even come close to proving that there are sex differences in central nervous system organization, they are sufficiently strong to suggest that this possibility can be entertained. Indeed, the special link between vocalization and attentional excitement in the infant girl may be a joint product of central nervous system organization wedded to special caretaking practices toward daughters. Since cultures are apt to adopt practices that are friendly to the biological attributes of the organism, both explanatory hypotheses may have some merit.[2]

Sex Differences in the Effects of Social Class. The covariation between educational level of the parents and indexes of growth and articulation of cognitive structure was consistently stronger for girls than boys. Duration of fixation at 8, 13, and 27 months, increases in fixation from 13 to 27 months, increases in vocalization from 8 to 13 months, quality of vocabulary, and Embedded Figures Test performance were all more closely associated with parental social class for girls than for boys. The independent study of 30 middle and 30 lower class, 10-month-old girls, mentioned in earlier chapters, affirms the strong influence of class on the female (Tulkin, unpublished). The middle class girl showed more vacillation in a conflict situation (i.e., when confronted with both an old toy and a new one, the middle class girl showed frequent visual shifting between the two). Furthermore, middle class girls showed differential responsivity to meaningful speech, when contrasted with their response to a preceding passage of meaningless speech. The middle class girl quieted more to the meaningful passage and maintained longer fixations on a stranger who sat beside her (as if the child believed the stranger was the source of the voice). The lower middle class girl did not show this differential reaction to the meaningful versus the nonmeaningful passage. Analogously, the upper middle class 8-month girls in our longitudinal study looked longer at the source of speech than the lower middle class girls.

Other investigators have reported closer covariation in females between social class and varied indexes of cognitive development. Hess and his colleagues (Hess, Shipman, Brophy, & Bear, 1968, 1969) gathered an exten-

---

[2] Western culture has produced many creative women poets and writers. But in the nonverbal art forms—music and painting—there are far fewer women than one would expect, considering their numbers in the language domains. Perhaps this asymmetry in choice of creative mode is the price that women pay for their initial left hemispheric advantage. Perhaps it is woman, not man, who is the intellectual specialist; woman, not man, who insists on interlacing sensory experience with meaning. These reversals of popular homilies join other myths that science has questioned. For it is the female who is more predictable, the female who is biologically more resistant to infirmity, and the female anatomy that is nature's preferred form. Man's *a priori* guesses about sex differences seem to reflect an understandable but excessive narcissism.

sive amount of test and observational data on a sample of 163 black mothers and their children, initially when the children were 4 years old and two years later when the children were in school. There was a stronger relation, at both ages, between the maternal intelligence test score or level of education, and the cognitive development of daughters than of sons. For example, the partial correlation between maternal verbal IQ and the 4-year old's IQ score, with maternal social class controlled, was .39 ($p < .001$) for daughters, but only .15 for sons. The same sex difference emerged even when this analysis was restricted to working class families. Moreover, maternal language ability, assessed when the child was of pre-school age, was a better predictor of reading proficiency two years later in daughters ($r = .50$) than in sons ($r = .25$). Since a mother's verbal skill is likely to covary with her sense of effectiveness in our culture, it is relevant to note that the mother's optimism about her future, obtained when her child was 4 years old, was a better predictor of reading achievement two years later for girls than for boys ($r = .44$ versus .06). The authors suggest,

Cognitive environment has a greater impact on girls' readiness for school than on boys' readiness for school . . . girls' scores are somewhat more closely related to crowding in the home and considerably more related to the use of home resources. Girls apparently are more influenced by the mother's feelings of effectiveness and optimism, her use of status-normative control strategies, the complexity and facility of her language and her affective support (as rated by the interviewer). (Hess, Shipman, Brophy, & Bear, 1969, p. 49.)

However, this sex difference only held for language and reading skills, not for arithmetic proficiency. The special effect of maternal ability and personality on the girl's cognitive development was clearest in the verbal domain.

A similar sex difference has been reported in a longitudinal study of Hawaiian infants. (Werner, 1969). Samples of 231 boys and 254 girls from the island of Kauai were given the Cattell Developmental Scale at 20 months of age and the Primary Mental Abilities Test at 10½ years of age. Both parental IQ and education were more highly correlated with girls' Cattell scores than with those of boys (r = 0.3 for girls; 0.1 for boys). Although this sex difference had diminished by age 10, an index of social class was still more strongly correlated with PMA IQ for girls than for boys ($r = .34$ versus .24). (Werner, 1969.)

Hindley's (1965) longitudinal study provides the closest parallel to the results reported here. Working and middle class English children were administered the Griffith's Infant Scale at 6 and 18 months and the Stanford-Binet Intelligence Scale at 3 and 5 years of age. The relation between social class and intelligence test quotients was higher for girls than for boys at all four ages. Moreover, there was no relation between social class and developmental quotient at 6 or 18 months for boys; but a substantial positive correlation for the 18 month old girls (Hindley, 1965). As in the present study, the covariation between social class and indexes of mental development increased with age and was slightly stronger for the female. Finally, the cross-age stabilities for the developmental quotients, over the period 6 months to 5 years, were consistently higher for girls than for boys. For example, the 6 to 18 month stability coefficients were .70 for girls but only .43 for boys. The 18-month to 5-year coefficients were .48 for girls and .34 for boys (Hindley, 1965). The remarkable similarity between these data on London children and the data gathered in Cambridge buttress our faith in the general validity of this sex difference.

This strange interaction between maternal education and girls' development may also hold true for patterns of overt behavior. In a recent study 34 boys and 33 girls of preschool age were observed in a variety of settings, including a Headstart group, a day care center, an experimental school, and a typical suburban nursery school. The child was observed three times for 20 minutes over a 3-month period. The behavioral variables included dependence, attention seeking, dominance, affection, and hostility toward both children or adults, as well as pride in mastery and role playing. None of the variables reliably differentiated lower from middle class boys, whereas four approached statistical significance for the girls. The middle class, in contrast to the lower class girls, sought adult attention more often but were less likely to direct peers or test adults. The middle class girls seemed to have a more positive attitude toward adults, while no such difference occurred for boys (Ogilvie, 1969).

The interpretation of sex differences in older children usually invokes the assumption of a stronger identification of the girl with the goals of the family. This dynamic may, indeed, operate with preschool and school age children, but it is clearly not operative at 8 or 12 months. At this very early age, we believe that there is greater variability across social class levels in maternal reactions to daughters than to sons. Most mothers in this culture, whether they be high school dropouts or college graduates, believe their sons will have to develop independence, responsibility, and a vocational skill. When lower and middle class mothers of 4-year olds were asked to teach their child a new task, mothers of both classes were more achievement oriented toward sons than toward daughters, adopting a more "businesslike" attitude toward boys than toward girls (Hess, Shipman, & Bear, 1968). Lower class mothers of daughters project their greater sense of impotence on to them and are less likely to stimulate, encourage, or reward their daughters' simple accomplishments. Observations of lower and middle class mothers of infants at 4, 10, and 27 months affirm this suggestion. Middle, in contrast to lower middle, mothers spend more time talking to and entertaining their daughters, and chide them more often for task incompetence.

It will be recalled from Chapter III that we made home observations of 90 members of the longitudinal sample when the children were 27-months old. A female observer visited the home on two occasions and recorded, for about five hours, units of interaction that focused on the child's violation of maternal standards for appropriate behavior and the mother's subsequent reactions to these violations. The data were in the form of descriptive statements of the interaction. These descriptions were typed and coded by two independent observers who had no knowledge of the social class of the mother and had never visited the home. Most of the variables did not yield dramatic sex by class interactions. However, whenever there was a class difference in maternal behavior, it was more likely to occur for daughters than sons. The most important difference, for our purposes, however, is that upper middle class mothers were more likely to note incompetent behavior and criticize it in daughters than in sons. If one computes all the incidents that provoked the mother to criticize or punish the child, less than 1% involved incompetence among lower middle boys, upper middle boys, or lower middle class girls. However, 2.4% of the maternal criticisms of the child involved this violation for the middle and upper middle class mothers. That is, *well-educated mothers of daughters were three times more likely than poorly educated ones to chide their daughter for not performing up to a standard held by the mother.* There was no comparable class difference for the mothers of sons. This difference was specific to task competence, for the well-educated mothers were generally more tolerant of other categories of violations in their daughters than were lower middle class mothers. It appears that mothers from a broad range of educational backgrounds are more divergent in their concern with proper behavioral and intellectual development in their daughters than their sons and this phenomenon would help to explain the greater covariation between maternal education and aspects of cognitive development among the girls.

A second factor, alluded to earlier, assumes less variability in temperamental dispositions among girls than boys, and implies that there are more infant boys who are extremely irritable, alert, active, or lethargic than girls. Infants who are at the extremes of a psychological dimension should be less influenced by specific caretaking experiences than those who are of normative disposition. It is more difficult to engage in long periods of reciprocal vocalization and joyful play with a highly mobile, highly apathetic, or highly irritable baby. The mother who initiates these caretaking actions will influence the child less than one who initiates the same sequence with a less extreme child. The analogy of the clay balls of variable malleability referred to in Chapter I is the image that captures this explanatory idea.[3] Support for the notion that social experience affects girls' cognitive development in a more orderly fashion is found in the relation of face-to-face contact between mother and infant in the home and fixation time to representations of faces. Observations of mothers and 3-month-old infants were made in the home and the amount of face-to-face contact quantified. Soon after the home observation, the infants were brought to the laboratory and shown both achromatic representations of faces and geometric stimuli, while fixation times were coded. There was a positive relation between face-to-face interaction and fixation time to the faces among girls $(r = .61, p < .01)$ but not for boys $(r = -.10)$ (Moss & Robson, 1967, 1968). However, the tendency to remain quiet and awake at 1 month and show *low irritability* at 3 months predicted fixation time for boys $(r = 0.5)$, but not for girls. Specific social experiences seemed to influence the attentional dynamics of girls; while congenital temperamental dimensions were more influential for boys (Moss & Robson, 1970). The effect of experience on attention (i.e., face-to-face contact) is more faithfully reflected in the infant female than the infant male. Perhaps the greater male variability in both maturational development and temperamental attributes is responsible for this difference.

CLASS DIFFERENCES

Despite the limited range of social class—as indexed by educational attainment—sampled in this study, meaningful differences emerged during the first year and were unequivocal by 27 months. This finding is to be contrasted with the absence of class differences during the first two years on the Piaget Object Scale or the Cattell Infant Intelligence Scale, neither of which focus on distribution of attention to discrepant schemata, but

[3] An elegant summary statistic that reflects the generally greater variability of boys' scores is derived from a discriminant analysis performed on the data gathered from the auditory episodes at 8 and 13 months. The analysis used 6 variables (looks at speaker, vocalization, and deceleration at 8 and 13 months) to trial 1 or trial 4. The log of the determinant of the variance-covariance matrix for each sex is an index of the dispersion of the scores and in both cases the boys' scores had slightly greater dispersion than girls. For trial 1, the log of the determinant was 15.01 for boys and 14.87 for girls $(F = 2.57, p < .05)$. For trial 4 the corresponding values were 14.67 and 13.16 $(F = 3.66, p < .05)$.

emphasize coordination of sensory-motor systems (Golden & Birns, 1967).

Social class is used here descriptively as a rough and indirect index of different categories of caretaking practices. The observed class differences in maternal behavior toward infants at 4, 10, and 27 months affirm the validity of this assumption. If we knew the critical caretaking parameters that mediated the differences in the infant's behavior we would select parents on these caretaking dimensions, rather than on social class. But we do not, and the psychological differences among the children are used to guide wise inferences about the caretaking practices that should be given theoretical emphasis. This strategy is common during the early period of a scientific discipline. Fifteenth century physics talked about the effects of heat on objects or solutions. Heat was not treated as an explanatory construct, but as a name for a set of unknown processes to be discovered.

One of the major dimensions that differentiates lower from middle class parents is the parents' faith that they can influence the child's mental development. Excerpts from interviews with some lower and middle class mothers of 10-month-old, firstborn daughters (Tulkin, in press) capture the greater sense of fatalism and impotence of the lower class mother, in contrast to the middle class mother's belief that she has the power to shape her infant's mind.

INTERVIEWER: Do you think there are things that mothers can either do or not do when kids are as young as she is that can make the kids smarter when they are older, or make their personalities different?

MOTHER: I don't think that they can make them smarter or dumber. I think they can change their personality. So, if we talk down in front of her—I don't do that—in stupid sentences, naturally, that's how she is going to talk. If we swear in front of her, that's how she's going to talk. If she ever swears when she's two years old, she heard it from us. Where else would she hear it? She's not out on the street playing. So she'll get our personality. As far as smartness, no, I don't think we have much to do with that. The school would. We teach her different things. But any baby can be taught to do something. If it's going to be a smart baby—kids in school now are always studying—but they are still a C student or a B student. Where other kids are just very smart, they can take everything in. It all depends on her. If she can take everything in and likes studying; some kids love studying but they are still a C student. So I think it's really up to her.

A second lower middle class mother admitted to the same fatalism.

MOTHER: I think it's good to play with her and show her different toys and games. It does make them curious and they do learn. But I don't think she'll be any smarter. If she's dumb, she's dumb. I don't know how to answer it, really . . . there's no way that I can change her. I mean if she will read books and play with different toys and learn things from different kinds of toys, she might grow up to be smart. Or she might be born with smartness, too. I think playing with games and toys—figuring what's there and what's that. . . . But I think that a baby is born with an intelligence.

This skepticism about being able to seriously influence the child's basic intellectual talents is contrasted with the exaggerated feeling of effectiveness of two upper middle class mothers.

MOTHER: I think you could teach your baby to coo or goo, or call you in some way at quite an early age if you responded to her crying. You'd have to be very careful and willing to experiment much more than I'm willing to do, but I do think it would be possible. At least the majority of children you could teach them to not cry.

INTERVIEWER: How did you see yourself as different from other mothers?

MOTHER: I hope that I would never yell at my kids and abuse my children as most of these people did. A steady stream of abuse seemed to be their control technique. I found that very difficult to live with because it was sort of all negative. I am sure that there were positive moments but they sort of came in between all the negative ones. I would try for the reverse. There's a great deal of yelling at the kids; there's relatively very little value placed on learning—but the kids have sort of learned to dislike school and the academic things.

INTERVIEWER: Is this a kind of intentional teaching, when they are taught to dislike school?

MOTHER: I think what happens is that there is no systematic effort to teach them to do the kinds of things that would result in their being successful in school. And so they fall behind a year. Like the twins next door. They are a year behind in school. Already they've fallen back a year. And the neighborhood culture is to hate school. I'm not saying that I would like their school but they don't seem to like any of the parts of school or consider them as pleasures. They have a different value scale.

A second mother captured the poetry of the reciprocal interaction between a parent and infant that, we believe, is a critical catalyst of cognitive growth.

INTERVIEWER: What are the things that you have so much fun doing?

MOTHER: Playing hide and go seek. My husband is worse than I am. He crawls around the house after her. He gets pretty serious about it. If an adult were around he would probably feel pretty silly. And the silly things, like trying to get them to laugh and things. It probably gets more ridiculous as they get older. Like maybe when she's two or three. To me, a person wouldn't be too much of a mother if she couldn't sit down and do foolish things. How could you not have fun with your own child? Not playing those little games they enjoy. I have more fun than she does, I think.

Social class is clearly not an explanatory construct. But the parent's feeling of effective power to control the environment and to sculpt her young child's interests and talents, which seems to covary with class membership, exerts a profound influence on broad classes of caretaking practices which, in turn, shape the child's behavioral and cognitive profile. This is but one dimension that seems to covary with class; we must discover the others.

The correlation between the infant's social class and his reactions to the laboratory episodes grew steadily as the child matured. There was little effect of class at 4 months, but clear effects at 27 months. The 27-month pattern provides clues to understanding the earlier data. Among girls, parental education covaried with richness of vocabulary, duration of attention, quality of performance on the Embedded Figures Test, and vacillation in the conflict situation. Education was not related to amount of spontaneous verbalization, deceleration, or smiling patterns. Class was most closely related to attentiveness, language, and problem solving competence, not to excitability, activity, or affectivity. Among boys each of these relations was diluted, although always in the same direction as the girls. Although parental education was not highly predictive of language competence and duration of attention among boys, it predicted proximity to mother during the free play episode. This observation is concordant with data gathered in the home, for well-educated mothers played much more with their sons than lower middle class mothers. Moreover, an independent sample of upper middle class 2-year-old boys remained closer to their mothers in a novel play situation than girls of comparable age and social class.

The infant is being continually influenced by the practices of his parents. These practices are a complex function of the parents' values which, of course, are shaped by their educational experiences. The public effect is subtle during the first half-year, but, by age 2, verbal competence, sustained attention, and inhibition—the hallmarks of white middle class values—are more salient for the middle than for the lower middle class white child.

CONCEPTUAL TEMPO

The belief that there is a stable disposition to invest long (versus short) epochs of attention in external events, independent of richness of cognitive structures, found only tentative support in the data. There was a small group of children who showed shallow habituation and high smiling to the faces at 4 months, a slow tempo of play at 8 and 27 months, and a reflective attitude on the Embedded Figures Test. These children approach a new problem situation by inhibiting task irrelevant actions and focusing attention on the event. They appear to be thinking about the material in front of them. The shallow habituation at 4 months presumably mirrors a sustained attempt to match the representation of faces to the delicately articulated schema developed during the first 16 weeks. The longer act sequences at 8 and 27 months may result from activation of mental representations of end states appropriate to objects in the play room. The connotative meaning of tempo implies an easy ability to immerse the self in an interesting event, and to retrieve structures appropriate to it. Some children's biology may make it easy for them to develop such a mental set, for tempo of play showed heritability at 8 months and was associated with a characteristic physique.

The continuity of this dimension is supported not only by the work of Pederson and Wender, who found analogous stability from 30 to 72 months, but also by the continued insistence of poets, novelists, and psychologists that an inhibition-excitability dimension captures one of the major dimensions of difference among people (Gottesman, 1966). Tempo is not viewed as synonymous with the classic meaning of introversion-extroversion, but may share some variance with it. Some individuals, children or adults, act on the world as it presents itself. One has the feeling they are dealing directly with experience, with the ideas that happen to be bubbling on the top of the mind. If the ideas generated are not appropriate to the situation, they are willing to leave that context and find another. The slow tempo child blocks action initially, scans the situation and his store of ideas, and searches for the most appropriate hypothesis. Generation of a faulty solution is followed by a second attempt, rather than the seeking of a new problem. This disposition is controlled by many independent factors, the most central of which is related to anxiety over error or failure. But the *a priori* hope that 10% of the variance for conceptual tempo at age 3 would be predicted by infant reaction patterns was just realized, and tempts us to posit a partial biological core to this complicated trait.

EPILOGUE

This investigation has implications for vital issues in contemporary psychology—class differences in mental development, biological determinants of behavior, and the usefulness of a longitudinal approach. The appearance of class differences in distribution of attention as early as 1 year may come as a surprise to some, for studies that have used traditional infant intelligence tests have not found social class differences before 18 months of age. The early emergence of social class differences gains in importance for the lower middle class subjects in this sample were from intact families, uncharacteristic of those normally residing in an urban ghetto. If language comprehension, sustained attention, and a reflective attitude continue to have some value in the public school setting, it may be wise to consider initiation of educational procedures with poor families during the first two years of life in order to prevent the lower class child from acquiring habits inimical to school progress. Those procedures may be administered in institutional settings if the caretaker-infant ratio is small enough, or in the home through semitherapeutic-educational sessions between mother and an adult whom she trusts. Both strategies should be tried. Investigators have begun to send trained paraprofessionals into the homes of mothers with young infants and to alter successfully the mother's practices with her child. It is too early to know if these procedures will affect permanent salutary changes in the child, but there is no indication that these interventions are undesirable.

A View of the Infant. The interpretations offered in this report reflect a conception of the young child different from more popular views. There are two independent prejudices about the nature of the child. Some observers see him as growing toward an ideal state that defines maturity; others see development as open ended, with no particular structure transcendent over another. A second dimension is captured by the antonyms active versus passive. Both Freud and Piaget are developmental idealists. They believe there is a special terminus that all children gradually approach, passing through a series of stages on the way. Formal operational thought, the ability to test systematically a set of relevant solution hypotheses and select the most appropriate, is the ideal in the Piagetian system. Genital maturity, with its accompanying freedom from repression and sexual anxiety, captures Freud's view of the ideal. The behaviorists, on the other hand, Watson, Hull, Miller, and Bandura, are nonevaluative. The child is not traveling in any particular direction. He is learning habits, attitudes, and motives in concordance with reinforcing agents. There is no press to postulate stages, for growth is continuous rather than discrete.

The child's passivity is the essence of the second dimension. Is the child, as Locke implied, shaped by events, or does he actively select the experiences he wishes to exploit, and regularly restructure the content of his mind, as Piaget implies. The major fault in the structure of classic behaviorism is its inability to deal with spontaneous restructuring of both thought and behavior. Although Piaget and Freud are both idealists, they diverge on this vector. Piaget argues for an active child. Freud, by contrast, has the infant buffeted by instinctual energy and the socializing actions of the environment. The child cannot avoid becoming trapped in conflicts that are necessities of the psychosexual stages. The behaviorists—Watson,

Miller, Skinner, Bandura—promote the view of a child of clay sculpted by the vicissitudes of contingent experiences. Few investigators side with the infant in the fourth cell—the active child who is not traveling toward any predestined Nirvana. The modern cognitivists, like Neisser and many existentialists, are friendly to this bias, which was clearly implied in several of our interpretations.

We suggested that the long fixation times after 1 year were the result of the child trying to explain the discrepant event, trying to restructure the scrambled face or form to the schema that he possesses. The 2-year old who actively generates some structure for a pile of blocks is likely to continue playing with them until that cognitive state is attained, or until he believes that it is not attainable. These sentences create the image of a child structuring his environment and attempting to understand it, but do not imply any particular terminus more desirable than another. Child and adult try to keep uncertainty low. Although adults may be more efficient, they are not freed of this burden. This image of the child does not deny the possibility of stages, but is not forced to postulate a hidden continuity across them or a logical relation among them. The image is of a small boat on a very large pond, rather than a car on a highway.

The Use of Longitudinal Studies. As in earlier work, the use of a longitudinal design has helped to uncover dynamic processes that could not have been discovered through cross-sectional investigations. Upper middle class girls showed larger increases in vocalization-verbalization from 8 to 13 months than lower middle class girls, yet class differences in spontaneous vocalization at each age were minimal. Since vocalization is under the control of many factors, the longitudinal design allows one to use each subject as his own control in order to tease out dynamic sequences. Similarly, the relevance of rate of habituation or early smiling at 4 months for the tempo cluster at 27 months or the relevance of 4-month irritability for precocity of cognitive structures at 1 year could only have been discovered with a longitudinal design. A most beautiful example of the profit of such an analysis was noted when vocalization at 4 months was combined with social class. The probability of spontaneous verbalization at 27 months was highest for upper middle class girls who were highly vocal at 4 months.

As long as the meaning of a behavior remains equivocal, longitudinal analyses can be helpful adjuncts to experimental studies in reducing our ignorance. Longitudinal analyses are especially critical when one is studying a time span during which the topography of behavior is changing rapidly. If some basic processes remain continuous, they can best be discovered through a combination of rigorous theory, bold inference and longitudinal data. The first longitudinal analysis conducted by the author dealt with data that covered the first 30 years. This one spanned less than 30 months. If there is a third, it will probably focus on the first 30 weeks. Each look at development narrows the time window and brings the lens closer to more specific phenomena. The successive steps necessary to learn more about man require inhuman patience and an insatiable appetite for fascination.

References

Acheson, R. N. Maturation of the skeleton. In F. Falkner (Ed.), *Human develop-ment*. Philadelphia: W. B. Saunders, 1966. Pp. 465–502.

Ainsworth, M. D. S. *Infancy in Uganda*. Baltimore: Johns Hopkins Press, 1967.

Allport, G. W. *Pattern and growth in personality*. New York: Holt, Rinehart & Winston, 1961.

Ambrose, A. J. The development of the smiling response in early infancy. In B. Foss (Ed.), *Determinants of infant behavior*. New York: John Wiley, 1961. Pp. 179–196.

Bandura, A. Vicarious processes: A case of no trial learning. In L. Berkowitz (Ed.), *Advances in experimental social psychology*. Vol. 2. New York: Academic Press, 1965.

Bandura, A., & Menlove, F. L. Factors determining vicarious extinction of avoidance behavior through symbolic modeling. *Journal of Personality and Social Psychology*, 1968, **8**, 99–108.

Bandura, A., & Walters, R. H. *Social learning and personality development*. New York: Rinehart & Winston, 1963.

Bartlett, F. C. *Remembering: A study in experimental and social psychology*. London: Cambridge University Press, 1932.

Bayley, N. Consistency and variability in the growth of intelligence from birth to 18 years. *Journal Genetic Psychology*, 1949, **75**, 165–196.

Bayley, N. Individual patterns of development. *Child Development*, 1956, **27**, 45–78.

Bayley, N. Developmental problems of the mentally retarded child. In I. Philips (Ed.), *Prediction and treatment of mental retardation*. New York: Basic Books, 1966. Pp. 85–110.

Bayley, N. *The Bayley Scale of Infant Development Manuals*. New York: The Psychological Corporation, 1969.

Berlyne, D. E. The influence of albedo and complexity of stimuli on visual fixation in the human infant. *British Journal of Psychology*, 1958, **49**, 315–318.

Berlyne, D. E. *Conflict, arousal and curiosity*. New York: McGraw-Hill, 1960.

Blest, A. D. The function of eye spot patterns in the lepidoptera. *Behavior*, 1957, **11**, 209–256.

Brackbill, Y. Extinction of the smiling response in infants as a function of reinforcement schedule. *Child Development*, 1958, **29**, 115–124.

Braine, M. D. S., Heimer, C. B., Wortis, H., & Freedman, A. M. Factors associated with impairment of the early development of prematures. *Monographs of the Society for Research in Child Development*, 1966, **31**, 1–92.

Broadbent, D. E. The role of auditory localization in attention and memory span. *Journal of Experimental Psychology*, 1954, **47**, 191–196.

Bronson, G. W. The development of fear in man and other animals. *Child Development*, 1968, **39**, 409–431. (a)

Bronson, G. W. The fear of novelty. *Psychological Bulletin*, 1968, **69**, 350–358. (b)

Bronson, W. C. Adult derivatives of emotional expressiveness and reactivity control: Developmental continuities from childhood and adulthood. *Child Development*, 1967, **38**, 801–818.

Bruner, J. S. *Processes of cognitive growth: Infancy.* Vol. III. Heinz Werner Lecture Series. Worcester, Mass.: Clark University Press, 1968.

Buhler, C. The social behavior of children. In C. A. Murchison (Ed.), *Handbook of child psychology.* (2nd ed.) Worcester, Mass.: Clark University Press, 1933.

Caldwell, B. M. The usefulness of the critical period hypothesis in the study of filiative behavior. *Merrill-Palmer Quarterly*, 1962, **8**, 229–242.

Cameron, J., Livson, N., & Bayley, N. Infant vocalizations and their relationship to mature intelligence. *Science*, 1967, **157**, 331–333.

Carpenter, G. C. Differential visual behavior to human and humanoid faces in early infancy. Presented at Merrill-Palmer Conference on Infancy. Detroit, February 1969.

Caudill, W., & Weinstein, H. Child care and infant behavior in Japanese and American urban middle class families. In R. Konig & R. Hill (Eds.), *Yearbook of the International Sociological Association*, 1966.

Caudill, W., & Weinstein, H. Maternal care and infant behavior in Japan and America. *Psychiatry*, 1969, **32**, 12–43.

Cazden, C. B. Subcultural differences in child language. *Merrill-Palmer Quarterly*, 1966, **12**, 185–219.

Charlesworth, W. R. Persistence of orienting and attending behavior in infants as a function of stimulus-locus uncertainty. *Child Development*, 1966, **37**, 473–490.

Cohen, S. Impulsivity in low achieving and high achieving lower class boys. Unpublished doctoral dissertation, Columbia University, 1969.

Collard, R. R. Social and play responses of first born and later born infants in an unfamiliar situation. *Child Development*, 1968, **39**, 325–334.

Collard, R. R. Age and sex differences in the exploratory and social behavior of infants. Unpublished manuscript, 1969, U. Massachusetts.

Collins, R. L. Inheritance of avoidance conditioning in mice. *Science*, 1964, **143**, 1188–1190.

Conel, J. L. The postnatal development of the human cerebral cortex. Vol. 3. *The cortex of the three month infant.* Cambridge, Mass.: Harvard University Press, 1947.

Conel, J. L. The postnatal development of the human cerebral cortex. Vol. 7. *The cortex of the four year child.* Cambridge, Mass.: Harvard University Press, 1963.

Davis, R. C., Buchwald, A. M., & Frankmann, R. W. Autonomic and muscular responses and their relation to simple stimuli. *Psychological Monographs,* 1955, **69,** (20, Whole No. 405).

Deese, J. Behavior and fact. *American Psychologist,* 1969, **24,** 515–522.

Denenberg, V. H. Critical periods, stimulus input, and emotional reactivity: A theory of infantile stimulation. *Psychological Review,* 1964, **71,** 335–351.

Denenberg, V. H. Animal studies on developmental determinants of behavioral adaptability. In O. J. Harvey (Ed.), *Experience, structure, and adaptability.* New York: Springer, 1966. Pp. 123–147.

Dodd, C. & Lewis, M. Attention distribution as a function of complexity and incongruity in the 24 month child. Paper presented at meeting of Eastern Psychological Association. Philadelphia, April 1969.

Drake, D. M. Perceptual correlates of impulsive and reflective behavior. Unpublished doctoral dissertation, Harvard University, 1968.

Dreyfus-Brisac, C., Samson, D., Blanc, C., & Monod, N. L'électroen-céphlograme de l'enfant normal de moins de 3 ans. *Etudes Néo-natales,* 1958, **7,** 143–175.

Dryman, I., Birch, H. G., & Korn, S. J. Verbalization and action in the problem solving of six year old children. Unpublished manuscript, 1969. Albert Einstein School of Medicine

Ellingson, R. J. Study of brain electrical activity in infants. In L. P. Lipsitt & C. C. Spiker (Eds.), *Advances in child development and behavior.* New York: Academic Press, 1967. Pp. 53–98.

Emde, R. N., & Koenig, K. L. Neonatal smiling and rapid eye movement states. *Journal of American Academy of Child Psychiatry,* 1969, **8,** 57–67.

Emmerich, W. Continuity and stability in early social development. *Child Development,* 1964, **35,** 311–332.

Etzel, B., & Gewirtz, J. Experimental modification of caretaker maintained high rate operant crying in an 8 and 20 week old infant (infans tyrannoteraus) extinction of crying with reinforcement of eye contact and smiling. *Journal of Experimental Child Psychology,* 1967, **5,** 303–317.

Fantz, R. L. Pattern vision in newborn infants. *Science,* 1963, **140,** 296–297.

Fantz, R. L. Visual experience in infants. *Science,* 1964, **146,** 668–670.

Fantz, R. L. Pattern discrimination and selective attention as determinants of perceptual development from birth. In A. H. Kidd & J. J. Rivoire (Eds.), *Perceptual development in children.* New York: International Universities Press, 1966.

Fantz, R. L. & Nevis, S. Pattern preferences in perceptual cognitive development in early infancy. *Merrill-Palmer Quarterly,* 1967, **13,** 77–108.

Feld, S. C. Longitudinal study of the origins of achievement strivings. *Journal of Personality and Social Psychology,* 1967, **7,** 408–414.

Finley, G. E. Visual attention, play, and satiation in young children: A cross cultural study. Unpublished doctoral dissertation, Harvard University, 1967.

Fischer, K. W. The effect of AHA reactions on heart rate. Paper presented at meeting of Society for Research in Child Development, Santa Monica, Calif., 1969.

Freedman, D. G. An ethological approach to the genetic study of human behavior. In S. G. Vandenberg (Ed.), *Methods and goals in human behavior genetics.* New York: Academic Press, 1965. Pp. 141–161.

Freedman, D. G., & Keller, B. Inheritance of behavior in infants. *Science,* 1963, **140,** 196–198.

Fuller, J. L. Experimental deprivation and later behavior. *Science,* 1967, **158,** 1645–1652.

Gardner, R. A., & Gardner, B. T. Teaching sign language to a chimpanzee. *Science,* 1969, **165,** 664–672.

Garn, S. M., Silverman, S. H., & Rohman, C. G. A rational approach to the assessment of skeletal maturation. In *Ann. Radiol.* (Paris), 1964, **7,** 297–307.

Gellermann, L. W. Change orders of alternating stimuli in visual discrimination experiments. *Journal of Genetic Psychology,* 1933, **54,** 231–237.

Gesell, A., & Amatruda, C. S. *Developmental diagnoses.* New York: Hoeber, 1941.

Gesell, A., & Thompson, H. *Infant behavior: Its genesis and growth.* New York: McGraw-Hill, 1934.

Gewirtz, J. L. The course of infant smiling in four child rearing environments in Israel. In B. M. Foss (Ed.), *Determinants of infant behavior.* III. London: Methuen & Co., 1965, Pp. 205–260.

Ghent, L. Developmental changes in tactual thresholds on dominant and non-dominant sides. *Journal of Comparative Physiological Psychology,* 1961, **54,** 670–673.

Golden, M., & Birns, B. Social class and cognitive development in infancy. Presented at Society for Research in Child Development meeting. New York City, March 1967.

Gordon, I. J. The Florida Parent Education Projects: Research Reports. Institute for Development of Human Resources. Gainesville, Fla: College of Education, University of Florida, 1969.

Gottesman, I. I. Heritability of personality. *Psychological Monographs,* 1963, **27,** No. 572.

Gottesman, I. I. Genetic variance in adaptive personality traits. *Journal of Child Psychology Psychiatry,* 1966, **7,** 199–208.

Graham, F. K., & Clifton, R. K. Heart rate change as a component of the orienting response. *Psychological Bulletin,* 1966, **65,** 305–320.

Haaf, R. A., & Bell, R. Q. A facial dimension in visual discrimination by human infants. *Child Development,* 1967, **38,** 893–899.

Haith, M. M. Response of the human newborn to visual movement. *Journal of Experimental Child Psychology,* 1966, **3,** 235–243.

Haith, M. M. Visual scanning in infants. Paper presented at regional meeting of Society for Research in Child Development. Clark University, Worcester, Mass., March 1968.

Hamburg, D. A., & Lunde, D. T. Sex hormones in the development of sex differences in human behavior. In E. E. Maccoby (Ed.), *The development of sex differences.* Stanford, Calif.: Stanford University Press, 1966. Pp. 1–24.

Harlow, H. F. The development of affection in primates. In E. L. Bliss (Ed.), *Roots of behavior.* New York: Harper, 1962.

Harlow, H. F., & Harlow, M. K. Learning to love. *American Scientist,* 1966, **54,** 244–272.

Hebb, D. O. On the nature of fear. *Psychological Review,* 1946, **53,** 259–276.

Hess, R. D., Shipman, V. C., Brophy, J. E., & Bear, R. M. The cognitive environments of urban preschool children. Report to the Graduate School of Education, University of Chicago, Chicago, 1968.

Hess, R. D., Shipman, V. C., Brophy, J. E., & Bear, R. M. The cognitive environments of urban preschool children: Follow-up phase. Chicago: The Graduate School of Education, University of Chicago, 1969.

Hindley, C. B. Stability and change in abilities up to five years: Group trends. *Journal Child Psychology Psychiatry,* 1965, **6,** 85–99.

Hubel, D. H., & Wiesel, T. N. Receptive fields of single neurons in the cat's striate cortex. *Journal of Physiology,* 1959, **148,** p. 574.

Hubel, D. H. & Wiesel, T. N. Receptive fields, binocular interaction, and the functional architecture in the cat's visual cortex. *Jorunal of Physiology,* 1962, **160,** 106–154.

Hull, C. L. *Essentials of behavior.* New Haven, Conn.: Yale University Press, 1951.

Hunt, J. McV. Motivation inherent in information processing and action. In O. J. Harvey (Ed.), *Motivation and social interaction: Cognitive determinants.* New York: Ronald Press, 1963.

Hunt, J. McV. Intrinsic motivation and its role in psychological development. In D. Levine (Ed.), *Nebraska symposium on motivation.* Lincoln: University of Nebraska Press, 1965.

James, W. *Principles of psychology.* Vol. 2. New York: Henry Holt. 1890.

Jay, P. The common langur of North India. In I. DeVore (Ed.), *Primate behavior.* New York: Holt, Rinehart & Winston, 1965. Pp. 197–249.

Jensen, G. D., Bobbitt, R. A., & Gordon, B. N. Sex differences in social interaction between infant monkeys and their mothers. In J. Wortis (Ed.), *Recent advances in biological psychiatry.* Vol. III. New York: Plenum Press (in press).

John, E. R., Chessler, P., Bartlett, F., & Victor, I. Observation learning in cats. *Science,* 1968, **159,** 1489–1491.

Jones, M. C. The development of early behavior patterns in young children. *Ped. Sem. J. Gent. Psychology,* 1926, **33,** 537–585.

Jurgens, U., Maurus, M., Ploog, D., & Winter, P. Vocalization in the squirrel monkey elicited by brain stimulation. *Experimental Brain Research,* 1967, **4,** 114–117.

Kagan, J. Individual differences in the resolution of response uncertainty. *Journal of Personality and Social Psychology*, 1965, **2**, 154–160.

Kagan, J. Developmental studies in reflection and analysis. In A. H. Kidd & J. L. Rivoire (Eds.), *Perceptual development in children*. New York: International Universities Press, 1966. Pp. 487–522.

Kagan, J. On the meaning of behavior: Illustrations from the infant. *Child Development*. 1969, **40**, 1121–1134.

Kagan, J. The determinants of attention in the infant. *American Scientist*. 1970, **58**, 298–306. (a)

Kagan, J. The distribution of attention in infancy. In D. H. Hamburg (Ed.), *Perception and its disorders*. Res. Publ. ARNMD. Vol. 48. Baltimore: Williams and Wilkins, 1970. Pp. 214–237. (b)

Kagan, J., & Moss, H. A. *Birth to maturity*. New York: Wiley, 1962.

Kagan, J., Pearson, L., & Welch, L. Conceptual impulsivity and inductive reasoning. *Child Development*, 1966, **37**, 583–594.

Kagan, J., & Rosman, B. L. Cardiac and respiratory correlates of attention and an analytic attitude. *Journal of Experimental Child Psychology*, 1964, **1**, 50–63.

Kagan, J., & Tulkin, S. Social class differences in child rearing practices. In H. R. Schaffer (Ed.), *CASDS-CIBA Symposium*. New York: Academic Press (in press).

Karmel, B. Z. Complexity, amount of contour and visually dependent behavior in hooded rats, domestic chicks, and human infants. *Journal of Comparative Physiological Psychology*, 1969, **69**, 649–657.

Karmel, B. Z., White, C. T., Cleaves, W. T., & Steinsiek, K. J. Pattern evoked potentials in infants. Paper presented at Eastern Psychological Association meeting. Atlantic City, N.J., April 1970.

Kaye, K. Unpublished research manuscript.

Kessen, W., Haith, M. M., & Salapatek, P. H. Human infancy: A bibliography and guide. In P. H. Mussen (Ed.), *Carmichael's Manual of Child Psychology*. Vol. I (3rd ed.) New York: Wiley, 1960. Pp. 287–446.

Kimura, D. Functional asymmetry of the brain in dichotic listening. *Cortex*, 1967, **III**, 163–178.

Knox, C., & Kimura, D. Cerebral processing of nonverbal sounds in boys and girls. *Neuropsychologia*, 1970, **8**, 227–237.

Koch, J. Conditioned orienting reactions in two month old infants. *British Journal of Psychology*, 1967, **58**, 105–110.

Kuffler, S. W. Neurons in the retina: Organization, inhibition, and excitation problems. *Cold Spring Harbor Symposium in Quantitative Biology*, 1952, **17**, 281–292.

Kuffler, S. W. Discharge patterns and functional organization of mammalian retina. *Journal of Physiology*, 1953, **16**, 37–68.

Lacey, J. I. Somatic response patterning in stress: Some revisions of activation theory. In M. H. Appley & R. Trumbull (Eds.), *Psychological stress: Issues in research*. New York: Appleton-Century-Crofts, 1967. Pp. 14–44.

Lancaster, J. B. Primate communication systems and the emergence of human language. In P. C. Jay (Ed.), *Primates*. New York: Holt, Rinehart & Winston, 1968. Pp. 439–457.

Lansdell, H. Sex differences in hemispheric asymmetries of the human brain. *Nature*, 1964, **203**, 550–551.

Lansdell, H. The use of factor scores from the Wechsler-Bellevue Scale of Intelligence in assessing patients with temporal lobe removals. *Cortex*, 1968, **IV**, 257–268.

Laroche, J. L., & Tcheng, F. *LeSourire du Nourrisson*. Louvain: Publications Universitaires, 1963.

Lenneberg, E. H. *Biological foundations of language*. New York: Wiley, 1967.

Levine, S. The psychophysiological effects of infantile stimulation. In E. L. Bliss (Ed.), *Roots of behavior*. New York: Harper, 1962. Pp. 246–253.

Lewis, M. Infants' responses to facial stimuli during the first year of life. *Developmental Psychology*, 1969, **2**, 75–86.

Lewis, M., & Goldberg, S. The acquisition and violation of expectancy: An experimental paradigm. *Journal Experimental Child Psychology*, 1969, **7**, 70–80.

Lewis, M. & Harwitz, M. The meaning of an orienting response: A study in the hierarchical order of attending. Research Bulletin 69–33. Princeon, N.J.: Educational Testing Service, April 1969.

Lewis, M., Kagan, J., Campbell, H., & Kalafat, J. The cardiac response as a correlate of attention in infants. *Child Development*, 1966, **37**, 63–72.

Littenberg, R., Tulkin, S. R., & Kagan, J. Cognitive components of separation anxiety. *Developmental Psychology*, 1971, (in press).

Maccoby, E. E. *The development of sex differences*. Stanford, Calif.: Stanford University Press, 1966.

Marler, P. R., & Hamilton, W. J. *Mechanisms of animal behavior*. New York: Wiley, 1966.

McCall, R. B., & Kagan, J. Attention in the infant: Effects of complexity, contour, perimeter, and familiarity. *Child Development*, 1967, **38**, 939–952.

McCall, R. B. & Kagan, J. Individual differences in the distribution of attention to stimulus discrepancy. *Developmental Psychology*, 1970, **2**, 90–98.

McCall, R. B. & Melson, W. H. Attention in infants as a function of the magnitude of discrepancy and habituation rate. *Psychon. Sci.*, 1969, **17**, 317–319.

McCall, R. B. & Melson, W. H. Amount of short term familiarization and the response to auditory discrepancies. *Child Develpm.*, 1970, **41**, 861–869.

McCall, R. B. & Melson, W. H. Complexity, contour, and area as determinants of attention in infants. *Developmental Psychology* 1970, **3**, 343–349.

Melson, W. H. & McCall, R. B. Attentional responses of 5 month girls to discrepant auditory stimuli. *Child Develpm.*, 1970, **41**, 1159–1171.

Miller, N. E. Learning of visceral and glandular responses. *Science*, 1969, **163**, 434–445.

Moltz, H., & Stettner, L. J. The influence of pattern-like deprivation on the critical period for imprinting. *Journal of Comparative and Physiological Psychology*, 1961, **54**, 279–283.

Moore, T. Language and intelligence: A longitudinal study of the first eight years. *Human Development,* 1967, **10**, 88–106.

Morgan, G. A. and Ricciuti, H. N. Infants' responses to strangers during the first year. In B. M. Foss (Ed.), *Determinants of infant behavior.* Vol. IV. London: Methuen, 1967.

Moss, H. A. Sex, age and state as determinants of mother-infant interaction. *Merrill-Palmer Quarterly,* 1967, **13**, 19–36.

Moss, H. A., & Robson, K. S. Maternal influences on early social-visual behavior. Presented at American Orthopsychiatric Association. New York City, 1967.

Moss, H. A. & Robson, K. S. Maternal influences in early social-visual behavior. *Child Development,* 1968, **39**, 401–408.

Moss, H. A. & Robson, K. S. The relation between the amount of time infants spend at various states and the development of visual behavior. *Child Development,* 1970, **41**, 509–517.

Moss, H. A., Robson, K. S., & Pedersen, F. Determinants of maternal stimulation of infants and consequences of treatment for later reactions to strangers. *Developmental Psychology,* 1969, **1**, 239–246.

Obrist, P. A., & Webb, R. A. Heart rate during conditioning in dogs: Relationship to somatic motor activity. *Psychophysiology,* 1967, **4**, 7–34.

Obrist, P. A., Sutterer, J. R., & Howard, J. L. Preparatory cardiac changes: A psychobiological approach. Unpublished manuscript, 1969.

Ogilvie, D. N. A conceptual framework for the evaluation of social behaviors of preschool children. Unpublished manuscript, Harvard Graduate School of Education, 1969.

Onufrock, C. Hereditary control during the first year. Unpublished manuscript, 1968.

Pedersen, F. A., & Bell, R. Q. Sex differences in preschool children without histories of complications of pregnancy and delivery. *Developmental Psychology,* 1970, **3**, 10–15.

Pedersen, F. A. & Wender, P. H. Early social correlates of cognitive functioning in six year old boys. *Child Development,* 1968, **39**, 185–194.

Piaget, J. *The origins of intelligence in children.* New York: International Universities Press, 1952.

Piaget, J. *The construction of reality in the child.* New York: Basic Books, 1954.

Ploog, D. Early communication processes in squirrel monkeys. In R. J. Robinson (Ed.), *Brain and behavior: Development in the fetus and infant.* New York: Academic Press, 1969. Pp. 269–298.

Pribram, K. H. The new neurology and the biology of emotion. *American Psychologist,* 1967, **22**, 830–838.

Radke Yarrow, M., Campbell, J. D., & Burton, R. V. Recollections of childhood. *Mongr. Soc. Res. Child Develpm.,* 1970, **35**, (No. 5), 1–83.

Reppucci, C. M. Hereditary influences upon distribution of attention in infancy. Unpublished doctoral dissertation, Harvard University, 1968.

Rheingold, H. L., & Eckerman, C. O. The infant separates himself from his mother *Science,* 1970, **168**, 78–90.

Riesen, A. H. Stimulation as a requirement for growth and function in behavioral development. In D. W. Fiske, & S. R. Maddi (Eds.), *Functions of varied experience*. Homewood, Ill.: Dorsey Press, 1961. Pp. 57–80.

Robbins, L. C. The accuracy of parental recall of aspects of child development and of child rearing practices. *Journal of Abnormal and Social Psychology*, 1963, **66**, 261–270.

Rosenblatt, J. S. Nonhormonal basis of maternal behavior in the rat. *Science*, 1967, **156**, 1512–1513.

Rosenzweig, M. R. Representations of the two ears at the auditory cortex. *American Journal of Physiology*, 1951, **167**, 147–158.

Russell, B. *An inquiry into meaning and truth*. London: Allen & Unwin, 1940.

Salapatek, P., & Kessen, W. Visual scanning of triangles by the human newborn. *Journal of Experimental Child Psychology*, 1966, **3**, 113–122.

Scarr, S. Genetic factors in activity motivation. *Child Development*, 1966, **37**, 663–673.

Schaffer, H. R. & Emerson, P. E. Patterns of response in early human development. *Journal of Child Psychology and Psychiatry*, 1964, **5**, 1–13.

Schaffer, H. R., & Parry, M. H. Perceptual-motor behavior in infancy as a function of age and stimulus familiarity. *British Journal of Psychology*, 1969, **60**, 1–9.

Shapiro, L. Play behavior of 18 and 28 month old children. Unpublished doctoral dissertation, Harvard University, 1970.

Scott, J. P., & Fuller, J. L. *Genetics and the social behavior of the dog*. Chicago: University of Chicago Press, 1965.

Soderling, B. The first smile: A developmental study. *Acta Pediatrica*, 1959, **48**, (Supplement 117), 78–82.

Solomon, R. L., & Turner, C. H. Discriminative classical conditioning in dogs paralyzed by curare can later control discriminative avoidance response in the normal state. *Psychological Review*, 1962, **69**, 202–219.

Super, C., Kagan, J., Morrison, F., & Haith M. An experimental test of the discrepancy hypothesis. *J. genet. Psychol.* (press).

Tanner, J. M. The regulation of human growth. *Child Development*, 1963, **34**, 817–848.

Tanner, J. M. Physical growth. In P. H. Mussen (Ed.), *Carmichael's Manual of Child Psychology*. Vol. I. (3rd ed.) New York: Wiley, 1970. Pp. 77–156.

Taylor, L. B. Backwardness in reading in brain dysfunction. Master's thesis, McGill University, 1961.

Tollman, J., & King, J. A. The effects of testosterone proprionate on aggression in male and female C-57 BL/10 mice. *British Journal of Animal Behavior*, 1956, **6**, 147–149.

Tolman, E. C. *Purposive behavior in animals and men*. New York: Appleton-Century-Crofts, 1932.

Tulkin, S. Social class differences in maternal practices and infant's psychological development. Unpublished manuscript.

Valenstein, E. S. Problems of measurement and interpretation with reinforcing brain stimulation. *Psychological Review,* 1964, **71,** 415–437.

Valenstein, E. S., Cox, V. C., & Kakolewski, J. W. Modification of motivated behavior elicited by electrical stimulation of the hypothalmus. *Science,* 1968, **159,** 1119–1121.

Valenstein, E. S., Cox, V. C. & Kakolewski, J. W. The hypothalamus and motivated behavior. In J. Tapp (Ed.), *Reinforcement.* New York: Academic Press, 1969,

Waldrop, M. F., & Bell, R. Q. Effects of family size and density on newborn characteristics. *American Journal of Orthopsychiatry,* 1966, **36,** 544–550.

Watson, J. S. Operant conditioning of visual fixation in infants under visual and auditory reinforcement. *Developmental Psychology,* 1969, **1,** 508–516.

Weiss, P. A. "Panta' rhei"—and so flow our nerves. *American Scientist,* 1969, **57,** 287–305.

Weizmann, F., Cohen, L. B., & Pratt, R. J. Novelty, familiarity, and the development of infant attention. Unpublished manuscript, 1969.

Werner, E. E. Sex differences in correlations between children's IQs and measures of parental ability and environment ratings. *Developmental Psychology,* 1969, **1,** 280–285.

White, S. H. Evidence for a hierarchical arrangement of learning processes. In L. P. Lipsitt & C. C. Spiker (Eds.), *Advances in child development and behavior.* Vol. 2. New York: Academic Press, 1966.

Wilcox, B. M. Visual preferences of human infants for representations of the human face. *Journal of Experimental Child Psychology,* 1969, **VII,** 10–20.

Yando, R., & Kagan, J. Differential reactions to increasing response uncertainty. *Cognitive Psychology,* 1970, **1,** 192–200.

Zelazo, P. R. Social reinforcement of vocalizations and smiling of three month old infants. Unpublished doctoral dissertation, University of Waterloo, 1967.

Zelazo, P. R. Smiling to social stimuli by three month old home reared infants. Presented at Society for Research in Child Development meeting. Santa Monica, Calif., March 1969. (a)

Zelazo, P. R. Differential three month old infant vocalizations to sex of strangers. Presented at International Congress of Psychology. London, July 1969. (b)

Zelazo, P. R., & Komer, J. M. Infants' smiling to nonsocial stimuli and the recognition hypothesis. *Child Develpm.* (Press).

Zigler, E., Levine, J., & Gould, L. Cognitive processes in the development of children's appreciation of humor. *Child Development,* 1966, **37,** 507–518.

Appendix

Table 1
Characteristics of Sample

	Mothers		Fathers	
	Boys	Girls	Boys	Girls
Age				
Mean	23.1	23.9	26.2	26.0
Median	23	23.5	25	25
Range	17–32	18–37	18–44	19–38
Education				
Eighth grade or less	2	1	3	2
Part high school	13	15	14	11
High school graduate	28	19	27	21
Training after high school	26	23	14	8
College graduate	12	18	11	16
Post graduate training	16	14	28	33

Table 2
Narrated Slides

Picture 1:	Boy and girl
Narration:	Hello, I'm Tommy. Hello, I'm Jane.
Picture 2:	Man and woman
Narration:	I'm the Mommy. I'm the Daddy.
Picture 3:	Man in a dress
Narration:	I'm the Daddy. I work on a train.
Picture 4:	Woman in kitchen
Narration:	I'm the Mommy. I cook the food.
Picture 5:	Girl
Narration:	Tommy, I want to play, "sprong yerf yaral quasal tass off."
Picture 6:	Boy
Narration:	I'm going to play with my blocks.
Picture 7:	Boy in air over his blocks
Narration:	I'm Tommy. I like to play with my blocks.
Picture 8:	Cat
Auditory:	Cat sounds
Picture 9:	Oversized cat with girl
Auditory:	Cat sounds
Picture 10:	Woman in car
Auditory:	Auto horn sounds
Picture 11:	Woman with head in hand
Narration:	I've just come home from the store.
Picture 12:	Woman at table
Narration:	I've fixed the lunch. Tommy and Jane come to lunch.
Picture 13:	Telephone
Auditory:	Auto horn sounds
Picture 14:	Fire engine
Auditory:	Fire engine sounds
Picture 15:	Boy
Narration:	I like to watch the fire engine going to the fire.
Picture 16:	Girl with mouth open
Auditory:	Dog barking
Picture 17:	Man getting out of car
Narration:	I've finished work and have come home for dinner.
Picture 18:	Man in chair
Narration:	I'm the Daddy. I've worked all day. (Woman's voice.)
Picture 19:	Woman setting table
Narration:	I've fixed the supper. Everyone come to supper.
Picture 20:	Man with four arms

Table 2 (*continued*)
Narrated Slides

Narration:	I'm hungry and ready to eat.
Picture 21:	Dog on street
Auditory:	Dog sounds
Picture 22:	Girl in bathtub
Narration:	I've gone to bed. Good night everyone.
Picture 23:	Man in bed
Narration:	I've gone to bed. Good night everyone.

Table 3
Vocabulary

Picture Recognition Test	Vocabulary Naming Test
Picture that examiner asks child to point to:	Picture that child must label:
1. Fork	1. Key
2. Apple	2. Scissors
3. Couch	3. Flower
4. Hat	4. Broken cup
5. Stove	5. Pin
6. Under	6. Policeman
7. Ring	7. Corn
8. Potatoes	8. Boots
9. Sitting	9. Chicken
10. Shirt	10. Stairs
11. Faucet	11. Boat
12. Buttons	12. Plug
13. Toothbrush	13. Zipper
14. Sandwich	14. Clock
15. Tail	15. Star
16. Smiling	
17. Letter	
18. Calendar	
19. Shelf	
20. Sneakers	
21. Fire hydrant	
22. Handle	

Table 4

Maximum Sample Sizes for Major Variables at 4, 8, 13, and 27 Months

	Boys	Girls
4 Months		
Fixation, smile, vocalization to two-dimensional faces	90	79
Deceleration to two-dimensional faces	60	54
Fixation, smile, vocalization to three-dimensional faces	79	71
Deceleration to three-dimensional faces	55	50
Activity to two-dimensional faces	36	30
Activity to three-dimensional faces	32	28
8 Months		
Fixation, vocalization, smile to two-dimensional faces	78	80
Deceleration to two-dimensional faces	68	75
Fixation, vocalization, smile to three-dimensional faces	68	66
Deceleration to three-dimensional faces	62	63
Orientation, vocalization to auditory	70	77
Deceleration to auditory	69	77
Activity to two-dimensional faces	35	31
Activity to three-dimensional faces	31	31
Activity to auditory	35	34
Free play	68	66
13 Months		
Fixation, vocalization, smile to HF I, HF II, faces, and auditory	85	75
Deceleration to HF I, HF II, faces and auditory	83	75
Activity to HF I, HF II, faces and auditory	56	55
Free play	85	75
27 Months		
Fixation, smile to slides	72	60
Deceleration to slides	54	51
Verbalization to slides	69	63
Fixation, smile to HF I	73	65
Verbalization to HF I	46	44
Fixation, smile to three-dimensional faces	72	65
Verbalization to three-dimensional faces	46	43
Response times to embedded figures test	71	64
Deceleration to embedded figures test	55	51
Affect to embedded figures test	57	48
Response time to conflict task	44	49
Free play	75	67
Vocabulary recognition and naming	62	53

Table 5

Mean Fixation Time at 4, 8, 13, and 27 Months to Visual Episodes[a]

		Boys		Girls	
		Mean	S.D.	Mean	S.D.
Two-Dimensional Faces—4 Months					
First fixation	PR	11.0	7.17	9.7	6.40
(Trials 1-2)	SR	11.5	6.84	9.8	6.51
	PS	8.6	6.37	7.4	6.28
	SS	7.7	6.20	7.6	5.81
First fixation, all trials		8.7	4.46	7.4	4.17
Total fixation, all trials		17.9	5.54	16.4	5.50
Three-Dimensional Faces—4 Months					
First fixation	Reg	9.6	6.41	9.2	7.04
(Trials 1-2)	Scr	10.5	6.98	10.3	7.01
	NE	6.8	4.67	6.4	4.85
	BL	5.0	3.36	5.0	3.19
First fixation, all trials		7.3	4.11	6.7	3.74
Total fixation, all trials		16.4	6.49	15.7	6.29
Two-Dimensional Faces—8 Months					
First fixation	PR	6.6	3.34	5.3	3.25
(Trials 1-2)	SR	6.0	2.95	5.1	2.54
	PS	5.0	2.56	3.9	2.11
	SS	5.0	2.85	4.3	2.27
First fixation, all trials		4.9	2.06	4.0	1.72
Total fixation, all trials		8.1	2.72	6.7	2.38
Three-Dimensional Faces—8 Months					
First fixation	Reg	5.7	2.90	5.8	3.34
(Trials 1-2)	Scr	6.5	3.92	6.7	3.87
	NE	5.6	2.74	5.5	2.65
	BL	4.4	2.35	4.0	1.98
First fixation, all trials		4.5	1.62	4.4	1.64
Total fixation, all trials		11.2	3.60	10.6	4.13
HF I—13 Months					
First fixation	Reg	5.9	2.72	6.1	2.73
(Trials 1-2)	Scr	6.0	2.82	5.8	2.33
	HBL	6.3	3.04	6.2	3.11
	FF	4.9	2.00	5.0	2.38
First fixation, all trials		5.3	1.80	5.2	1.90
Total fixation, all trials		8.5	2.95	8.2	2.82
Three-Dimensional Faces—13 Months					
First fixation	Reg	5.3	3.30	5.1	2.95
(Trials 1-2)	Scr	5.0	3.33	4.8	2.96
	EO	4.6	2.78	4.6	2.71
	NE	4.3	2.78	4.5	3.04
	BL	4.4	2.03	4.4	2.23
First fixation, all trials		4.1	1.74	4.1	1.60
Total fixation, all trials		7.2	2.71	6.9	2.12

Table 5 (*continued*)

Mean Fixation Time at 4, 8, 13, and 27 Months to Visual Episodes[a]

		Boys		Girls	
		Mean	S.D.	Mean	S.D.
HF II–13 Months					
First fixation	3H	6.3	3.93	6.6	3.87
(Trials 1-2)	HH	6.1	7.86	4.9	2.53
	AH	7.3	6.72	6.5	3.67
First fixation, all trials		5.3	4.39	5.1	2.01
Total fixation, all trials		7.5	3.49	7.7	3.35
HFI–27 Months					
First fixation					
(Trials 1-2)	Reg	8.3	4.61	6.6	3.77
	Scr	9.1	4.99	8.8	5.22
	HBL	9.3	5.20	7.8	4.53
	FF	6.0	2.71	5.7	3.17
First fixation, all trials		8.1	3.11	7.2	3.07
Three-Dimensional Faces–27 Months					
First fixation					
(Trial 1-2)	Reg	5.7	4.26	5.5	3.40
	Scr	7.7	5.58	8.3	5.13
	NE	5.5	3.43	5.6	4.25
	BL	5.5	2.95	4.7	3.55
	EO	5.5	3.62	5.1	3.56
First fixation, all trials		6.0	2.83	5.9	2.87
Narrated Slides					
First fixation to all 23 scenes		7.0	2.03	6.4	2.07

Key. Reg, Regular; Scr, Scrambled; NE, No eyes; BL, Blank; EO, Eyes only.
PR, Photo regular; SR, Schematic regular; PS, Photo scrambled: SS, Schematic scrambled.
HF I, Human Forms I; HF II, Human Forms II; HH, Human head; 3H 3 heads; AH, Animal head; HBL, Head between legs; FF, Free form.

[a]The mean scores for individual stimuli are for the first two trials. Fixation time to the first two trials was used in most of the statistical analyses because many infants become bored, or irritable, after 8 to 10 trials.

Table 6

Intercorrelations of Fixation Times at 4 Months

	Two-Dimensional Faces						Three-Dimensional Faces					
	PR	SR	PS	SS	First Fixation All	Total Fixation All	Reg	Scr	NE	BL	First Fixation All	Total Fixation All
Two-dimensional faces												
First fixation PR	—	.50b	.52b	.56b	.78b	.56b	.20	.30a	.28a	.11	.29a	.23
SR	.44b	—	.67b	.54b	.75b	.44b	.13	.12	.22	−.08	.11	.00
PS	.52b	.52b	—	.48b	.77b	.57b	.15	.07	.14	.08	.10	.11
SS	.48b	.72b	.57b	—	.74b	.61b	.14	.18	.25a	.09	.24a	.18
First fixation, all trials	.73b	.69b	.74b	.72b	—	.76b	.19	.20	.26a	.04	.23	.21
Total fixation, all trials	.60b	.63b	.64b	.58b	.85b	—	.17	.17	.23	.26a	.27a	.39b
Three-dimensional faces												
First fixation Reg	.20	.16	.35b	.19	.33b	.35b	—	.57b	.63b	.57b	.80b	.57b
Scr	.16	.16	.30a	.23a	.26a	.25a	.68b	—	.57b	.62b	.75b	.58b
NE	.42b	.37b	.40b	.28a	.42b	.41b	.65b	.56b	—	.38b	.83b	.53b
BL	.13	.22a	.22	.11	.27a	.28a	.62b	.50b	.58b	—	.64b	.60b
First fixation, all trials	.22	.21	.32b	.19	.30b	.30b	.81b	.79b	.74b	.78b	—	.76b
Total fixation, all trials	.26a	.23a	.31b	.16	.32b	.37b	.71b	.58b	.64b	.68b	.82b	—

Key. PR, Photo regular; SR, Schematic regular; PS, Photo scrambled; SS, Schematic scrambled; Reg, Regular; Scr, Scrambled; NE, No eyes; and BL, Blank.

Note. Girls to right and above diagonal; boys to left and below diagonal.

[a] $p < .05$.
[b] $p < .01$.

Table 7

Intercorrelations of Fixation Times at 8 Months

	PR	SR	PS	SS	First Fixation All	Total Fixation All	Reg	Scr	NE	BL	First Fixation All	Total Fixation All
Two-dimensional faces												
First fixation PR	—	.39[b]	.41[b]	.69[b]	.80[b]	.62[b]	.18	.10	-.03	.07	.11	.13
SR	.36[b]	—	.51[b]	.39[b]	.66[b]	.56[b]	.13	-.04	-.01	-.07	-.05	.09
PS	.62[b]	.42[b]	—	.49[b]	.64[b]	.64[b]	.16	.03	.02	-.08	.03	.07
SS	.48[b]	.32[b]	.71[b]	—	.73[b]	.58[b]	.03	-.01	-.11	.01	.00	.05
First fixation, all trials	.73[b]	.29[a]	.83[b]	.74[b]	—	.79[b]	.21	.17	.07	-.01	.19	.27[a]
Total fixation, all trials	.50[b]	.40[b]	.66[b]	.62[b]	.78[b]	—	.26[a]	.11	.10	-.00	.16	.36[b]
Three-dimensional faces												
First fixation Reg	.37[b]	.37[b]	.45[b]	.24[a]	.47[b]	.31[a]	—	.43[b]	.53[b]	.43[b]	.62[b]	.56[b]
Scr	.21	.25[a]	.18	.23	.26[a]	.18	.43[b]	—	.69[b]	.39[b]	.84[b]	.66[b]
NE	.24[a]	.06	.25[a]	.28[a]	.36[b]	.16	.38[b]	.43[b]	—	.45[b]	.80[b]	.65[b]
BL	.39[b]	.59[b]	.55[b]	.57[b]	.65[b]	.46[b]	.51[b]	.48[b]	.35[b]	—	.62[b]	.46[b]
First fixation, all trials	.28[a]	.40[b]	.38[b]	.34[b]	.48[b]	.29[a]	.67[b]	.74[b]	.61[b]	.63[b]	—	.84[b]
Total fixation, all trials	.21	.39[b]	.36[b]	.33[b]	.46[b]	.37[b]	.54[b]	.51[b]	.42[b]	.59[b]	.42[b]	—

Note. Girls to right and above diagonal; boys to left and below diagonal.

[a] $p < .05$.
[b] $p < .01$.

Table 8

Intercorrelations for Fixation Time at 13 Months

	1	2	3	4	5	6	7
1. HF I First fixation	—	.86[b]	.47[b]	.42[b]	.57[b]	.53[b]	.20
2. HF I Total fixation	.82[b]	—	.47[b]	.54[b]	.48[b]	.53[b]	.13
3. Three-dimensional faces First fixation	.45[b]	.34[b]	—	.85[b]	.21	.35[b]	.30[b]
4. Three-dimensional faces Total fixation	.36[b]	.40[b]	.77[b]	—	.31[b]	.50[b]	.25[a]
5. HF II First fixation	.46[b]	.47[b]	.29[a]	.34[b]	—	.73[b]	.06
6. HF II Total fixation	.39[b]	.51[b]	.11	.26[a]	.81[b]	—	.15
7. Orientation to speaker: auditory	.42[b]	.28[a]	.27[a]	.14	.25[a]	.09	—

Note. Boys to right and above diagonal; girls to left and below diagonal.

[a] $p < .05$
[b] $p < .01$

Table 9
Correlations of Fixation Time with Deceleration at 13 Months

	Boys											
	First Fixation											
	HF I				Three-Dimensional Faces					HF II		
Deceleration	Reg	Scr	HBL	FF	Reg	Scr	EO	NE	BL	3H	HH	AH
HF I												
Reg	.18	.04	.05	.14	-.03	.07	.17	.00	.03	.14	.03	.22[a]
Scr	-.11	-.06	-.07	-.04	-.24[a]	-.07	.08	-.05	-.06	-.09	-.07	-.13
HBL	.18	.07	.11	.04	.18	.10	.26[a]	.22[a]	-.05	.04	.07	.00
FF	.08	-.04	.05	.25[a]	.02	.00	.16	.18	-.08	.05	-.02	.04
Three-Dimensional faces												
Reg	.19	.17	.31[b]	.24[a]	.13	.15	.14	-.03	.27[a]	.16	.16	.13
Scr	.04	-.01	.12	.11	-.07	.26[a]	.05	-.10	.10	.01	-.03	.01
EO	.00	-.04	-.04	.22	.08	.15	.30[b]	.17	.19	.02	-.03	.05
NE	.16	.13	.21	.24[a]	.23[a]	.31[b]	.38[b]	.33[b]	.38[b]	.31[b]	.11	.15
BL	.12	.10	.20	.25[a]	.14	.19	.15	.10	.35[b]	.19	.34[b]	.36[b]
HF II												
3H	.03	.02	.09	.06	.00	-.06	.13	-.03	-.03	.32[b]	.12	.18
HH	.34[b]	.13	.17	.09	.16	.06	.28[b]	.03	.22[a]	.30[b]	.20	.20
AH	.20	.19	.22[a]	.23[a]	.06	.03	.18	-.02	.26[a]	.38[b]	.20	.27[a]

Table 9 (*continued*)

	Girls											
	First Fixation											
	HF I				Three-Dimensional Faces					HF II		
Deceleration	Reg	Scr	HBL	FF	Reg	Scr	EO	NE	BL	3H	HH	AH
HF I												
Reg	.24	.08	.16	.04	.24	-.01	.13	.22	-.13	.26a	.18	-.04
Scr	.07	.11	.16	.09	.10	-.11	.15	-.25a	-.04	.17	.20	.16
HBL	-.14	-.20	-.02	-.16	.28a	-.16	-.05	-.17	.01	-.12	-.22	-.07
FF	.00	.01	.21	.29a	.25a	-.07	.30a	-.21	.01	.19	.17	.21
Three-Dimensional faces												
Reg	-.19	-.09	-.07	-.10	.29a	-.08	.03	-.03	.14	-.09	.01	.11
Scr	.02	.16	-.03	.09	.32b	.16	.09	.03	.17	.20	.22	.19
EO	-.21	-.21	-.04	.00	.08	-.26a	.25a	-.21	.00	.08	.12	.12
NE	-.11	.09	.20	.29a	.23	.18	.11	.18	.17	.15	.12	.08
BL	-.12	.00	.08	.00	.02	-.04	.14	-.11	.17	-.10	.09	.27
HF II												
3H	.35b	.35b	.43b	.30a	.33b	.11	.37b	-.15	.05	.66b	.46b	.39b
HH	.09	.04	.11	.04	.09	.11	.03	-.02	.09	.47b	.41b	.13
AH	.26a	.15	.27a	.18	.17	.11	.34b	-.02	.18	.33b	.23	.41b

a $p < .05$.
b $p < .01$.

Table 10

Activity Correlates of First and Total Fixation at 13 months

13 Months	HF I				Three-Dimensional Faces				HF II			
	First Fixation		Total Fixation		First Fixation		Total Fixation		First Fixation		Total Fixation	
	B	G	B	G	B	G	B	G	B	G	B	G
Twist HF I	-.21	-.45b	-.27a	-.45b	.18	-.23	-.20	-.12	-.61b	-.14	-.49b	-.26
Quiet HF I	.58b	.61b	.64b	.61b	.54b	.15	.57b	.21	.14	.36b	.35b	.40b
Twist Three-dimensional faces	.07	-.24	-.05	-.33a	.06	-.27	-.11	-.22	-.09	-.17	-.12	-.21
Quiet Three-dimensional faces	.37b	.22	.44b	.41b	.66b	.43b	.73b	.62b	.15	.35a	.29a	.34a
Twist HF II	-.25	-.04	-.24	-.19	-.17	-.03	-.21	.00	-.21	-.05	-.26a	-.27
Quiet HF II	.49b	.00	.50b	.14	.48b	.09	.53b	.18	.43b	.39a	.60b	.41b

[a] $p < .05$.
[b] $p < .01$.

Table 11

Intercorrelations of Fixation Times at 27 Months

	Human Forms	Three-Dimensional Faces	Narrated Slides	
	First Fixation All	First Fixation All	Normal	Discrepant
Human Forms				
First fixation, all trials	—	.60[b]	.49[b]	.39[b]
Three-Dimensional Faces				
First fixation, all trials	.52[b]	—	.46[b]	.48[b]
Narrated Slides				
Normal scenes	.34[b]	.46[b]	—	.76[b]
Discrepant scenes	.20	.26[a]	.63[b]	—

Note. Girls to right and above diagonal; boys to left and below diagonal.

[a]$p < .05$.
[b]$p < .01$.

Table 12

Correlations Between Parental Educational Level and Fixation Time

	Boys		Girls	
4 Months				
Two-Dimensional Faces				
First fixation, all trials	−.02		.19	
Total fixation, all trials	.03		.19	
Three-Dimensional Faces				
First fixation, all trials	.06		.02	
Total fixation, all trials	.11		.07	
8 Months				
Two-Dimensional Faces				
First fixation, all trials	.11		.27[a]	
Total fixation, all trials	.08		.28[a]	
Three-Dimensional Faces				
First fixation, all trials	.01		.15	
Total fixation, all trials	.06		.24	
13 Months	First Fixation	Total Fixation	First Fixation	Total Fixation
Human Forms I				
Reg	.20	.18	.18	.29[a]
Scr	.25[a]	.19	.32[b]	.27[a]
HBL	.17	.20	.28[a]	.29[a]
FF	.14	.28[a]	.24[a]	.23[a]
All trials	.23[a]	.28[a]	.30[b]	.34[b]
Three-Dimensional Faces				
Reg	.17	.14	.09	−.02
Scr	.25[a]	.29[a]	−.02	.09
EO	.18	.18	.20	.18
NE	.30[b]	.38[b]	.20	.19
BL	.06	.09	−.10	.16
All trials	.21	.25[a]	.17	.20
Human Forms II				
3H	.13	.09	.28[a]	.36[b]
HH	.00	.17	.25[a]	.33[b]
AH	−.06	.21	.09	.32[b]
All trials	.01	.21	.30[a]	.36[b]
27 Months				
Human Forms I				
Reg	.35[b]	.25[a]	.44[b]	.43[b]
Scr	−.16	.14	−.04	.08
HBL	.19	.28[a]	.16	.03
FF	−.09	.11	.50[b]	.40[b]
All trials	.14	.28[a]	.35[b]	.32[a]

Table 12 (*continued*)
Correlations Between Parental Educational Level and Fixation Time

	First Fixation	Total Fixation	First Fixation	Total Fixation
Three-Dimensional Faces				
Reg	.18	−.15	.11	.02
Scr	.06	−.26[a]	.24	.37[b]
NE	.09	−.07	.21	.38[b]
EO	.10	.04	.32[a]	.18
BL	.08	.06	.21	.22
All trials	−.15	−.12	.33[b]	.32[b]
Narrated Slides				
All scenes	.29[a]	.27[a]	.32[a]	.37[b]

[a] $p < .05$.
[b] $p < .01$.

Table 13
Two-Year-Old Correlates of Increase in First Fixation Between 13 and 27 Months

	Human Forms I (First Fixation 27–13)		Three-Dimensional Faces (First Fixation 27–13)	
27 Months	Boys	Girls	Boys	Girls
Educational level	.06	.20	−.04	.31[a]
Vocabulary recognition	.10	.08	.05	.22
Vocabulary naming	.08	.15	−.04	.33[a]
Verbalization to:				
HFI	.03	.11	.07	.39[a]
Three-dimensional faces	.03	.33[a]	.23	.58[b]

[a] $p < .05$.
[b] $p < .01$.

Table 14a

Stability of Fixation Time from 8 to 13 Months
Predictor: Fixation to Two-Dimensional Faces at 8 Months

| | Two Dimensional Faces—8 Months | | | |
| | First Fixation All Trials | | Total Fixation All Trials | |
13 Months	B	G	B	G
HF I				
First fixation, all	.17	.21	.18	.23
Total fixation, all	.20	.22	.27[a]	.29[a]
HF II				
First fixation, all	.24[a]	.29[a]	.14	.25[a]
Total fixation, all	.19	.22	.15	.18
Three-Dimensional Faces				
First fixation, all	.20	.26[a]	.20	.44[b]
Total fixation, all	.15	.27[a]	.23	.41[b]

[a] $p < .05$.
[b] $p < .01$.

Table 14b

Stability of Fixation Time from 8 to 13 Months
Predictor: Fixation Time to Three-Dimensional Faces at 8 Months

| | Three-Dimensional Faces—8 Months | | | |
| | First Fixation All Trials | | Total Fixation All Trials | |
13 Months	B	G	B	G
HF I				
First fixation, all	.17	.06	.10	.11
Total fixation, all	.18	.02	.16	.09
HF II				
First fixation, all	.36[b]	.11	.24	.14
Total fixation, all	.26[a]	.04	.25	.08
Three-Dimensional Faces				
First fixation, all	.19	.24	.17	.30[a]
Total fixation, all	.02	.48[b]	.08	.51[b]

[a] $p < .05$.
[b] $p < .01$.

Table 15a

Correlations Between Fixation Times to Human Forms I at 13 Months and Fixation Times at 27 Months

13 Months Human Forms I	Human Forms I First Fixation All	Three-Dimensional Faces First Fixation All	Narrated Slides First Fixation All	Narrated Slides Total Fixation All	Normal Scenes First Fixation	Discrepant Scenes First Fixation
	Boys (27 Months)					
First fixation, all trials	.04	.26[a]	.26[a]	.20	.28[a]	.17
Total fixation, all trials	.00	.24[a]	.28[a]	.24[a]	.29	.20
	Girls (27 Months)					
First fixation, all trials	.26[a]	.23	.21	.17	.24	.15
Total fixation, all trials	.19	.31[a]	.17	.18	.19	.12

[a] $p < .05$.

Table 15b
Correlations Between Fixation Times to Human Forms II at 13 Months and Fixation Time at 27 Months

13 Months Human Forms II	Boys (27 Months)					
	Human Forms I First Fixation All	Three-Dimensional Faces First Fixation All	Narrated Slides First Fixation All	Narrated Slides Total Fixation All	Normal Scenes First Fixation	Discrepant Scenes First Fixation
First fixation, all trials	.23	.32b	.24a	.15	.21	.23
Total fixation, all trials	.22	.32b	.32b	.25a	.30a	.28a
Girls (27 Months)						
First fixation, all trials	.11	.12	.28a	.22	.26	.26
Total fixation, all trials	.15	.15	.19	.14	.17	.19

$^a p < .05.$
$^b p < .01.$

Table 15c
Correlations Between Fixation Times to Three-Dimensional Faces at 13 Months and Fixation Times at 27 Months

13 Months Three-Dimensional Faces	Boys (27 Months)					
	Human Forms I First Fixation All	Three-Dimensional Faces First Fixation All	Narrated Slides First Fixation All	Narrated Slides Total Fixation All	Normal Scenes First Fixation	Discrepant Scenes First Fixation
First fixation, all trials	.08	.20	.31[b]	.28[a]	.34[b]	.21
Total fixation, all trials	.05	.14	.25[a]	.28[a]	.28[a]	.17
Girls (27 Months)						
First fixation, all trials	.21	.13	.11	.06	.16	.05
Total fixation, all trials	.08	.01	.09	.07	.10	.06

[a] $p < .05$.
[b] $p < .01$.

Table 16a

Derivatives of Fixation Time to Two-Dimensional Faces at 8 Months
Predictor: Eight Months Fixation Time to Two-Dimensional Faces

13 Months	First Fixation All		Total Fixation All	
	B	G	B	G
Human Forms I				
Twist: stimulus on	.17	−.22	.09	−.08
Twist: stimulus off	.04	−.17	−.05	−.19
Quiet to stimulus	.08	.19	.09	.11
Lean forward	.19	.16	.09	.07
Auditory				
Twist: stimulus on	.00	−.05	−.16	−.24
Twist: stimulus off	.07	.11	−.05	−.04
Quiet to stimulus	.26	.17	.25	.12
Lean forward	.00	.60[b]	−.04	.34[a]
Three-Dimensional Faces				
Twist: stimulus on	−.18	−.06	−.23	−.21
Twist: stimulus off	.14	−.03	.04	−.19
Quiet to stimulus	.22	.21	.16	.36[a]
Lean forward	−.10	−.03	−.14	.01
Human Forms II				
Twist: stimulus on	−.09	.00	−.19	−.10
Twist: stimulus off	−.19	−.06	−.36[a]	−.15
Quiet to stimulus	.11	.35[a]	.08	.18
Lean forward	−.02	.34[a]	.00	.21
Ratings				
Activity	−.21	−.26	−.22	−.21
Alert	.31[a]	.23	.36[a]	.33[a]
Speed of habituation	−.29[a]	−.24	−.28[a]	−.30[a]

[a] $p < .05$.
[b] $p < .01$.

Table 16b
Derivatives of Fixation Time to Three-Dimensional Faces at 8 Months
Predictor: Eight Months Fixation Time to Three-Dimensional Faces

13 Months	First Fixation All		Total Fixation All	
	B	G	B	G
Human Forms I				
Twist: stimulus on	.10	.22	.23	.18
Twist: stimulus off	−.11	.03	.00	−.09
Quiet to stimulus	.18	−.03	.05	.02
Lean forward	.18	−.07	.27	−.08
Auditory				
Twist: stimulus on	−.19	−.03	−.05	−.12
Twist: stimulus off	−.08	.12	.09	−.06
Quiet to stimulus	.34[a]	−.13	.22	−.09
Lean forward	−.02	.11	−.08	.28
Three-Dimensional Faces				
Twist: stimulus on	.05	−.21	.04	−.16
Twist: stimulus off	.09	−.17	.11	−.22
Quiet to stimulus	.16	.15	.09	.16
Lean forward	−.11	−.01	−.10	−.10
Human Forms II				
Twist: stimulus on	−.03	−.32	−.15	−.17
Twist: stimulus off	−.01	.08	−.12	.05
Quiet to stimulus	.31[a]	.19	.18	.21
Lean forward	−.04	.38[a]	−.06	.37[a]
Ratings				
Active	−.16	−.14	.03	−.15
Alert	.27	.37[a]	.18	.35[a]
Speed of habituation	−.48[b]	−.23	−.32[a]	−.23

[a]$p < .05.$
[b]$p < .01.$

Table 17

Stability of Orientation to Speaker from 8 to 13 Months

Predictor: Orientation at 8 Months

13 Months Orientation to Speaker	LL		HL		LH		HH		All	
	B	G	B	G	B	G	B	G	B	G
LL	.11	.06	.26[a]	.04	.15	.04	.17	.04	.20	.04
HL	.01	.32[a]	.21	.29[a]	.12	.27[a]	.20	.27[a]	.16	.30[a]
LH	.15	.36[b]	.37[b]	.34[b]	.29[a]	.24	.41[b]	.39[b]	.36[b]	.35[b]
HH	.12	.36[b]	.29[a]	.40[b]	.20	.31[a]	.31[b]	.34[b]	.27[a]	.37[b]
All	.12	.31[a]	.32[b]	.30[a]	.22	.24	.32[b]	.29[a]	.29[a]	.30[a]

Key. LL, Low meaning, low inflection; HL, High meaning, low inflection; LH, Low meaning, high inflection; HH, High meaning, high inflection.

[a] $p < .05$.
[b] $p < .01$.

Table 18
Mean Vocalization Time Across 4, 8, and 13 Months

	Boys		Girls	
	Mean	S.D.	Mean	S.D.
4 Months				
Two-Dimensional Faces				
PR	2.5	3.56	2.3	3.01
SR	2.4	2.78	1.9	2.38
PS (Trials 1-2)	2.3	2.94	2.1	2.60
SS	2.3	2.89	2.1	2.78
All 16 Trials	2.4	2.35	2.1	1.84
Three-Dimensional Faces				
Reg	2.5	3.02	3.0	3.90
Scr	2.5	3.26	2.0	2.81
NE (Trials 1-2)	2.0	2.28	2.0	2.77
BL	1.6	2.32	2.3	2.67
All 16 trials	2.4	2.51	2.3	2.40
8 Months				
Two-Dimensional Faces				
PR	0.9	1.41	0.6	1.22
SR	0.7	1.37	0.8	1.32
PS (Trials 1-2)	0.7	0.89	0.5	1.08
SS	0.8	1.36	0.6	1.11
All 16 trials	0.9	0.93	0.7	0.99
Three-Dimensional Faces				
Reg	1.5	2.25	1.8	2.67
Scr	1.2	1.56	1.8	2.49
NE (Trials 1-2)	1.5	2.09	1.5	2.02
BL	0.9	1.61	1.4	1.79
All 16 trials	1.3	1.38	1.7	1.67
Auditory "OFF"				
LL	0.8	1.16	0.9	1.42
HL	1.0	1.42	0.8	1.05
LH (Trials 1-3)	0.7	0.91	0.8	1.05
HH	1.2	1.39	0.9	1.11
All 12 trials	0.9	0.98	0.8	0.93
13 Months				
HF I				
Reg	1.1	1.50	1.2	1.70
Scr	1.2	1.21	1.3	1.99
HBL (Trials 1-2)	1.2	1.64	1.3	1.91
FF	1.0	1.26	0.9	1.28
All 12 trials	1.2	1.18	1.2	1.32
Three-Dimensional Faces				
Reg	1.2	1.47	1.5	1.97
Scr	1.4	1.68	1.4	1.56
EO (Trials 1-2)	1.3	1.71	1.8	2.12

Table 18 (continued)

| | Boys | | Girls | |
	Mean	S.D.	Mean	S.D.
NE	1.1	1.40	1.4	2.10
BL	1.1	1.76	1.5	2.23
All 15 trials	1.4	1.22	1.5	1.51
HF II				
3H	2.0	2.53	1.6	1.93
HH (Trials 1-2)	2.2	3.02	1.6	2.37
AH	2.5	2.70	1.8	2.60
All 12 trials	2.3	1.61	2.1	1.67
Auditory "OFF"				
LL	1.1	1.31	0.7	1.17
HL	1.1	1.00	0.9	1.27
LH (Trials 1-3)	1.0	1.11	0.9	1.47
HH	1.2	1.2	1.2	1.67
All 12 trials	1.2	1.47	1.0	1.24

Table 19

Interepisode Consistency of Vocalization at 8 Months

| | | | | Vocalization to Two-Dimensional Faces | | | | | | |
| | PR | | SR | | PS | | SS | | | |
8 Months	B	G	B	G	B	G	B	G
Vocalization Three-Dimensional Faces								
Reg	.37b	−.06	.13	.18	.29a	.27a	.32b	.34b
(Trials 1-2) Scr	.34b	.02	.23	.15	.37b	.08	.48b	.25a
NE	.30a	.03	.13	.15	.27a	.19	.47b	.26a
BL	−.11	.18	−.06	.31a	−.02	.35b	.02	.46b
Vocalization Auditory−Off								
LL	−.08	.35b	−.05	.38b	.30a	.25a	.05	.36b
(Trials 1-3) HL	.02	.06	.00	.08	.19	−.03	.11	.11
LH	.03	−.01	.00	.20	.10	.16	.05	.16
HH	.03	.24a	.03	.31b	.10	.29a	.15	.28a

| | | | | Vocalization to Three-Dimensional Faces | | | | |
| | Reg | | Scr | | NE | | BL | |
	B	G	B	G	B	G	B	G
Vocalization Auditory−Off								
LL	.00	.23	−.04	.49b	.02	.52b	.06	.43b
(Trials 1-3) HL	.06	.27a	.15	.55b	.16	.50b	.20	.40b
LH	.38b	.35b	.25a	.62b	.34b	.49b	.32a	.47b
HH	.12	.43b	.04	.43b	.09	.60b	.43b	.47b

[a] $p < .05$.
[b] $p < .01$.

Table 20

Correlations Between Deceleration and Voc Off (by Trial) at 8 Months

Boys

Vocalization Following Termination

Deceleration	LL TR 1	LL TR 2	HL TR 1	HL TR 2	HL TR 3	LH TR 1
Dec. LL TR 1,	-.071	-.058	-.071	-.032	-.018	-.046
Dec. LL TR 2,	-.081	-.073	-.056	-.059	.005	-.157
Dec. LL TR 3,	.245[a]	.150	-.005	.029	.017	-.035
Dec. HL TR 1,	.054	-.070	.002	.005	.005	-.050
Dec. HL TR 2,	.011	.031	.010	.118	.062	.299[a]
Dec. HL TR 3,	.019	.074	.036	.266[a]	.031	.143
Dec. LH TR 1,	.005	-.053	-.041	-.003	.078	.122
Dec. LH TR 2,	.009	-.082	.026	.021	.194	.215
Dec. LH TR 3,	.209	.156	.089	-.009	.091	.410[b]
Dec. HH TR 1,	-.124	-.130	.046	.039	.085	-.006
Dec. HH TR 2,	.101	.101	.020	.022	-.011	.073
Dec. HH TR 3,	.157	.010	.081	.137	.112	.040

Deceleration	LH TR 2	LH TR 3	HH TR 1	HH TR 2	HH TR 3
Dec. LL TR 1,	-.059	-.069	.099	-.158	-.093
Dec. LL TR 2,	.064	-.043	-.111	-.082	-.018
Dec. LL TR 3,	.016	.042	.006	.111	.028
Dec. HL TR 1,	-.014	-.181	-.020	-.042	.118
Dec. HL TR 2,	.024	-.031	.027	.062	.176
Dec. HL TR 3,	-.026	-.075	-.085	-.126	-.148
Dec. LH TR 1,	-.028	-.106	-.007	-.118	-.066
Dec. LH TR 2,	.196	-.056	.024	.014	.123
Dec. LH TR 3,	.108	.200	.126	.094	.203
Dec. HH TR 1,	-.040	-.205	-.045	.020	-.053
Dec. HH TR 2,	.016	-.124	-.030	.169	-.069
Dec. HH TR 3,	.064	-.134	-.125	.181	.087

Table 20 (continued)

Girls

	LL TR 1	LL TR 2	HL TR 1	HL TR 2	HL TR 3	LH TR 1
Dec. LL TR 1,	.021	.087	-.012	.099	.121	-.006
Dec. LL TR 2,	.200	.364[b]	.111	.574[b]	.140	.287[a]
Dec. LL TR 3,	.008	.193	.304[b]	.384[b]	.185	.335[b]
Dec. HL TR 1,	.150	.254[a]	.178	.213	.018	.065
Dec. HL TR 2,	.134	.268[a]	.033	.347[b]	.053	.131
Dec. HL TR 3,	.058	.116	.035	.272[a]	-.067	.194
Dec. LH TR 1,	.058	.305[b]	.020	.332[b]	.089	.133
Dec. LH TR 2,	-.186	.063	-.118	.270[a]	.132	.053
Dec. LH TR 3,	.037	-.003	-.093	.203	.068	.218
Dec. HH TR 1,	.059	.051	-.155	.364[b]	-.097	.151
Dec. HH TR 2,	.176	.348[b]	.167	.472[b]	.008	.335[b]
Dec. HH TR 3,	.008	.255[a]	-.079	.240[a]	.242[a]	.025

	LH TR 2	LH TR 3	HH TR 1	HH TR 2	HH TR 3
Dec. LL TR 1,	.076	.116	.003	.131	.214
Dec. LL TR 2,	.343[b]	.037	.292[b]	.250[a]	.361[b]
Dec. LL TR 3,	.048	.051	.069	.071	.096
Dec. HL TR 1,	-.013	-.010	.097	.262[a]	.179
Dec. HL TR 2,	.031	-.009	.139	.178	.055
Dec. HL TR 3,	-.005	-.014	.083	.270[a]	.195
Dec. LH TR 1,	.114	.190	.185	.305[b]	.278[a]
Dec. LH TR 2,	.131	.042	.073	.009	.000
Dec. LH TR 3,	-.006	.014	.014	-.038	.101
Dec. HH TR 1,	.009	.141	.105	.190	.290[a]
Dec. HH TR 2,	.248[a]	-.015	.205	.291[a]	.222
Dec. HH TR 3,	.327[b]	.233[a]	.064	.043	.338[b]

[a] $p < .05.$
[b] $p < .01.$

Table 21

Intercorrelation of Vocalization at 13 Months

13 Months

Total Vocalization to:

Total Vocalization to:	First Stimulus HF I	All Stimuli HF I	First Stimulus HF II	All Stimuli HF II	First Stimulus Three-Dimensional	All Stimuli Three-Dimensional	First Stimulus Off Auditory	All Stimuli Off Auditory
First stimulus HF I	—	.56b	-.18	-.05	.26a	.12	.12	.12
All stimuli HF I	.46b	—	.12	.13	.43b	.37b	.11	.26a
First stimulus HF II	.19	-.01	—	.48b	.31a	.55b	-.11	-.02
All stimuli HF II	.06	.00	.58b	—	.14	.52b	.08	.03
First stimulus Three-dimensional	.20	.35b	.14	.19	—	.69b	.04	.39b
All stimuli Three-dimensional	.08	.16	.18	.45b	.38b	—	-.02	.34b
First stimulus Off auditory	.17	.37b	-.06	.14	.36b	.31b	—	.25a
All stimuli Off auditory	.00	.17	-.06	.25a	.10	.20	.14	—

Note. Girls above and to right of diagonal; boys below and to left of diagonal

[a] $p < .05$.
[b] $p < .01$.

Table 22

Intercorrelations Among Verbalization Measures at 27 Months

	Voc. R	Voc. N	Normal Sl. Voc.	Disc. Sl. Voc.	Slides S. Voc.	Slides Adv. Voc.	HF I No. Words	Three-Dimensional Faces No. Words	Play Adapt.	Play (1-3)	Play (4-6)	Play All
Vocabulary recognition	—	.77[b]	.35[a]	.44[b]	.31[a]	.49[b]	.44[b]	.56[b]	.31[a]	.53[b]	.37[b]	.48[b]
Vocabulary naming	.61[a]	—	.21	.30[a]	.20	.37[b]	.37[a]	.52[b]	.45[b]	.51[b]	.38[b]	.48[b]
Normal slides voc.	.29[a]	.17	—	.86[b]	.81[b]	.58[b]	.51[b]	.33[a]	.35[b]	.44[b]	.23	.35[b]
Discrepant slides voc.	.33[a]	.22	.90[b]	—	.79[b]	.58[b]	.46[b]	.26	.41[b]	.46[b]	.29[a]	.40[b]
Slides simple voc.	.07	-.01	.81[b]	.73[b]	—	.32[a]	.24	.10	.29[a]	.32[a]	.17	.26[a]
Slides advanced voc.	.36[b]	.23	.72[b]	.77[b]	.46[b]	—	.44[b]	.42[b]	.43[b]	.46[b]	.29[a]	.40[b]
Human forms I No. words	.42[b]	.33[a]	.34[a]	.45[b]	.31	.38[a]	—	.66[b]	.60[b]	.66[b]	.55[b]	.64[b]
Three-Dimensional faces No. words	.09	.30	.21	.28	.13	.28	.58[b]	—	.37[a]	.44[b]	.43[b]	.47[b]
Play adaptation	.36[b]	.32[a]	.29[a]	.25[a]	.25[a]	.39[b]	.27	.11	—	.70[b]	.58[b]	.68[b]
Play (1-3)	.37[b]	.18	.25[a]	.24[a]	.12	.37[b]	.24	.17	.17	—	.75[b]	.93[b]
Play (4-6)	.37[b]	.42[b]	.02	.06	-.06	.20	.28	.03	.39[b]	.60[b]	—	.91[b]
Play all	.42[b]	.35[b]	.14	.16	.03	.31[a]	.29[a]	.10	.53[b]	.88[b]	.94[b]	—

Note. Girls above and to right of diagonal; boys below and to left of diagonal.

[a] $p < .05$.
[b] $p < .01$.

Table 23

Correlation Between Social Class and Vocalization-Verbalization: 4 Through 27 Months

	Boys	Girls
4 Months		
Two-dimensional faces: all stimuli	.05	−.03
Three-dimensional faces: all stimuli	.14	.07
8 Months		
Two-dimensional faces: all stimuli	.07	.01
Three-dimensional faces: all stimuli	.03	.09
Voc. off auditory: all stimuli	.17	.09
13 Months		
HF I: all stimuli	.14	.10
Three-dimensional faces: all stimuli	.15	−.03
Voc. off auditory: all stimuli	.15	−.02
HF II: all stimuli	.22[a]	.03
27 Months		
Slides: advanced verbalizations	.17	.27[a]
HF I: total verbalization	.08	.34[a]
Three-dimensional faces: total verbalization	−.03	.37[a]
Free play adapt.	.16	.13
Minutes 1-15	.11	.30[a]
Minutes 16-30	.16	.15
Total time	.15	.23
Slides: no. normal scenes verbalize	.19	.10
No. discrep. scenes verbalize	.09	.14
Vocabulary:		
Recognition	.19	.52[b]
Naming	.24	.52[b]

[a] $p < .05$.
[b] $p < .01$.

Table 24
Stability of Vocalization 4, 8, and 13 Months

		4 Months Two-Dimensional Faces				8 Months Two-Dimensional Faces			
		Tr 1		Tr 1-16		Tr 1		Tr 1-16	
		B	G	B	G	B	G	B	G
8 Months									
Two-dimensional faces	Tr 1	-.05	-.14	.03	-.08				
	Tr 1-16	-.09	-.03	.04	.02				
Three-dimensional faces	Tr 1	-.10	.03	-.03	.21				
	Tr 1-16	-.04	.06	.02	.00				
Auditory	Tr 1	.12	.08	.30[a]	.09				
	Tr 1-12	.01	-.07	.12	.01				
13 Months									
HF I	Tr 1	-.08	-.01	.00	.24	.02	.04	.07	.19
	Tr 1-12	.04	.01	-.02	.23	-.07	.15	.03	.28[a]
Three-dimensional faces	Tr 1	.01	.00	-.02	.26	.02	.48[b]	.03	.24
	Tr 1-15	-.07	-.15	-.06	.03	.12	.47[b]	-.02	.30[a]
HF II	Tr 1	.03	.05	.13	-.02	.09	.32[a]	.20	.13
	Tr 1-12	.01	-.16	.06	-.19	-.01	.14	.11	.21
Auditory	Tr 1	-.02	-.13	-.02	-.16	-.09	.07	.01	.11
	Tr 1-12	-.07	-.11	-.08	.00	.03	.24[a]	.08	.37[b]

Table 24 (*continued*)
Stability of Vocalization 4, 8, and 13 Months

		8 Months Three-Dimensional Faces				8 Months Auditory			
		Tr 1		Tr 1-16		Tr 1		Tr 1-12	
		B	G	B	G	B	G	B	G
13 Months									
HF I	Tr 1	.17	.11	.28[a]	.02	.03	-.01	.14	-.02
	Tr 1-12	.03	.11	.39[b]	.39[b]	.00	.28[a]	.25[a]	.34[b]
Three-dimensional faces	Tr 1	-.07	.51[b]	-.07	.43[b]	.06	.45[b]	-.02	.27[a]
	Tr 1-15	-.06	.32[a]	-.15	.47[b]	.03	.29[a]	.06	.46[b]
HF II	Tr 1	-.03	.10	.06	.32[a]	.18	.30[a]	.15	.27[a]
	Tr 1-12	-.02	.06	.00	.26[a]	.09	.12	.26[a]	.28[a]
Auditory	Tr 1	-.07	.08	-.02	.28[a]	.12	.09	.16	.32[a]
	Tr 1-12	.03	.13	.14	.21	.05	.19	.18	.28[a]

Table 24 (*continued*)

| | 13 Months HF I | | | | 13 Months Three-Dimensional Faces | | | |
| | Tr 1 | | Tr 1-12 | | Tr 1 | | Tr 1-15 | |
	B	G	B	G	B	G	B	G
27 Months								
Slides								
Verbal discrepant	-.07	.10	-.09	.01	.09	.13	.11	.06
Verbal nondiscrepant	-.14	.05	-.19	.06	.12	.16	.16	.15
HF I								
Verbalization	-.15	.28	-.09	.39[a]	.13	.43[b]	-.20	.37
Three-dimensional faces								
Verbalization	.21	.40[a]	-.19	.47[b]	.21	.23	-.01	.07
Free play								
Verbalization: Adaptation	-.06	.27[a]	.13	.30[a]	.23	.38[b]	.31[b]	.39[b]
Minutes 1-15	.01	.26[a]	.23	.15	.09	.34[a]	.26[a]	.16
Minutes 16-30	-.03	.32[a]	-.01	.34[b]	.04	.32[a]	.14	.17
Vocabulary recognition	-.26[a]	.23	-.14	-.10	.23	.01	.22	-.18
Vocabulary naming	.12	.16	-.04	.02	.21	-.09	.15	-.23

Table 24 (*continued*)

Stability of Vocalization 4, 8, and 13 Months

	13 Months HF II				13 Months Auditory			
	Tr 1		Tr 1-12		Tr 1		Tr 1-12	
	B	G	B	G	B	G	B	G
27 Months								
Slides								
Verbal discrepant	.16	−.14	.19	−.02	−.08	.17	−.13	−.07
Verbal nondiscrepant	.16	−.14	.25[a]	.01	−.01	.27[a]	−.09	.04
HF I								
Verbalization	.09	.18	−.13	.12	−.01	.02	−.16	.21
Three-dimensional faces								
Verbalization	.05	−.18	−.07	−.14	−.03	.12	−.06	.14
Free play adaptation	.07	.15	.19	.19	.21	.19	.25[a]	.16
Minutes 1-15	.10	−.06	.15	.08	.13	.09	.19	.10
Minutes 16-30	.06	−.05	.11	.11	.02	−.03	.09	.23
Vocabulary recognition	.08	−.26	.14	−.27	−.03	−.04	.02	−.05
Vocabulary naming	.05	−.17	.18	−.10	.05	−.04	.12	−.19

Table 24 (*continued*)

	4 Months Two-Dimensional Faces				8 Months Two-Dimensional Faces			
	Tr 1		Tr1-16		Tr 1		Tr1-16	
	B	G	B	G	B	G	B	G
27 Months								
Slides								
Verbal discrepant	.00	−.01	.30[a]	.00	.27[a]	−.06	.32[a]	−.04
Verbal nondiscrepant	.04	.17	.35[b]	.12	.40[b]	.08	.36[b]	.13
HF 1								
Verbalization	−.06	.02	.09	.26	−.04	.16	.01	.17
Three-dimensional faces								
Verbalization	−.20	−.05	−.06	.18	−.08	.01	−.04	.41[b]
Free play adaptation	.04	−.09	−.01	.13	.23	.13	.23	.14
Minutes 1-15	.02	−.03	−.12	.17	.20	−.04	.15	−.06
Minutes 16-30	.06	−.15	−.04	.08	−.01	.00	−.13	.11
Vocabulary recognition	.02	−.17	.07	.04	.03	−.14	−.03	−.27
Vocabulary naming	−.08	−.18	.02	.05	−.06	.05	−.11	−.06

Table 24 (continued)
Stability of Vocalization 4, 8, and 13 Months

| | 8 Months Three-Dimensional Faces | | | | 8 Months Auditory | | | |
| | Tr 1 | | Tr 1-16 | | Tr 1 | | Tr 1-12 | |
	B	G	B	G	B	G	B	G
27 Months								
Slides								
Verbal discrepant	.34[a]	−.09	.22	.03	.17	.01	.12	−.10
Verbal nondiscrepant	.27[a]	−.01	.12	.26	.11	.12	.11	−.01
HF I								
Verbalization	−.01	.12	−.01	.31	.20	.07	.26	.03
Three-dimensional faces								
Verbalization	.33	−.12	−.01	.27	.13	.12	.11	.08
Free play adaptation	−.03	.05	−.06	.11	.01	.14	.05	.28[a]
Minutes 1-15	.17	.14	.02	.11	.04	.22	.07	.16
Minutes 16-30	−.06	.07	−.18	−.06	.07	.17	−.06	.05
Vocabulary recognition	.20	−.26	−.12	−.22	.36[b]	−.08	.17	−.19
Vocabulary naming	.19	−.11	−.08	−.20	.24	−.03	.10	−.03

[a] p < .05.
[a] p < .01.

Table 25

Differences Between Infants with Equally Long Fixations to PR (or SR) at 4 Months but Differing in Vocalization to PR (or SR) at 4 Months

Boys

Variables	PR4 Months				SR4 Months			
	N = 23 High voc.	N = 21 Low voc.	t	p	N = 23 High voc.	N = 21 Low voc.	t	p
Auditory: Orientation to speaker at 8 months								
LL	3.6	9.4			2.1	10.7	1.99	=.06
HL	6.0	5.4			2.6	8.0	1.95	=.06
LH	8.0	7.9			3.9	9.4	1.73	=.09
HH	8.1	4.8			4.5	9.9		

Girls

Variables	PR4 Months				SR4 Months			
	N = 22 High voc.	N = 18 Low voc.	t	p	N = 25 High voc.	N = 15 Low voc.	t	p
Auditory: Orientation to speaker at 8 months								
LL	5.8	3.4			8.9	2.5	2.36	<.05
HL	6.5	2.1	1.72	=.10	8.7	1.6	2.73	<.01
LH	7.6	1.8	2.12	=.05	9.6	1.7	2.80	<.01
HH	7.8	4.4			9.8	3.5	1.93	=.06

Table 26

Mean Time Orientation to Speaker for Ss High Versus Low on Vocalization to PR or SR at 8 Months, but Equally Long on Fixation Time to PR or SR at 8 Months

8 Months		Boys				Girls			
		PR High voc. $N = 21$	PR Low voc. $N = 18$	SR High voc. $N = 22$	SR Low voc. $N = 14$	PR High voc. $N = 17$	PR Low voc. $N = 17$	SR High voc. $N = 19$	SR Low voc. $N = 21$
Orientation to speaker	LL	2.5	6.7[a]	3.2	4.8	8.4	3.6	7.3	5.6
	HL	1.5	7.7[a]	3.9	7.3	8.3	2.4[a]	7.3	5.1
	LH	2.1	8.1[a]	5.3	6.6	9.5	4.0	7.5	6.5
	HH	2.3	11.5[a]	5.3	8.3	9.5	3.5	8.8	5.1

[a]Difference between high versus low vocalization groups statistically significant at $p < .05$ or better.

Table 27

Social Class Differences in Behavior with Vocalization at 4 Months Controlled

| | Girls | | | | | | | | |
| | Low Voc. at 4 | | | Middle Voc. at 4 | | | High Voc. at 4 | | |
	LMC + MC$_1$ $N = 10$	MC$_2$ + UMC $N = 13$	Class Diff. p	LMC + MC$_1$ $N = 7$	MC$_2$ + UMC $N = 16$	Class Diff. p	LMC + MC$_1$ $N = 10$	MC$_2$ + UMC $N = 12$	Class Diff. p
Vocalization									
Two-dimensional faces at 8	0.5	1.1		0.6	0.6		0.5	0.9	
Three-dimensional faces at 8	1.1	1.7		1.9	1.4		1.8	1.9	
Three-dimensional faces at 13	1.8	1.1		1.6	1.6		1.5	1.7	
Human Forms I at 13	0.5	0.9		0.8	1.3		1.1	2.3	< .10
Human Forms II at 13	1.6	2.4		2.3	2.3		1.5	1.4	
Auditory at 8	0.8	0.8		0.6	0.9		0.8	1.1	
Auditory at 13	0.7	0.6		1.8	1.1		0.5	1.2	< .05
27 Months									
Vocabulary recognition	12.9	14.4	= .07	12.2	15.8	= .08	12.7	16.7	< .05
Vocabulary naming	7.0	9.9		6.9	10.9	= .01	8.0	10.0	
Speech quality	4.4	4.3		3.6	5.2	= .01	4.8	4.8	
Speech quantity	4.4	4.5		3.3	4.5	= .08	4.5	4.3	
Slides scaled verbalization	1.4	1.5		1.5	1.9		1.4	2.2	= .05
Free play verbalization	214	146		116	202	< .05	181	235	

Table 27 (*continued*)
Social Class Differences in Behavior with Vocalization at 4 Months Controlled

	Boys								
	Low Voc. at 4			Middle Voc. at 4			High Voc. at 4		
	LMC + MC$_1$ $N = 9$	MC$_2$ + UMC $N = 13$	Class Diff. p	LMC + MC$_1$ $N = 13$	MC$_2$ + UMC $N = 13$	Class Diff. p	LMC + MC$_1$ $N = 10$	MC$_2$ + UMC $N = 15$	Class Diff. p
Vocalization									
Two-dimesional faces at 8	0.6	0.6		1.2	1.4		0.7	1.0	
Three-dimesional faces at 8	1.2	0.9		1.2	2.1		1.7	1.0	
Three-dimensional faces at 13	1.5	1.7		1.9	1.3		0.9	1.1	
Human Forms I at 13	1.3	1.1		0.9	1.6		1.1	1.2	
Human Forms II at 13	1.9	1.9		2.2	2.7		1.2	1.7	
Auditory at 8	0.6	0.9		0.8	1.4		1.0	1.0	
Auditory at 13	0.7	1.7	<.01	1.1	0.7		1.0	1.1	
27 Months									
Vocabulary recognition	12.6	14.7		14.0	12.8		14.6	15.0	
Vocabulary naming	9.8	10.2		8.9	9.1		9.7	11.3	
Speech quality	5.1	5.2		4.3	4.3		4.8	4.0	
Speech quantity	5.0	4.6		4.7	5.2		4.6	4.5	
Free play verbalization	169	177		182	196		168	176	

Table 28

Deceleration to First Fixation or to Auditory Component (Percent of Group with Deceleration $\geq$ 6 bpm)

	Deceleration to Auditory				Deceleration to First Fixation		
No.	Scene	Boys (Percent)	Girls (Percent)	No.	Scene	Boys (Percent)	Girls (Percent)
16	Girl bark	73	48	10	Mom – car horn	53	53
10	Mom – car horn	60	66	11	Woman, no head	53	61
22	Girl in tub	57	46	20	Man, 4 arms	51	37
3	Man in dress	56	59	18	Man, female voice	47	38
5	Girl nonsense	55	54	16	Girl bark	45	25
11	Woman, no head	55	53	22	Girl in tub	42	38
2	Man and woman	50	50	5	Girl nonsense	42	40
21	Dog	48	43	7	Boy in air	41	32
8	Cat	48	52	23	Man in bed	41	56
9	Big cat	48	43	1	Boy and girl	40	34
14	Fire engine	47	59	4	Woman in kitchen	39	49
18	Man, female voice	47	32	3	Man in dress	38	42
4	Woman in kitchen	46	29	15	Boy	36	40
23	Man in bed	45	34	8	Cat	36	33
7	Boy in air	42	25	14	Fire engine	34	33
12	Woman at table	42	32	12	Woman at table	33	36
20	Man, 4 arms	42	25	9	Big cat	31	49
17	Man, car	41	37	2	Man and woman	30	52
19	Woman table	35	32	13	Telephone	30	27
13	Telephone	34	48	19	Woman table	28	21
15	Boy	25	28	21	Dog	28	40
1	Boy and girl	24	28	17	Man, car	27	38
6	Boy	16	21	6	Boy	22	21

Table 29

Percent of Infants in Each Class Displaying Decelerations of 6 or More Beats to Faces at 4 Months

			LC	MC_1	MC_2	UMC	$x^2/6df$	p
			Boys					
PR	Trial	1	33	53	33	63		
		2	33	41	25	63		
		3	20	38	17	60	14.07	< .05
SR	Trial	1	26	59	64	25	11.66	< .10
		2	20	41	25	31		
		3	26	47	25	40		
PS	Trial	1	27	41	25	31		
		2	13	24	17	33		
		3	6	6	9	27		
SS	Trial	1	20	35	17	38		
		2	20	18	9	13		
		3	0	20	33	20		
Reg	Trial	1	25	40	40	35		
		2	33	13	30	29		
		3	18	40	9	29	11.00	< .10
Scr	Trial	1	16	47	46	41		
		2	16	20	55	59	12.58	< .05
		3	9	40	18	13		
NE	Trial	1	9	60	55	35		
		2	16	20	18	29		
		3	36	27	30	33		
BL	Trial	1	18	40	9	29		
		2	0	33	9	29		
		3	0	13	18	27		
			Girls					
PR	Trial	1	40	46	39	60		
		2	30	25	46	27		
		3	37	25	31	21		
SR	Trial	1	40	50	31	27		
		2	20	33	39	33		
		3	12	21	39	23		
PS	Trial	1	0	25	23	33	10.57	= .10
		2	20	25	15	33	12.24	= .05
		3	12	20	15	36		
SS	Trial	1	30	44	39	31		
		2	10	13	31	13		
		3	13	14	31	29		

Table 29 (*continued*)
Percent of Infants in Each Class Displaying Decelerations of 6 or More Beats to Faces at 4 Months

				Girls				
			LC	MC_1	MC_2	UMC	$x^2/6df$	p
Reg	Trial	1	36	33	88	63	13.86	< .05
		2	9	33	75	38	16.58	< .01
		3	9	31	13	17		
Scr	Trial	1	36	27	37	38		
		2	18	40	50	25		
		3	18	14	25	55	13.13	< .05
NE	Trial	1	36	20	25	44		
		2	18	27	25	31		
		3	18	29	38	18		
BL	Trial	1	9	27	50	31		
		2	0	20	50	25	10.56	= .10
		3	0	14	25	25	11.06	< .10

Table 30

Intercorrelations of Deceleration Measures at 4 Months

	Two-Dimensional Faces: Deceleration						Three-Dimensional Faces: Deceleration					
	Tr 1	PR	SR	PS	SS	Mean Max. Decel.[c]	Tr 1	Reg	Scr	NE	BL	Mean Max. Decel.
Deceleration to two-dimensional faces												
Trial 1	—	.08	.66[b]	.38[b]	.22	.31[a]	-.26	.03	-.11	-.34[a]	.29[a]	-.03
Deceleration to PR	.26[a]	—	.40[b]	.42[b]	.47[b]	.67[b]	.04	.41[b]	.01	.14	.08	.32[a]
SR	.75[b]	.48[b]	—	.61[b]	.39[b]	.66[b]	-.26	.16	-.15	-.36[a]	.18	.11
PS	.35[b]	.50[b]	.69[b]	—	.42[b]	.75[b]	-.13	.37[a]	.14	-.10	.39[b]	.26
SS	.33[a]	.49[b]	.54[b]	.35[b]	—	.66[b]	-.14	.32[a]	.02	.01	.22	.33[a]
Mean max. deceleration	.47[b]	.68[b]	.77[b]	.69[b]	.77[b]	—	-.21	.41[b]	-.07	-.11	.34[a]	.30[a]
Deceleration to three-dimensional faces												
Trial 1	.43[b]	.38[b]	.41[b]	.36[b]	.40[b]	.42[b]	.00	-.06	.19	.68[b]	-.04	.22
Deceleration to Reg	.03	.25	.08	.08	.35[a]	.24	.32[a]	—	.26	.16	.48[b]	.59[b]
Scr	.17	.26	.27[a]	.27[a]	.20	.29[a]	.83[b]	.32[a]	—	.48[b]	.29[a]	.70[b]
NE	.46[b]	.31[a]	.34[a]	.34[a]	.31[a]	.35[b]	.32[a]	-.01	.34[a]	—	.11	.56[b]
BL	.24	.34[a]	.22	.22	.46[b]	.44[b]	.32[a]	.13	.28[a]	.07	—	.45[b]
Mean max. deceleration	.38[b]	.46[b]	.37[b]	.37[b]	.58[b]	.56[b]	.64[b]	.48[b]	.68[b]	.64[b]	.43[b]	—

Note. Girls to right and above diagonal; boys to left and below diagonal

[a] $p < .05$.

[b] $p < .01$.

[c] Mean maximal deceleration is the mean of the single longest deceleration to each of the four stimuli in the series.

Table 31

Intercorrelations of Deceleration Measures at 8 Months

		Deceleration–Two-Dimensional Faces					
		Tr 1	PR	SR	PS	SS	Mean Max.
Deceleration to Two-Dimensional Faces							
Trial 1		—	.29[a]	.86[b]	.49[b]	.46[b]	.67[b]
Deceleration	PR	.22	—	.41[b]	.38[b]	.52[b]	.63[b]
	SR	.76[b]	.26[a]	—	.55[b]	.55[b]	.78[b]
	PS	.25[a]	.24[a]	.28[a]	—	.63[b]	.71[b]
	SS	.31[b]	.27[a]	.26[a]	.40[b]	—	.78[b]
Mean max.		.51[b]	.39[b]	.62[b]	.62[b]	.60[b]	—
Deceleration to Three-Dimensional Faces							
Trial 1		.02	.30[a]	.14	−.07	.21	.20
Deceleration	Reg	.04	.26[a]	.21	.12	.09	.27[a]
	Scr	.26[a]	.16	.20	−.02	−.07	.13
	NE	.09	.28[a]	.22	.01	.24	.32[a]
	BL	.14	.00	.11	.02	.11	.08
Mean max.		.20	.19	.26[a]	.13	.14	.41[b]
Deceleration to Auditory							
Trial 1		−.06	−.04	−.01	.04	.09	.12
Deceleration	LL	−.04	−.12	−.05	.12	.13	.10
	HL	.04	.08	.12	.13	.09	.23
	LH	.22	.16	.21	.08	−.07	.16
	HH	.06	.12	.03	.10	.23	.28[a]
Mean max.		.15	.00	.16	.14	.17	.30[a]

Table 31 (*continued*)

Intercorrelations of Deceleration Measures at 8 Months

		Deceleration–Three-Dimensional Faces					
		Tr 1	Reg	Scr	NE	BL	Mean Max.
Deceleration to Two-Dimensional Faces							
Trial 1		.02	.08	.06	−.02	.01	.06
Deceleration	PR	.12	.09	.37[b]	.05	.00	.16
	SR	−.08	.18	.10	−.05	.03	.08
	PS	−.05	.39[b]	.16	−.06	.10	.10
	SS	.18	.33[b]	.41[b]	.12	.16	.26[a]
Mean max.		.10	.29[a]	.32[a]	.11	.11	.21
Deceleration to Three-Dimensional Faces							
Trial 1		—	.23	.42[b]	.83[b]	.40[b]	.49[b]
Deceleration	Reg	.39[b]	—	.45[b]	.28[a]	.44[b]	.61[b]
	Scr	.17	.25[a]	—	.43[b]	.45[b]	.62[b]
	NE	.89[b]	.55[b]	.25[a]	—	.41[b]	.56[b]
	BL	.12	.36[b]	.45[b]	.28[a]	—	.58[b]
Mean max.		.50[b]	.63[b]	.62[b]	.62[b]	.64[b]	—
Deceleration to Auditory							
Trial 1		.11	.28[a]	.05	.16	.24	.32[a]
Deceleration	LL	.10	.36[b]	.06	.17	.29[a]	.32[a]
	HL	.16	.25	.13	.24	.27[a]	.28[a]
	LH	.23	.36[b]	.10	.37[b]	.30[a]	.32[a]
	HH	.20	.27[a]	.02	.32[a]	.31[a]	.26[a]
Mean max.		.21	.44[b]	.15	.36[b]	.42[b]	.44[b]

Table 31 (*continued*)

Intercorrelations of Deceleration Measures at 8 Months

		Tr 1	LL	HL	LH	HH	Mean Max.
				Deceleration–Auditory			
Deceleration to Two-Dimensional Faces							
Trial 1		.19	.20	.31[b]	.27[a]	.18	.28[a]
Deceleration	PR	.10	.18	.33[b]	.27[a]	.29[a]	.31[b]
	SR	.12	.17	.40[b]	.33[b]	.25[a]	.35[b]
	PS	.01	.16	.26[a]	.36[b]	.28[a]	.31[b]
	SS	.11	.21	.27[a]	.26[a]	.30[b]	.30[b]
Mean max.		.14	.24[a]	.44[b]	.36[b]	.37[b]	.44[b]
Deceleration to Three-Dimensional Faces							
Trial 1		.16	.14	.07	.08	.14	.18
Deceleration	Reg	−.05	.09	.16	.20	.04	.15
	Scr	.14	.25[a]	.21	.28[a]	.14	.24
	NE	.12	.09	.10	.09	.17	.18
	BL	−.04	−.05	−.11	.09	−.02	.01
Mean max.		.16	.25[a]	.22	.28[a]	.22	.31[b]
Deceleration to Auditory							
Trial 1		—	.79[b]	.19	.20	.31[b]	.54[b]
Deceleration	LL	.79[b]	—	.34[b]	.40[b]	.47[b]	.71[b]
	HL	.25[a]	.40[b]	—	.45[b]	.41[b]	.64[b]
	LH	.22	.28[a]	.37[b]	—	.42[b]	.75[b]
	HH	.35[b]	.42[b]	.33[b]	.52[b]	—	.72[b]
Mean max.		.57[b]	.71[b]	.66[b]	.68[b]	.73[b]	—

Note. Girls to right and above diagonal; boys to left and below diagonal.

[a] $p < .05$.

[b] $p < .01$.

Table 32

Intercorrelations of Deceleration Measures at 13 Months

		Deceleration—Human Forms I						Deceleration—Human Forms II				
		Tr 1	Reg	HBL	Scr	FF	Mean Max.	Tr 1	3H	HH	AH	Mean Max.
Deceleration to Human Forms I												
Trial I		—	.39[b]	.40[b]	.40[b]	.30[a]	.76[b]	.14	.25[a]	.09	.16	.25[a]
Deceleration	Reg	.52[b]	—	.15	.44[b]	.47[b]	.61[b]	.22	.26[a]	.10	.22	.33[b]
	HBL	.11	.36[b]	—	.51[b]	.21	.16	.02	-.05	-.07	.12	.17
	Scr	.46[b]	.29[b]	.35[b]	—	.66[b]	.72[b]	.26[a]	.31[b]	.13	.32[b]	.25
	FF	.20	.22[a]	.23[a]	.13	—	.74[b]	.15	.39[b]	.14	.38[b]	.33[b]
Mean max.		.48[b]	.69[b]	.69[b]	.58[b]	.48[b]	—	.29[a]	.33[b]	.16	.34[b]	.35[b]
Deceleration to Human Forms II												
Trial 1		.07	.12	.22[a]	.13	.04	.15	—	.66[b]	.71[b]	.40[b]	.21
Deceleration	3H	.17	.14	.19	.09	-.08	.25	.39[b]	—	.59[b]	.36[b]	.15
	HH	.07	.16	.18	.12	-.03	.19	.47[b]	.31[b]	—	.29[a]	.05
	AH	.30[b]	.23[a]	.10	.19	-.02	.18	.26[a]	.42[b]	.33[b]	—	.03
Mean max.		.29[b]	.29[b]	.33[b]	.30[b]	.32[b]	.47[b]	.18	.36[b]	.34[b]	.47[b]	—

Table 32 (continued)

	Deceleration—Three-Dimensional Faces							Deceleration—Auditory					
	Tr 1	Reg	Scr	EO	NE	BL	Mean Max.	Tr 1	LL	HL	LH	HH	Mean Max.
Deceleration to Three-Dimensional Faces													
Trial 1	—	.12	.23	.58[b]	.30[a]	.48[b]	.40[b]	.27[a]	.26[a]	.17	−.05	.07	.18
Deceleration Reg	.12	—	.03	.35[b]	.07	.21	.11	−.07	.03	.15	−.14	−.02	−.02
Scr	.10	.16	—	.08	.35[b]	.13	.26	−.10	.05	.23	−.08	.01	.13
EO	.50[b]	.04	.26[a]	—	.15	.22	.35[b]	.31[a]	.28[a]	.20	.00	.02	.17
NE	.43[b]	.01	.13	.17	—	.21	.22	.06	.11	.22	.01	.12	.15
BL	.38[b]	.27[a]	.17	.25[a]	.16	—	.26[a]	.11	.19	.03	.01	.15	.14
Mean max.	.32[b]	.36[b]	.20	.23[a]	.04	.56[b]	—	.19	.29[a]	.34[b]	−.02	.33[b]	.37[b]
Deceleration to Auditory													
Trial 1	.15	.01	.10	.16	.08	.32[b]	.26[a]	—	.85[b]	.28[a]	.32[b]	.25[a]	.63[b]
Deceleration LL	.17	−.06	.09	.18	.09	.28[a]	.31[b]	.91[b]	—	.44[b]	.34[b]	.37[b]	.72[b]
HL	−.06	.12	.26[a]	.18	−.16	.35[b]	.45[b]	.42[b]	.38[b]	—	.33[b]	.56[b]	.74[b]
LH	.10	.12	.01	.20	−.08	.08	.27[a]	.36[b]	.27[a]	.50[b]	—	.48[b]	.64[b]
HH	.14	.26[a]	−.06	−.00	−.10	.32[b]	.49[b]	.30[b]	.27[a]	.31[b]	.36[b]	—	.71[b]
Mean max.	.12	.12	.20	.31[b]	−.08	.32[b]	.43[b]	.71[b]	.66[b]	.69[b]	.66[b]	.49[b]	—

Table 32 (*continued*)

Intercorrelations of Deceleration Measures at 13 Months

	Boys										
	Deceleration–Human Forms I						Deceleration–Human Forms II				
	Tr 1	Reg	HBL	Scr	FF	Mean Max.	Tr 1	3H	HH	AH	Mean Max.
Deceleration to Three-Dimensional Faces											
Trial 1	.09	.20	.32b	.30b	.06	.34b	.23a	.32b	.46b	.08	.47b
Deceleration Reg	.12	.17	.22	.28a	.06	.25a	.21	.12	.36b	.30b	.41b
Scr	-.00	.08	.07	.16	.14	.16	.03	.12	.06	.18	.58b
EO	.20	.18	.20	.23a	.28b	.33b	.22	.15	.30b	.12	.61b
NE	.18	.22	.32b	.10	.15	.28a	.16	.14	.05	-.06	.40b
BL	.15	.16	.14	.10	.19	.21	.06	.36b	.31b	.60b	.67b
Mean max.	.27a	-.24a	.17	-.23a	-.01	.30b	.39b	.70b	.62b	.78b	.53b
Deceleration to Auditory											
Trial 1	.21	.14	.14	.22a	.14	.28a	-.00	.21	.04	.26a	.37b
Deceleration LL	.22a	.11	.11	.16	.14	.23a	.04	.21	.09	.32b	.34b
HL	.26a	.12	.09	.23a	.19	.28a	-.01	.27a	.07	.46b	.38b
LH	.25a	.22a	.11	.21	.38b	.38b	-.01	.12	.12	.14	.20
HH	.24a	.26a	.15	.20	.21	.33b	.02	.31b	.36b	.34b	.19
Mean max.	.40b	.34b	.16	.33b	.31b	.47b	.02	.30b	.13	.34b	.45b

Table 32 (*continued*)

		Girls												
		Deceleration–Three-Dimensional Faces							Deceleration–Auditory					
		Tr 1	Reg	Scr	EO	NE	BL	Mean Max.	Tr 1	LL	HL	LH	HH	Mean Max.
Deceleration to Human Forms I														
Trial 1		.19	−.00	.31b	.30a	.24	.24	.36b	.31a	.38b	.30a	.20	.22	.37b
Deceleration	Reg	.35b	.03	.37b	.22	.26a	.13	.37b	.20	.28a	.38b	.21	.22	.34b
	HBL	.16	.14	.02	.16	−.04	.24	.05	.28a	.33b	.27a	.23	.18	.31
	Scr	.41b	−.09	.40b	.19	.08	.27a	.52b	.17	.30a	.34b	.19	.28a	.38b
	FF	.48b	.05	.34b	.47b	.16	.24a	.49b	.36b	.42b	.22	.08	.14	.34b
Mean max.		.39b	.34b	.32b	.49b	.12	.26a	.50b	.36b	.45b	.46b	.26a	.29a	.49b
Deceleration to Human Forms II														
Trial I		.10	.08	.02	.14	.27a	.19	.65b	.15	.22	.20	.22	.34b	.29a
Deceleration	3H	.27a	.06	.17	.26a	.15	.22	.70b	.16	.15	.15	.10	.08	.19
	HH	.14	−.01	.02	.05	.10	.04	.64b	.09	.07	.11	.01	.27a	.19
	AH	.33b	.02	.06	.41b	.13	.17	.66b	.25a	.36b	.26a	.06	.36b	.34b
Mean max.		.45b	.73b	.41b	.51b	.44b	.47b	.31a	.12	.24	.32b	−.06	.07	.18

Note. Girls to right and above diagonal; boys to left and below diagonal.

[a] $p < .05$.
[b] $p < .01$.

Table 33

Correlation of Deceleration to Two Dimensional and Three Dimensional Faces at 4 Months with Deceleration at 8 Months

	Boys				
Two Dimensional Faces 4 Months	Two Dimensional Faces: Deceleration at 8 Months				
	PR	SR	PS	SS	Mean Max.
PR	.31[a]	.20	.25	.09	.48[b]
SR	.28	.17	.27	.07	.40[b]
PS	.36[a]	.09	.26	−.03	.30[a]
SS	.30[a]	.32[a]	.16	.19	.46[b]
Mean max.	.30[a]	.34[a]	.40[b]	.13	.59[b]
Three Dimensional Faces 4 Months	Three Dimensional Faces at 8 Months				
	Reg	Scr	NE	BL	Mean Max.
Reg	.06	−.07	.05	.15	.12
Scr	.03	.26	.08	.08	.16
NE	.18	−.02	.46[b]	−.03	.17
BL	.12	.34[a]	.33[a]	.23	.31
Mean max.	.27	.21	.43[b]	.23	.41[b]
	Girls				
Two Dimensional Faces 4 Months	Two-Dimensional Faces at 8 Months				
	PR	SR	PS	SS	Mean Max.
PR	.05	−.06	.26	−.01	.03
SR	.15	.10	.19	.18	.07
PS	.03	−.06	.26	.03	.01
SS	.06	−.18	.25	−.01	−.04
Mean max.	.01	−.03	.24	.10	−.02
Three Dimensional Faces 4 Months	Three-Dimensional Faces at 8 Months				
	Reg	Scr	NE	BL	Mean Max.
Reg	.18	−.06	−.13	−.18	−.19
Scr	−.01	−.14	.14	−.02	.03
NE	.17	−.12	.26	.02	−.01
BL	.08	.26	.12	.15	.27
Mean max.	.33[a]	−.09	.07	.00	.02

[a] $p < .05$.
[b] $p < .01$.

Table 34

Correlations of Deceleration at 8 Months with Deceleration at 13 Months

Three Dimen-sional faces 8 Months	Three-Dimensional Faces (13 Months)					
	Girls					
	Reg	Scr	EO	NE	BL	Mean Max.
Reg	−.06	.01	.22	.18	−.26	.02
Scr	−.17	.20	.16	.34[a]	−.01	.08
NE	−.09	.22	.13	.28[a]	.04	−.06
BL	−.13	.01	.05	.19	−.09	−.06
Mean Max.	−.03	−.04	.18	.29[a]	−.03	.03
	Boys					
Reg	.06	.07	−.06	−.11	−.05	.07
Scr	−.08	.10	−.06	−.04	−.12	.16
NE	.10	.08	.01	.04	−.16	.04
BL	−.08	.05	−.08	.04	.03	.16
Mean Max.	.06	.11	−.04	.06	−.04	.31[a]

Auditory 8 Months	Auditory (13 Months)				
	Girls				
	LL	HL	LH	HH	Mean Max.
LL	.12	.28[a]	.31[a]	.20	.26[a]
HL	.05	.06	.34[b]	.16	.26
LH	.16	.20	.19	.33[b]	.33[b]
HH	.18	.21	.38[b]	.30[a]	.37[b]
Mean max.	.21	.29[a]	.32[a]	.30[a]	.41[b]
	Boys				
LH	.14	.13	.07	.07	.15
HH	.13	.21	.15	.17	.31[a]
LH	.07	.16	.22	.27[a]	.20
HH	.14	.30[a]	.32[b]	.18	.32[b]
Mean max.	.17	.27[a]	.23	.18	.33[b]

[a] $p < .05$
[b] $p < .01$

Table 35

Stability of Deceleration Measures from 13 to 27 Months

	Boys (27 Months)							
	Slides		EFT	EFT	EFT	EFT	EFT	EFT
13 Months	Disc Scenes	Non-disc Scenes	DHB_1	DHB_2	DHB_3	CCF_1	CCF_2	CCF_3
Deceleration to Human Forms I								
Reg	.06	.24	−.04	−.05	.26	.11	.14	.12
HBL	.13	.36[b]	.18	.01	.21	−.02	.39[b]	.29[a]
FF	−.10	.25	.04	−.09	.19	−.01	−.20	−.02
Scr	.00	−.07	.20	.09	.24	−.25	.32[a]	.20
Mean max.	.01	.24	.14	−.05	.37[b]	−.04	.26	.22
Deceleration to Auditory								
LL	.16	.02	.28	.01	.10	−.06	.09	.00
HL	.15	.16	−.01	.15	.21	−.16	.11	.24
LH	.06	.22	.05	−.06	.18	.20	.06	−.15
HH	.04	−.03	−.06	−.17	.09	.03	.01	.00
Mean max.	.10	.20	.15	−.03	.25	.04	.11	.06
Deceleration to Three-Dimensional Faces								
Reg	.15	.20	.00	.05	−.10	.03	−.07	.25
Scr	.32[a]	.33[a]	.27	.03	.17	−.14	.09	.34[a]
EO	.05	.14	.28[a]	.10	.19	.03	.23	.37[b]
NE	.13	.19	.19	−.10	.02	−.01	.18	.17
BL	−.12	−.07	−.12	−.11	.01	−.02	−.03	.50[b]
Mean max.	.12	.15	.04	−.02	−.02	.08	.07	.19
Deceleration to Human Forms II								
3H	.23	.27[a]	.11	−.08	.04	.09	.23	.00
HH	−.05	−.01	.14	−.01	−.10	.08	.03	−.07
AH	.12	.01	−.07	.22	−.05	.01	.07	.20
Mean max.	.12	.28[a]	.22	.00	.30[a]	.03	.15	.45[b]

Table 35 (*continued*)
Stability of Deceleration Measures from 13 to 27 Months

					Girls (27 Months)				
	Slides		EFT	EFT	EFT	EFT	EFT	EFT
13 Months	Disc Scenes	Non-Disc Scenes	DHB_1	DHB_2	DHB_3	CCF_1	CCF_2	CCF_3
Deceleration to Human Forms I								
Reg	.17	.21	−.08	.09	.24	−.03	−.03	.03
HBL	−.01	.27	−.10	.05	−.18	.13	.25	−.20
FF	−.10	.21	−.11	.22	.17	−.09	−.04	.18
Scr	−.25	−.12	.01	.00	.08	−.17	.03	−.04
Mean max.	−.08	.23	−.06	.19	.13	−.03	.10	−.07
Deceleration to Auditory								
LL	.22	.26	−.30[a]	.02	−.19	−.03	−.02	.09
HL	.13	.10	−.14	.01	.02	−.10	.21	−.06
LH	.04	.05	−.07	−.04	−.17	.05	.18	.17
HH	.32[a]	.33[a]	.14	−.03	.16	.00	.20	−.05
Mean max.	.20	.26	−.09	.04	.06	.06	.15	.09
Deceleration to Three-Dimensional Faces								
Reg	−.02	.30[a]	.15	.10	−.01	−.11	.01	.14
Scr	−.04	−.08	.13	−.04	.28	.32[a]	−.05	−.10
EO	−.00	.31[a]	.03	.40[b]	.23	−.05	.21	.28
NE	.00	−.08	.03	.12	.07	.19	−.06	.04
BL	.20	.37[a]	−.08	.11	−.02	.19	.17	−.02
Mean max.	.03	.17	−.04	.02	.23	−.21	−.12	.08
Deceleration to Human Forms II								
3H	−.13	.04	−.05	−.12	.04	−.23	−.13	.08
HH	−.08	.12	.11	.12	.14	−.20	.15	−.04
AH	.18	.23	.10	.06	.17	−.14	−.07	.12
Mean max.	.10	.26	.13	.29	.22	.17	.05	.09

[a] $p < .05$.
[b] $p < .01$.

Table 36
Correlations of First Trial Reactions

| | | 4 Months | | | | 8 Months | | | | | |
| | | Two-Dimensional Faces | | Three-Dimensional Faces | | Two-Dimensional Faces | | Three-Dimensional Faces | | Auditory | |
13 Months		Voc.	Decel.	Voc.	Decel.	Voc.	Decel.	Voc.	Decel.	Voc.	Decel.
HF I Voc.	B	.19	-.10	.26[a]	-.08	.01	.08	.17	-.10	.03	.16
	G	.32[b]	-.26	.02	.00	.05	-.05	.11	-.03	-.11	-.02
Decel.	B	.02	.33[a]	.16	.46[b]	-.02	.07	-.05	.26[a]	-.01	.19
	G	.08	.20	-.16	.08	-.04	.18	.00	.34[a]	.08	.31[a]
Three Voc.	B	.01	.21	-.05	.41[b]	.03	.16	-.07	.16	.06	.06
Dimen-	G	.25	.28	.03	-.11	.48[b]	.02	.51[b]	-.10	.45[b]	.20
sional Faces Decel.	B	-.03	-.04	-.07	.29	.16	.13	-.12	.05	-.21	.19
	G	.08	.51[b]	-.21	-.10	-.05	.23	-.17	.16	-.07	.25
HF II Voc.	B	-.18	-.24	-.10	-.16	-.07	-.07	.07	-.34[a]	-.04	-.14
	G	-.12	.17	-.04	.17	.27	.11	.30	-.14	.78[b]	-.12
Decel.	B	-.11	.23	-.06	.44[a]	.05	-.05	-.16	.35[a]	.39[b]	.43[b]
	G	-.03	.06	-.11	.10	.27	.07	.18	-.04	.06	.08
Aud- Voc.	B	.00	-.10	.05	.14	-.09	.34[b]	-.06	-.06	.11	.11
itory	G	-.16	-.01	-.01	.01	.06	-.11	.08	.11	.09	-.13
Decel.	B	-.21	-.26	-.23	-.14	-.21	.52[b]	-.19	.12	.05	.09
	G	-.03	.31	-.07	-.37	-.13	.31	.07	.23	.35[a]	.23

[a] p < .05.
[b] p < .01.

Table 37
Predictive Validity of Combined Fixation and Deceleration Patterns at 13 Months for 27-Month Variables

27 Months		HF I at 13 months					HF II at 13 months				
		L-L	L-H	H-L	H-H	F/p	L-L	L-H	H-L	H-H	F/p
Educational level	B	2.1	2.7	2.7	2.7		2.3	2.6	2.6	2.8	
	G	2.4	2.2	3.3	2.9	2.90/< .05	2.4	2.2	3.7	2.9	4.76/< .01
Vocabulary	B	11.6	11.6	11.6	12.8		11.7	10.8	11.6	12.9	
Total score	G	10.9	10.0	13.7	11.9	2.95/< .05	10.5	10.6	15.1	11.9	3.78/< .01
HF I: First fix	B	6.9	8.2	8.3	9.2		10.1	8.8	8.8	10.5	
	G	7.1	8.7	8.9	10.4		7.5	8.1	12.3	9.0	2.87/< .05
Slides: First fix	B	6.0	6.6	8.1	7.2	4.17/< .01	6.6	6.7	7.1	7.1	
All stimuli	G	6.5	6.3	6.8	6.5		6.6	5.1	7.6	7.0	2.82/< .05
Slides: Fixation time: disc minus nondisc scenes	B	1.6	-.3	1.4	1.5		0.8	1.7	0.5	2.2	
	G	1.4	0.3	1.6	-.8	2.13/< .10	0.3	-.8	4.1	-.6	3.30/< .05
Slides	B	0.7	2.0	1.5	3.0		1.1	1.9	1.3	2.9	
Verbalization	G	1.2	1.0	2.7	2.7		.8	.7	5.4	1.9	4.76/< .01

Key. L-L, Below median on fixation time and deceleration at 13 months; L-H, Below median on fixation time and above median on deceleration; H-L, Above median on fixation time and below median on deceleration; H-H, Above median on fixation time and above median on deceleration.

Table 38

Mobility and Tempo of Play at 8 and 13 Months

	Boys Mean	Girls Mean
8 Months		
Number squares traversed		
Min. 1–4	1.9	1.7
Min. 5–8	2.6	2.0
Min. 9–12	2.4	2.3
Min. 13–15	1.6	1.6
Total Min. 1–15	8.4	7.8
Number act changes		
Min. 1–4	7.1	8.5
Min. 5–8	6.8	7.8
Min. 9–12	6.4	7.0
Min. 13–15	4.3	4.5
Total Min. 1–15	24.5	27.1
13 Months		
Number squares traversed		
Min. 1–4	15.8	15.9
Min. 5–8	14.7	15.4
Min. 9–12	15.5	14.4
Min. 13–17	14.7	11.6
Total Min. 1–17	60.7	57.3
Number act changes		
Min. 1–4	10.2	10.4
Min. 5–8	8.2	7.7
Min. 9–12	6.6	6.4
Min. 13–17	7.5	7.1
Total Min. 1–17	32.7	31.9

Table 39
Primary Play Measures at 27 Months

	Boys Mean	Girls Mean
Total SDA's	32.1	30.1
Number acts	75.9	68.1
Number SDAs: 0-20 seconds duration	13.3	12.9
Greater than 120 seconds duration	3.0	2.7
SDA: Q_3	65.6	65.0
Mean 3 longest SDA's	198.8	204.2
Verbalization (adaptation period)	48.5	46.5
Verbalization: total playtime	174.3	189.0
Contact with mother (seconds)	37.5	93.9
Squares near mother (proximity)	449.3	514.7
Smiles	9.3	8.1
Look at mother (seconds)	90.7	112.5

Table 40
Mean squares and acts by age, sex and social class

	Boys		Girls	
	Squares	Acts	Squares	Acts
8 Months				
(15 min.)				
LMC	11.8	25.8	10.9	32.1
MC_1	10.1	27.7	8.1	27.4
MC_2	7.4	25.8	5.6	25.4
UMC	6.0	20.1	8.1	25.6
13 Months				
(17 min.)				
LMC	62.2	30.2	71.5	25.5
MC_1	60.3	34.1	53.9	32.8
MC_2	66.8	31.5	62.0	36.4
UMC	68.7	34.1	56.0	31.9
27 Months				
(30 min.)				
LMC	139.4	63.1	179.7	60.1
MC_1	181.5	84.6	164.2	71.8
MC_2	211.8	81.5	207.6	76.2
UMC	153.1	70.4	154.7	65.8
	$F = 3.71$	$F = 6.80$		
	$p < .05$	$p < .001$		

Table 41a

Stability of Mobility (Squares Traversed) from 8 to 13 Months

13 Months	Boys (8 Months)				
	1–15 Min.	1–4 Min.	5–8 Min.	9–12 Min.	13–15 Min.
Min. 1–17	.20	−.04	.16	.19	−.17
Min. 1–4	.30[a]	.15	.25[a]	.23	.26[a]
Min. 5–8	.33[b]	.11	.29[a]	.25[a]	.28[a]
Min. 9–12	.14	−.06	.10	.15	.07
Min. 13–17	−.04	−.24[a]	−.03	.04	.05
	Girls (8 Months)				
Min. 1–17	.31[a]	.37[b]	.26[a]	.12	.42[b]
Min. 1–4	.20	.27[a]	.17	.00	.27[a]
Min. 5–8	.31[a]	.36[b]	.27[a]	.10	.38[b]
Min. 9–12	.36[b]	.35[b]	.25[a]	.17	.46[b]
Min. 13–17	.10	.09	.06	.13	.20

[a] $p < .05$; two tails.
[b] $p < .01$; two tails.

Table 41b

Stability of Mobility (Squares Traversed) from 13 to 27 Months

Number of Squares; Free Play 27 Months	Boys				
	Number of Squares at 13 Months				
	Total	1–4 Min.	5–8 Min.	9–12 Min.	13–17 Min.
Adaptation	.36[b]	.30[b]	.17	.31[b]	.24[a]
Min. 1–15	.06	−.06	−.04	.14	.10
Min. 16–30	.15	.15	.07	.17	.05
Total time	.12	.06	.01	.18	.08
	Girls				
Adaptation	.20	.24	.24	.18	−.15
Min. 1–15	.08	−.05	.12	.12	−.03
Min. 16–30	.07	.11	.13	.01	−.01
Total time	.08	.03	.15	.09	−.02

[a] $p < .05$.
[b] $p < .01$.

Table 42

Stability of Tempo from 8 and 13 to 27 Months

| 27 Months | Number of Acts | | | |
| | 8 Months | | 13 Months | |
	Boys	Girls	Boys	Girls
No. acts	.05	−.07	−.03	.29[a]
No. SDA < 20 seconds	.11	−.07	−.13	.05
> 120 seconds	−.12	−.11	.28[a]	.03
SDA: Q_3 value	−.26[a]	.00	.09	−.13

[a]$p < .05$.

Table 43

Difference in Behavior at 27 Months for Fast and Slow Tempo Children (Based on Free Play) at 27 Months

27-Month Variables	Boys				Girls			
	Fast Tempo	Slow Tempo	t	p	Fast Tempo	Slow Tempo	t	p
Vocabulary score	11.9	13.9	2.05	< .05	12.4	12.7		
First fixation: HF I	10.6	10.0			7.1	10.9	2.22	< .05
First fixation: Three-dimensional faces	6.9	9.3	1.76	< .10	5.3	8.7	2.30	< .05
First fixation: Slides	6.6	8.3	2.78	< .01	5.9	7.7	2.27	< .01
First fixation: average standard score, HF I, Three-dimensional faces, slides	−.04	+.45	1.96	< .05	−.24	+.55	2.31	< .05
Embedded Figures Test, response time								
DHB: easy items	3.5	3.8			2.9	4.5	3.48	< .01
CCI: hard items	5.0	5.9			4.6	6.0	1.91	< .10

Table 43 (*continued*)

27-Month Variables	Boys				Girls			
	Fast Tempo	Slow Tempo	t	p	Fast Tempo	Slow Tempo	t	p
Embedded Figures Test, percent correct								
DHB: easy items	65.0	68.7			61.5	81.6	2.12	< .05
CCF: hard items	61.5	61.2			61.6	75.8		
Conflict task: response time to 5 criteria trials								
Neg. 1 ⎫ Response	1.8	1.5			1.5	1.7		
Pos. 1 ⎬ time to	4.1	4.4			2.7	4.5	1.67	= .11
Neg. 2 ⎬ conflict	2.0	2.3			2.1	3.3	1.75	< .10
Pos. 2 ⎭ trials	2.2	2.6			3.3	3.9		
	1.7	2.2			1.9	2.7	1.78	< .10
All 4 lights	3.2	2.6			2.1	4.8	3.80	< .001

Table 44

Differences in Infancy Between Fast and Slow Tempo Children (Based on Q_3 and SDAs Over Two Minutes in Free Play at 27 Months)

	Boys			Girls		
	Fast Tempo	Slow Tempo	p	Fast Tempo	Slow Tempo	p
4 Months						
First fixation to two-dimensional faces:						
Trials 1–4	10.3	8.6		8.1	10.6	
5–8	8.0	9.1		6.1	8.4	
9–12	5.2	9.7	< .01	4.6	8.0	< .10
13–16	4.5	8.3	< .10	5.5	6.6	
Habituation ratio: First fixation	.71	.52	< .05	.64	.61	
Smiles						
PR	1.4	4.6	< .05	2.5	4.8	
SR	1.0	3.0		1.7	4.0	
All stimuli	3.5	9.6	< .10	6.9	15.3	

Table 44 (*continued*)

	Boys			Girls		
	Fast Tempo	Slow Tempo	p	Fast Tempo	Slow Tempo	p
8 Months						
First fixation to two-dimensional faces:						
Trials 1–4	5.8	7.2		3.9	5.1	<.10
5–8	3.8	5.6	<.01	3.5	4.6	
9–12	3.9	4.5		3.2	3.4	
13–16	3.4	4.4		2.8	3.7	
Habituation ratio: first fixation	.64	.64		.59	.58	
Smiles						
PR	1.0	2.0		0.8	1.3	
SR	0.8	1.4		0.6	1.2	
All stimuli	2.6	6.3	<.10	2.2	4.0	
No. acts in free play	25.0	18.1	<.10	26.8	21.3	
13 Months						
Activity						
Twist, HF I (during stimuli)	2.8	1.1	<.05	2.6	2.7	
Twist, HF I (intertrial interval)	2.4	1.1	<.05	2.6	2.0	
Wave, three-dimensional faces (during stimuli)	1.9	0.7	<.01	0.8	1.4	
Wave, three-dimensional faces (intertrial interval)	1.5	0.6	<.10	0.5	1.2	

Table 45
Difference Between Impulsive and Reflective Children (Based on EFT)

	Boys			Girls		
	Impulsive N = 19	Reflective N = 21	p	Impulsive N = 22	Reflective N = 15	p
4 Months						
First fixation: two-dimensional faces	8.1	9.2		6.4	9.7	= .06
Habituation ratio	0.67	0.56		0.65	0.66	
8 Months						
First fixation: two-dimensional faces	3.9	5.1	< .10	5.0	4.4	
Habituation ratio	0.68	0.65		0.64	0.61	
Number of acts	31.8	23.7	= .12	27.9	28.0	
13 Months						
HF I, twist (during stimuli)	2.6	1.0	< .05	2.6	2.5	
Auditory, twist (during)	2.7	1.8		2.1	2.5	
Three-dimensional faces, twist (during stimuli)	4.2	2.3	= .06	3.2	4.2	
HF II, twist (during stimuli)	3.4	1.8	< .05	2.5	2.2	
27 Months						
Conflict task						
Response time, Neg. 1	3.1	4.9		2.2	4.2	< .05
Response time, Pos. 1	1.6	2.9	< .05	1.8	2.6	< .05
Response time, Neg. 2	2.4	2.9		2.3	3.4	
Response time, Pos. 2	1.6	2.7	< .05	1.6	2.6	< .001
All 4 lights	3.4	3.2		2.7	3.3	
Free play Q_3	62.0	73.0		53.0	67.0	< .10
Time near mother (adaptation)	73.0	80.0		44.0	107.0	< .01
Minutes 1–15	187.0	181.0		216.0	267.0	
Minutes 16–30	183.0	318.0	< .05	248.0	346.0	
Educational level	2.4	2.8		2.6	2.7	

Table 46

Relation of Tempo During Infancy to Tempo at 27 Months (Boys) (Numbers Refer to Number of Children)

	Fast Tempo in Infancy (Rapid Habituation at 4 Months; Many Acts at 8 Months)	Slow Tempo in Infancy (Shallow Habituation at 4 Months; Few Acts at 8 Months)
27 Months		
Fast tempo in play at 27	13	4
Slow tempo in play at 27	4	16
	$\chi^2 = 9.7, p < .01$	
Impulsive on EFT at 27	7	3
Reflective on EFT at 27	3	7
	$p = .08$, Fisher's exact test	
Fast tempo and impulsive at 27	6	1
Slow tempo and reflective at 27	1	6
	$p < .05$, Fisher's exact test	

272

Table 47
Mean Number of Smiles (All Trials)

	Sum Smiles	Mean	Mean
4 Months Two-dimensional faces,	PR	3.5	2.6
	SR	2.1	2.0
Three-dimensional faces,	all trials	7.2	7.0
	Reg	3.0	2.0
	all trials	6.4	5.3
8 Months Two-dimensional faces,	PR	1.6	1.0
	SR	1.0	0.8
Three-dimensional faces,	all trials	4.2	2.8
	Reg	1.0	0.7
	all trials	2.4	1.8
13 Months			
HF I, all trials		1.2	1.2
HF II, all trials		0.9	1.0
Three-dimensional faces,	all trials	0.8	1.5
27 Months			
HF I		5.1	6.0
	Three-dimensional faces	3.1	4.0
	Slides	9.4	9.5

Table 48a
Stability of Smiling at 4, 8, and 13 Months

| | 4 Months | | | | | |
| | PR | | SR | | Reg | |
	Boys	Girls	Boys	Girls	Boys	Girls
8 Months						
PR	.16	.19	.22	.14	.09	.00
SR	.00	.00	.04	.04	.00	.11
Reg	.02	.10	.00	.11	.09	-.11

| | 4 Months | | | | | |
| | PR | | SR | | Reg | |
	Boys	Girls	Boys	Girls	Boys	Girls
13 Months						
HF I	.12	.16	.08	.16	.03	-.02
HF II	.04	.06	.15	.15	.23	.03
Three-dimensional faces	.04	.29[a]	.13	.36[b]	.33[b]	.10
Auditory	.20	-.09	.33[b]	-.04	.28[a]	.27[a]

| | 8 Months | | | | | | | |
| | PR | | SR | | Reg | | Aud | |
	Boys	Girls	Boys	Girls	Boys	Girls	Boys	Girls
13 Months								
HF I	-.01	.33[b]	-.03	.15	.01	.15	.01	.11
HF II	.00	.29[a]	.06	.32[b]	.08	.42[b]	.16	-.06
Three-dimensional faces	.02	-.11	.04	-.07	.03	.12	.17	-.06

[a] p < .05.
[b] p < .01.

Table 48b

Stability of Smile—Affect

27 Months	4 Months					
	PR		SR		Reg	
	Boys	Girls	Boys	Girls	Boys	Girls
EFT affect: all items	.26[a]	.32[a]	.11	.30[a]	.28[a]	-.04
HF I	.00	.08	-.04	.03	-.03	-.17
Three-dimensional faces	.00	-.18	-.03	-.12	-.02	.07
Slides	-.05	-.23	.01	-.27	-.08	-.03
Free play	.08	.18	.06	.14	.19	.05

$^a p < .05.$

Table 48c

Stability of Smile—8 to 27 Months

27 Months	8 Months							
	PR		SR		Reg		Aud	
	Boys	Girls	Boys	Girls	Boys	Girls	Boys	Girls
EFT affect: all	.01	.00	.39[a]	.05	.17	.03	.19	.00
Free play: all	-.02	.00	.04	-.01	.12	.27	-.04	-.13
Human Forms I	-.06	.02	-.01	-.02	.07	-.06	-.03	.18
Three-dimensional faces	-.21	.00	-.13	.01	.07	-.11	-.01	.21
Slides	.02	.12	.04	.11	.14	.00	.24	-.11

$^a p < .05.$

Table 48d

Stability of Smile—13 to 27 Months

| | 13 Months—Three-Dimensional Faces | | | | | | | | | | | |
| | Reg | | Scr | | EO | | NE | | BL | | All | |
27 Months	Boys	Girls	Boys	Girls	Boys	Girls	Boys	Girls	Boys	Girls	Boys	Girls
EFT affect: all	-.05	.12	-.11	.20	-.12	.30[a]	-.03	.22	-.12	.28[a]	-.13	.27[a]
HF I: all	-.24[a]	.19	-.19	.40[b]	.04	.10	-.08	.25	.11	.27[a]	-.20	.30[a]
Three-dimensional faces: all	-.21	.35[b]	-.09	.28[a]	.00	.21	-.15	.28[a]	-.08	.17	-.22	.33[a]
Slides: all	-.16	.07	.24	.07	-.11	-.04	-.04	.14	.14	.06	-.12	.06
Free play: all	-.11	.24	-.13	.43[b]	.04	.18	-.13	.21	.05	.25	-.11	.35[b]

| | 13 Months | | | | | |
| | HF 1 All | | HF II All | | Auditory | |
	Boys	Girls	Boys	Girls	Boys	Girls
EFT affect: all	.15	.00	-.10	.11	-.13	.06
HF I: all	-.02	.32[a]	-.13	.10	.00	.21
Three-dimensional faces: all	-.14	.33[b]	-.15	.08	-.07	.34[b]
Slides: all	.07	.17	-.09	.10	-.07	.33[a]
Free play: all	-.14	-.05	-.15	.13	.23[a]	.07

[a] $p < .05$.
[b] $p < .01$.

275

Table 49
Physique at 27 Months and Smiling

| | 27 Months | | | | | |
| | Ponderance | | Height | | Weight | |
Smiles	B	G	B	G	B	G
Two-dimensional faces at 4 months	.00	−.38[b]	.05	−.32[a]	.06	.33[a]
Two-dimensional faces at 8 months	−.09	−.43[b]	−.04	−.35[b]	.02	.38[b]
Human Forms I at 13 months	.00	−.14	.06	−.13	.10	.10
Human Forms I at 27 months	.04	−.04	.11	−.08	.10	−.04
Free play at 27 months	.20	−.15	.22	−.22	.06	−.09
Embedded Figures Test at 27 months	.04	−.01	.09	−.08	.16	−.13

[a] $p < .05$.
[b] $p < .01$.

Table 50
Relation of Body Proportions at 4, 8, 13, and 27 Months to Affect on Embedded Figures Test at 27 Months

| | Boys | | | | | | | |
| | Height | | | | Weight | | | |
EFT Affect	4	8	13	27	4	8	13	27
Easy items	.26[a]	.35[b]	.28[a]	.03	.27[a]	.33[a]	.34[b]	.20
Moderate items	.28[a]	.35[b]	.25[a]	.06	.30[a]	.27[a]	.24	.18
Hard items	.29	.36[b]	.25[a]	.09	.23	.21	.22	.10
	Girls							
Easy items	−.03	.05	.10	−.12	−.06	−.21	−.21	−.07
Moderate items	−.01	.07	.07	−.02	.05	−.17	−.15	−.08
Hard items	−.01	.09	.10	−.13	−.01	−.05	−.08	.04

[a] $p < .05$.
[b] $p < .01$.

Table 51

Percent of Group Showing Fear at 8 and 13 Months

	Boys _N_ = 73			Girls _N_ = 73			Pooled (B and G) _N_ = 146		
Age	8	13	8 and 13	8	13	8 and 13	8	13	8 and 13
Lower middle class	8	8	8	26	19	6	17	13	7
Middle class$_1$	23	4	4	17	17	0	20	11	2
Middle class$_2$	12	25	6	13	26	13	13	26	9
Upper middle class	38	32	16	40	37	8	39	35	12

Table 52

Proportion of Infants in Each Social Class Group Who Cried, Fretted, or Did Neither to Separation at 8 Months

	LMC		MC$_1$		MC$_2$		UMC	
	B	G	B	G	B	G	B	G
Cry	20	17	22	13	55	45	26	27
Fret	10	8	13	37	27	22	39	13
No distress	70	75	65	50	18	33	35	50

Table 53

Two-Year Derivatives of Fear to Faces at 8 Months

27-Month Variables	Boys			Girls		
	Fear	No Fear	p	Fear	No Fear	p
Vocabulary score	10.2	13.2	<.05	12.9	11.5	
Verbalization to						
Slides	3.7	5.0		6.1	2.6	<.05
HF I	17.2	18.2		37.5	10.4	<.01
Three-dimensional faces	6.8	33.4	<.05	31.1	17.1	<.01
Free play (adaptation)	44.0	54.0		61.0	34.0	<.05
Minutes 1–15	62.0	56.0		113.0	84.0	
Minutes 16–30	103.0	75.0		134.0	81.0	<.05

Table 54

Intercorrelations Among Postural and Activity Variables at 13 Months

	Human Forms I			
	Twist On	Twist Off	Lean Forward	Quiet
HF I				
Twist on	—	.54[b]	.19	−.13
Off	.61[b]	—	.06	−.22
Lean forward	−.15	−.01	—	.05
Quiet	−.36[b]	−.35[b]	.12	—
Aud				
Twist on	.29[a]	.14	.08	−.02
Off	.29[a]	.43[b]	.24	.04
Lean forward	−.02	−.07	.40[b]	.06
Quiet	−.29[a]	.03	−.03	.34[a]

Table 54 (*continued*)

Intercorrelations Among Postural and Activity Variables at 13 Months

	Human Forms I			
	Twist On	Twist Off	Lean Forward	Quiet
Three-Dim. Faces				
Twist on	.43[b]	.49[b]	.07	−.30[a]
Off	.21	.42[b]	.18	−.05
Lean forward	−.16	−.15	.57[b]	.15
Quiet	−.23	−.49[b]	.10	.46[b]
HF II				
Twist on	.35[a]	.31[a]	.01	−.30
Off	.22	.23	−.01	−.21
Lean forward	.06	−.24	.16	.18
Quiet	−.11	−.41[b]	.07	.37[a]
	Auditory			
HF I				
Twist on	.39[b]	.51[b]	−.01	−.07
Off	.24	.45[b]	−.27	−.20
Lean forward	.02	.02	.18	.03
Quiet	−.17	.01	.25	.59[b]
Aud				
Twist on	−	.36[b]	.06	−.24
Off	.40[b]	−	.04	.02
Lean forward	.04	.11	−	.29[a]
Quiet	−.35[a]	−.25	.11	−
Three-Dim. Faces				
Twist on	.32[a]	.53[b]	.09	−.23
Off	.34[a]	.29	.11	−.14
Lean forward	.19	.10	.17	−.28
Quiet	−.08	−.14	.24	.24
HF II				
Twist on	.26	.36[a]	.15	−.30
Off	.36[a]	.31	.00	−.27
Lean forward	.16	.01	.52[b]	.06
Quiet	−.03	−.12	.33[a]	.22
	Three Dimensional Faces			
	Twist On	Twist Off	Lean Forward	Quiet
HF I				
Twist on	.28[a]	.16	.16	−.07
Off	.23	.01	−.11	−.20
Lean forward	.15	−.03	.34[a]	−.02
Quiet	.13	.02	.13	.65[b]

Table 54 (*continued*)

Intercorrelations Among Postural and Activity Variables at 13 Months

	Three Dimensional Faces			
	Twist On	Twist Off	Lean Forward	Quiet
Aud				
Twist on	.11	.06	.07	−.16
Off	.47[b]	.23	.08	.01
Lean forward	.22	.02	.29[a]	.33[a]
Quiet	.06	.03	.11	.73[b]
Three-Dim. Faces				
Twist on	—	.11	.23	−.04
Off	.59[b]	—	.21	.02
Lean forward	−.10	.01	—	.08
Quiet	−.33[a]	−.08	.13	—
HF II				
Twist on	.61[b]	.29	−.21	−.21
Off	.39[a]	.31[a]	−.23	−.20
Lean forward	−.05	.00	−.01	.18
Quiet	−.18	−.14	.00	.24
	Human Forms II			
HF I				
Twist on	.37[b]	.31[a]	−.05	−.10
Off	.30[a]	.12	−.17	−.23
Lean forward	−.10	.20	−.03	−.01
Quiet	−.22	−.02	.26	.58[b]
Aud				
Twist on	.20	.08	−.05	−.21
Off	.52[b]	.35[b]	−.10	.01
Lean forward	−.02	.29[a]	.06	.24
Quiet	.02	.05	.14	.54[b]
Three-Dim. Faces				
Twist on	.45[b]	.46[b]	.00	.10
Off	.17	.28[a]	−.04	−.02
Lean forward	−.04	.12	.09	.05
Quiet	−.03	.04	.12	.66[b]
HF II				
Twist on	—	.42[b]	−.09	−.08
Off	.62[b]	—	−.08	.08
Lean forward	−.10	−.02	—	.13
Quiet	−.10	.04	.42[b]	—

Note 1. Boys to right of diagonal; girls to left of diagonal.

Note 2. On = during stimulus presentation; off = during interstimulus interval.

[a]$p < .05$.

[b]$p < .01$.

Table 55
Correlates of Quieting at 13 Months

13 Months	Quiet HF I		Quiet Auditory		Quiet Three-Dimensional Faces		Quiet HF II	
	B	G	B	G	B	G	B	G
HF I, first fixation (all trials)	.58[b]	.61[b]	.39[b]	.18	.37[b]	.22	.49[b]	.00
HF I, total fixation (all)	.64[b]	.61[b]	.39[b]	.17	.44[b]	.41[b]	.50[b]	.06
HF I, smiles	−.28[a]	−.20	−.12	−.05	−.20	.31[a]	.03	.07
Three-dimensional faces, first fixation (all)	.54[b]	.15	.52[b]	.09	.66[b]	.43[b]	.48[b]	.09
Three-dimensional faces, total fixation (all)	.57[b]	.21	.52[b]	−.06	.73[b]	.62[b]	.53[b]	.18
Three-dimensional faces, smiles	−.28[a]	−.03	−.16	−.27	−.19	.17	−.12	.04
HF II, first fixation (all)	.14	.36[b]	−.03	.03	.15	.35[a]	.44[b]	.39[a]
HF II, total fixation (all)	.35[b]	.40[b]	.16	−.13	.29[a]	.34[a]	.60[b]	.41[b]
Free Play: Squares	−.27[a]	.00	−.25	−.39[b]	−.22	−.15	−.24	−.22
Free Play: Act changes	−.34[a]	−.11	−.18	−.07	−.32[a]	.13	−.15	−.23
Auditory: Orientation to speaker	.00	.05	.31[a]	.34[a]	.23	.12	.14	−.11
Educational level	.19	.35[b]	.20	.32[a]	.15	.23	.04	.19

[a] $p < .05$.
[b] $p < .01$.

Table 56

Correlates of Twisting at 13 Months

13 Months	HF I Twist On B	HF I Twist On G	HF I Twist Off B	HF I Twist Off G	Auditory Twist On B	Auditory Twist On G	Auditory Twist Off B	Auditory Twist Off G
Educ. level	.05	-.15	.02	-.15	.05	-.11	.10	.00
First fix., HF I	-.21	-.45[b]	-.37[b]	-.34[b]	-.22	-.14	.00	-.11
Total fix., HF I	-.27[a]	-.45[b]	-.32[a]	-.38[b]	-.23	-.14	.08	-.14
Orient. to speaker; aud.	.29[a]	-.09	-.12	.04	-.11	.09	-.03	.03
First fix., three-dim.	-.18	-.23	-.23	-.09	-.06	-.12	.00	-.03
Total fix., three-dim.	-.20	-.12	-.30[a]	-.19	-.10	-.11	.00	-.08
First fix., HF II	.04	-.14	-.21	-.25	-.15	-.11	-.17	-.17
Total fix., HF II	.09	-.26	-.14	-.40[b]	-.08	-.09	-.11	-.20
Squares, play	.23	.27	.31[a]	.25	.01	.12	.10	.25
Acts, play	.05	.09	.00	.14	.00	.11	-.01	-.01

Table 56 (*continued*)

13 Months	Three-Dimensional Faces				HF II			
	Twist On		Twist Off		Twist On		Twist Off	
	B	G	B	G	B	G	B	G
Educ. Level	-.02	-.20	.18	-.26	.14	-.13	.00	-.40[b]
First fix., HF I	.07	-.24	-.18	-.13	-.25	-.04	.00	-.20
Total fix., HF I	-.05	-.33[a]	-.17	-.17	-.24	-.19	-.14	-.26
Orient. to speaker; aud.	-.09	-.11	-.12	-.25	-.07	.08	.05	-.15
First fix., three-dim.	.06	-.27	-.09	-.17	-.16	-.03	-.07	.00
Total fix., three-dim.	-.11	-.22	-.07	-.28	-.21	.00	-.07	.05
First fix., HF II	-.09	-.17	-.05	-.25	-.21	-.05	-.06	-.20
Total fix., HF II	-.11	-.25	-.06	-.20	-.26[a]	-.27	.05	-.34[a]
Squares, play	.12	-.19	-.07	-.02	.27[a]	-.05	.28[a]	.01
Acts, play	.08	-.10	-.08	-.21	.05	-.35[a]	-.10	-.31[a]

[a] $p < .05$.
[b] $p < .01$.

Table 57
Correlates of Leaning Forward at 13 Months

13 Months	HF I B	HF I G	Auditory B	Auditory G	Three-Dimensional B	Three-Dimensional G	HF II B	HF II G
Educ. level	.05	-.11	.03	.22	.06	-.11	.07	.39b
First fix., HF I	.10	.28a	.25	.11	.16	.03	.17	.17
Deceleration, HF I Reg	.29a	.62b	-.01	.45b	.10	.54b	.04	.10
Scr	.15	.55b	.04	.30a	.13	.50b	-.01	-.08
HBL	.28a	.18	.05	.01	.40b	.13	-.08	-.16
FF	.21	.45b	.17	.44b	.22	.37a	.00	-.02
Orient. to speaker auditory (all)								
Deceleration LL	.11	-.15	.22	.05	.24	-.19	.25a	.10
HL	.08	.24	.09	.11	.08	.16	.19	.10
LH	.01	.17	-.12	.18	-.08	.34a	-.16	.01
HH	.23a	.14	.16	.09	.16	.07	-.03	.01
Auditory	.21	-.07	.09	.08	.23	.09	.11	-.01

Table 57 (*continued*)

13 Months		HF I		Auditory		Three-Dimensional		HF II	
		B	G	B	G	B	G	B	G
First fix. three-dim. (all)		.03	-.01	.25	.48[b]	.20	-.09	.00	.10
Deceleration, three-dim.	Reg	.21	.23	.25	.18	.35[b]	.35[a]	-.06	-.04
	Scr	.32[a]	.21	.07	.41[b]	.32[a]	.46[b]	.30[a]	.02
	EO	.20	.33[a]	-.03	.24	.05	-.07	.01	.14
	NE	.13	.23	.33[a]	.21	.35[b]	.55[b]	.07	-.05
	BL	-.01	.43[b]	.04	.15	.34[a]	.27	.06	-.01
HF II, First fix. (all)		.01	.05	.01	.27	.07	.10	.09	.37[a]
Deceleration	3H	.30[a]	.20	.11	.36[a]	.26[a]	.12	.11	.13
	HH	.29[a]	-.06	.11	.23	.20	-.17	.21	.01
	AH	.18	.35[a]	.18	.35[a]	.32[a]	.43[b]	.00	.05
Smiles, HF I (all)		.25	.01	-.11	.31[a]	.00	-.16	-.10	.47[b]
Smiles, auditory (all)		-.15	-.17	-.18	.02	.02	-.12	-.02	-.03
Smiles, three-dim. (all)		.00	-.11	-.09	.25	.40[b]	-.03	-.14	.26
Smiles, HF II (all)		-.19	-.06	-.10	.45[b]	-.03	-.11	.14	.35[a]

[a] $p < .05$.
[b] $p < .01$.

285

Table 58

Predictive Correlates of Activity at 13 Months (all episodes)

	Twist On		Twist Off	
	B	G	B	G
27 Months				
Embedded Figures Test				
% correct DHB	−.08	−.19	−.31[a]	−.19
% correct CCF	−.35[a]	−.09	−.48[b]	−.05
Embedded Figures Test				
Response time DHB	−.11	.19	−.23	.19
Response time CCF	−.14	.27	−.19	.34[a]
Free play Q_3	−.11	−.13	.12	−.11
Number of acts < 20 seconds	.08	−.01	−.22	.01
Number of acts > 120 seconds	−.29[a]	−.07	−.16	−.04

Key. DHB, dog-horse-bird - first 3 series; CCF, cat-car-flower - second 3 series.
[a]$p < .05$.
[b]$p < .01$.

Table 59

Average Scores to Visual Stimuli

	First fixation		Deceleration		Smiles		Vocalization	
	Boys	Girls	Boys	Girls	Boys	Girls	Boys	Girls
4 Months								
Two-dimensional faces:								
PR	11.0	9.7	5.9	5.5	3.5	2.6	2.5	2.3
SR	11.5	9.8	5.5	4.5	2.1	2.0	2.4	2.0
PS	8.6	7.4	4.3	3.6	0.8	1.6	2.3	2.2
SS	7.7	7.6	3.7	3.8	0.8	1.2	2.3	2.1
Three-dimensional faces:								
Reg	9.6	9.2	4.3	5.7	3.0	2.0	2.4	3.0
Scr	10.5	10.3	5.0	5.0	1.6	0.4	2.5	2.1
NE	7.6	7.5	4.3	3.8	1.6	0.4	2.0	2.0
BL	4.9	5.0	3.2	3.0	0.4	0.2	2.5	2.3

287

Table 59 (*continued*)
Average Scores to Visual Stimuli

	First fixation		Deceleration		Smiles		Vocalization	
	Boys	Girls	Boys	Girls	Boys	Girls	Boys	Girls
8 Months								
Two-dimensional faces:								
PR	6.6	5.3	3.3	3.1	1.6	0.9	0.9	0.6
SR	6.0	5.1	3.7	2.9	0.9	0.8	0.7	0.8
PS	5.0	3.9	2.6	2.4	0.8	0.4	0.7	0.5
SS	5.0	4.3	2.9	2.8	0.8	0.8	0.8	0.6
Three-dimensional faces:								
Reg	5.7	5.8	3.6	3.4	0.9	0.6	1.6	1.6
Scr	6.5	6.7	3.3	3.7	0.8	0.4	1.1	1.8
NE	5.6	5.5	3.4	3.3	0.8	0.4	1.5	1.5
BL	4.4	4.0	2.7	2.4	0.1	(0.0)	0.9	1.4
13 Months								
Human Forms I:								
Reg	5.9	6.2	3.8	3.9	0.3	0.5	1.1	1.2
HBL	6.3	6.2	3.8	3.3	0.3	0.2	1.2	1.3
Scr	6.0	5.8	3.7	3.1	0.4	0.4	1.0	1.3
FF	4.9	5.0	2.6	3.4	0.2	0.1	1.0	0.9

Table 60

Summary of Selected Stability Coefficients

Predictive Relation	Fixation		Deceleration (Mean Max.)		Smile (all Trials)		Vocalization (All Trials)	
	B	G	B	G	B	G	B	G
Two-dim. faces at 8 to HF I at 13	.27[b]	.29[b]	.24	.04	−.01	.33[b,d]	.03	.28[b]
Two-dim. faces at 8 to three-dim. faces at 13	.23	.41[c]	.07	.09	−.02	.11[d]	−.02	.30[b]
Three-dim. faces at 8 to three-dim. faces at 13	.08	.51[c]	.31[b]	.03	.03	.12[e]	−.15	.47[c]
Auditory at 8 to auditory at 13	.29[b]	.30[b]	.33[c]	.41[c]	.28[b]	−.10	.18	.28[b]
HF I at 13 to HF I at 27	.04	.26[b]	no data		−.02	.32[b]	−.09	.39[b]
Three-dim. faces at 13 to three-dim. faces at 27	.20	.13	no data		−.22	.33[b]	−.01	.07

[a]The 8 to 13 month coefficients are for total fixation, all trials; the 13 to 27 month coefficients for first fixation, all trials.
[b]$p < .05$.
[c]$p < .01$.
[d]PR at 8 months as predictor.
[e]Reg at 8 months as predictor.

Author Index

Subject Index